KU-099-588

PRAISE FOR VISUAL BOOKS...

"This is absolutely the best computer-related book I have ever bought. Thank you so much for this fantastic text. Simply the best computer book series I have ever seen. I will look for, recommend, and purchase more of the same."

—David E. Prince (NeoNome.com)

"I have several of your Visual books and they are the best I have ever used."

—Stanley Clark (Crawfordville, FL)

"I just want to let you know that I really enjoy all your books. I'm a strong visual learner. You really know how to get people addicted to learning! I'm a very satisfied Visual customer. Keep up the excellent work!"

—Helen Lee (Calgary, Alberta, Canada)

"I have several books from the Visual series and have always found them to be valuable resources."

—Stephen P. Miller (Ballston Spa, NY)

"This book is PERFECT for me — it's highly visual and gets right to the point. What I like most about it is that each page presents a new task that you can try verbatim or, alternatively, take the ideas and build your own examples. Also, this book isn't bogged down with trying to 'tell all' — it gets right to the point. This is an EXCELLENT, EXCELLENT, EXCELLENT book and I look forward to purchasing other books in the series."

—Tom Dierickx (Malta, IL)

"I have quite a few of your Visual books and have been very pleased with all of them. I love the way the lessons are presented!"

—Mary Jane Newman (Yorba Linda, CA)

"I am an avid fan of your Visual books. If I need to learn anything, I just buy one of your books and learn the topic in no time. Wonders! I have even trained my friends to give me Visual books as gifts."

—Illona Bergstrom (Aventura, FL)

"I just had to let you and your company know how great I think your books are. I just purchased my third Visual book (my first two are dog-eared now!) and, once again, your product has surpassed my expectations. The expertise, thought, and effort that go into each book are obvious, and I sincerely appreciate your efforts."

—Tracey Moore (Memphis, TN)

"Compliments to the chef!! Your books are extraordinary! Or, simply put, extra-ordinary, meaning way above the rest! THANK YOU THANK YOU THANK YOU! I buy them for friends, family, and colleagues."

—Christine J. Manfrin (Castle Rock, CO)

"I write to extend my thanks and appreciation for your books. They are clear, easy to follow, and straight to the point. Keep up the good work! I bought several of your books and they are just right! No regrets! I will always buy your books because they are the best."

—Seward Kollie (Dakar, Senegal)

"I am an avid purchaser and reader of the Visual series, and they are the greatest computer books I've seen. Thank you very much for the hard work, effort, and dedication that you put into this series."

—Alex Diaz (Las Vegas, NV)

Credits

Project Editor
Dana Rhodes Lesh

Sr. Acquisitions Editor
Jody Lefevere

Copy Editor
Dana Rhodes Lesh

Technical Editor
Robin Sease

Editorial Manager
Robyn Siesky

Business Manager
Amy Knies

Sr. Marketing Manager
Sandy Smith

Permissions Editor
Laura Moss

Manufacturing
Allan Conley
Linda Cook
Paul Gilchrist
Jennifer Guynn

Book Design
Kathryn Rickard

Production Coordinator
Erin Smith

Layout & Graphics
Jennifer Mayberry
Amanda Spagnuolo
Christine Williams

Screen Artist
Jill A. Proll

Cover Illustration
Kristin Corley

Proofreader
Sean Medlock

Quality Control
John Greenough
Jessica Kramer

Indexer
Potomac Indexing, LLC

**Vice President and Executive
Group Publisher**
Richard Swadley

Vice President and Publisher
Barry Pruett

Composition Director
Debbie Stailey

XML

Your visual blueprint™ for building expert Web sites with XML, CSS, XHTML, and XSLT

UNIVERSITY OF WOLVERHAMPTON
LEARNING & INFORMATION
SERVICES SCIT

ACC. NO. 2443324	CLASS S23
CONTROL NO. 047193383x	005.
DATE 15. JUL 2008	SITE WV	133
		XML/
		HUD

by Rob Huddleston

BICENTENNIAL 1807 WILEY 2007 BICENTENNIAL

Wiley Publishing, Inc.

XML: Your visual blueprint™ for building expert Web sites with XML, CSS, XHTML, and XSLT

Published by
Wiley Publishing, Inc.
111 River Street
Hoboken, NJ 07030-5774

Published simultaneously in Canada

Copyright © 2008 by Wiley Publishing, Inc., Indianapolis, Indiana

No part of this publication may be reproduced, stored in a retrieval system or transmitted in any form or by any means, electronic, mechanical, photocopying, recording, scanning or otherwise, except as permitted under Sections 107 or 108 of the 1976 United States Copyright Act, without either the prior written permission of the Publisher, or authorization through payment of the appropriate per-copy fee to the Copyright Clearance Center, 222 Rosewood Drive, Danvers, MA 01923, (978)750-8400, fax (978)646-8600. Requests to the Publisher for permission should be addressed to the Legal Department, Wiley Publishing, Inc., 10475 Crosspoint Blvd., Indianapolis, IN 46256, (317)572-3447, fax (317)572-4355, online: www.wiley.com/go/permissions.

Library of Congress Control Number: 2006939489

ISBN: 978-0-471-93383-0

Manufactured in the United States of America

10 9 8 7 6 5 4 3 2 1

Trademark Acknowledgments

Wiley, the Wiley Publishing logo, Visual, the Visual logo, Simplified, Master VISUALLY, Teach Yourself VISUALLY, Visual Blueprint, Read Less - Learn More and related trade dress are trademarks or registered trademarks of John Wiley & Sons, Inc. and/or its affiliates. All other trademarks are the property of their respective owners. Wiley Publishing, Inc. is not associated with any product or vendor mentioned in this book.

LIMIT OF LIABILITY/DISCLAIMER OF WARRANTY: THE PUBLISHER AND THE AUTHOR MAKE NO REPRESENTATIONS OR WARRANTIES WITH RESPECT TO THE ACCURACY OR COMPLETENESS OF THE CONTENTS OF THIS WORK AND SPECIFICALLY DISCLAIM ALL WARRANTIES, INCLUDING WITHOUT LIMITATION WARRANTIES OF FITNESS FOR A PARTICULAR PURPOSE. NO WARRANTY MAY BE CREATED OR EXTENDED BY SALES OR PROMOTIONAL MATERIALS. THE ADVICE AND STRATEGIES CONTAINED HEREIN MAY NOT BE SUITABLE FOR EVERY SITUATION. THIS WORK IS SOLD WITH THE UNDERSTANDING THAT THE PUBLISHER IS NOT ENGAGED IN RENDERING LEGAL, ACCOUNTING, OR OTHER PROFESSIONAL SERVICES. IF PROFESSIONAL ASSISTANCE IS REQUIRED, THE SERVICES OF A COMPETENT PROFESSIONAL PERSON SHOULD BE SOUGHT. NEITHER THE PUBLISHER NOR THE AUTHOR SHALL BE LIABLE FOR DAMAGES ARISING HEREFROM. THE FACT THAT AN ORGANIZATION OR WEBSITE IS REFERRED TO IN THIS WORK AS A CITATION AND/OR A POTENTIAL SOURCE OF FURTHER INFORMATION DOES NOT MEAN THAT THE AUTHOR OR THE PUBLISHER ENDORSES THE INFORMATION THE ORGANIZATION OR WEBSITE MAY PROVIDE OR RECOMMENDATIONS IT MAY MAKE. FURTHER, READERS SHOULD BE AWARE THAT INTERNET WEBSITES LISTED IN THIS WORK MAY HAVE CHANGED OR DISAPPEARED BETWEEN WHEN THIS WORK WAS WRITTEN AND WHEN IT IS READ.

FOR PURPOSES OF ILLUSTRATING THE CONCEPTS AND TECHNIQUES DESCRIBED IN THIS BOOK, THE AUTHOR HAS CREATED VARIOUS NAMES, COMPANY NAMES, MAILING, E-MAIL AND INTERNET ADDRESSES, PHONE AND FAX NUMBERS AND SIMILAR INFORMATION, ALL OF WHICH ARE FICTITIOUS. ANY RESEMBLANCE OF THESE FICTITIOUS NAMES, ADDRESSES, PHONE AND FAX NUMBERS AND SIMILAR INFORMATION TO ANY ACTUAL PERSON, COMPANY AND/OR ORGANIZATION IS UNINTENTIONAL AND PURELY COINCIDENTAL.

Contact Us

For general information on our other products and services, please contact our Customer Care Department within the U.S. at (800)762-2974, outside the U.S. at (317)572-3993 or fax (317)572-4002.

For technical support, please visit www.wiley.com/techsupport.

St. Basil's Cathedral, Moscow

The graceful spires and onion domes crowning St. Basil's Cathedral represent, for many, the enigma that is Russia. For Russians, this glorious edifice has long symbolized their history and culture. Commissioned in 1555 by Ivan the Terrible to commemorate his conquest of Kazan, the cathedral still reigns over Red Square despite the efforts of both Napoleon and Josef Stalin to destroy it. Legend claims that the brutal Ivan had the architect, Postnik Yakovlev, blinded so that he could never create an equal masterpiece. Learn more about Russian architecture, lore, and legend in Frommer's *Moscow & St. Petersburg,* available wherever books are sold and at www.frommers.com.

Sales

Contact Wiley
at (800) 762-2974
or (317) 572-4002.

About the Author

Rob Huddleston has been developing Web pages and applications since 1994. Since 1999, he has been a full-time instructor and has taught Web and graphic design to thousands of students. Rob is an Adobe User Group Manager and was recently named as an Adobe Community Expert for his volunteer work answering user questions in online forums. Rob lives in Northern California with his wife and two children.

Author's Acknowledgments

To my wife and best friend, Kelley. None of what I do would be possible without you. I will always love you.

I want to thank Dana Lesh, my project editor; Robin Sease, my technical editor; and Jody Lefevere, my acquisitions editor, for your patience and guidance in completing this book, as well as all of the other wonderful people at Wiley.

My parents have been a constant source of inspiration throughout my life. It is not possible to thank them enough. Thank you to Matt Boehmer, Seth Duffey, Stephanie Liese, and Sue Mathison for the occasional tip and for keeping me motivated on the project.

And thank you to Jess and Xander, just for being you.

TABLE OF CONTENTS

TABLE OF CONTENTS

TABLE OF CONTENTS

HOW TO USE THIS BOOK

XML: Your visual blueprint for building expert Web sites with XML, CSS, XHTML, and XSLT uses clear, descriptive examples to show you how to use XML to create powerful, flexible Web pages. If you are already familiar with XML, you can use this book as a quick reference for many XML tasks.

I suggest that you read this book in order, from beginning to end, as each chapter builds on the concepts from those that precede it. However, the book is structured so that you can also skip sections that cover topics with which you are already familiar.

Who Needs This Book

This book is for the experienced computer user who wants to find out more about XML. It is also for more experienced XML users who want to expand their knowledge of the different features that XML has to offer.

Book Organization

XML: Your visual blueprint for building expert Web sites with XML, CSS, XHTML, and XSLT has 13 chapters and 5 appendixes:

Chapter 1, "Getting Started with XML," introduces the basic concepts and syntaxes of the XML language, along with companion languages such as the XML Schema Definition language, the Extensible Style Sheet Language, XPath, XHTML, and CSS. It will show you how to view XML and discusses best practices of writing XML.

Chapter 2, "Creating XML Documents," gets you started with coding your first XML document. It shows how to add additional information to the document including attributes, entities, and data. It also introduces the concept of namespaces.

Chapter 3, "Defining the Structure of XML with Schemas," shows you how to use XML schemas to define the structure of your XML documents so that others can use them. It covers the World Wide Web Consortium's official XML Schema, shows how to validate your XML documents

against a schema, and demonstrates the powerful, visual schema builder included with the Altova XMLSpy editor.

Chapter 4, "Using Other Validation Schemas," discusses Document Type Definitions, an older method of defining the validity of the document but one that is still in widespread use, and RELAX NG, a different schema language that provides an alternative to the World Wide Web Consortium's official language.

Chapter 5, "Generating XML from Existing Data," shows how you can use popular programs such as Microsoft Excel or Microsoft Access to automatically generate XML and schemas from data that you already have.

Chapter 6, "Learning XHTML Basics," covers the XHTML language for creating Web pages. It shows the differences between HTML and XHTML and teaches best practices for modern Web designers to create Web pages.

Chapter 7, "Transforming XML to XHTML with XSLT," introduces the details of the powerful Extensible Style Sheet Language transformations, which enable you to take your XML documents and convert them to XHTML for display in a Web browser.

Chapter 8, "Formatting Your Web Site Using CSS," covers the cascading style sheets language, a powerful, robust formatting language for the Web. It shows you how to format text, use color, apply background images, and lay out your page using CSS.

Chapter 9, "Translating Legacy HTML to XHTML," discusses methods by which you can convert documents written in older versions of HTML to the new standard, XHTML. It shows you how to use two powerful tools — HTML Tidy and Adobe Dreamweaver — to convert your pages quickly and easily.

Chapter 10, "Designing and Building Your Web Site," covers best practices for planning and implementing Web sites.

Chapter 11, "Publishing Your Web Site," shows how to sign up with a Web host, buy a domain name, and upload your site to the Web.

Chapter 12, "Testing and Debugging," teaches you how to validate your XHTML and CSS to be sure that you do not have typos or otherwise invalid code; shows Firebug, a free debugging tool for the Mozilla Firefox browser; and describes how to test your site to ensure that it is accessible to users with disabilities.

Chapter 13, "Integrating Your Web Site with Other Web Sites," shows how to use Really Simple Syndication to allow others to subscribe to your site, display photos with Flickr, embed video with YouTube, share links with del.icio.us, and display a Google map or advertising.

Appendix A is a complete XHTML reference.

Appendix B is a CSS reference.

Appendix C is an XSD reference.

Appendix D is an XSLT reference.

Appendix E is an XPath reference.

What You Need to Use This Book

To perform the tasks in this book, you need a computer with a Web browser such as Microsoft Internet Explorer or Mozilla Firefox and a text editor. Many of the examples are shown using Altova XMLSpy but can be performed in any text editor, such as Notepad. Several examples require Adobe Dreamweaver or an active Internet connection to complete.

The Conventions in This Book

A number of styles have been used throughout *XML: Your visual blueprint for building expert Web sites with XML, CSS, XHTML, and XSLT* to designate different types of information.

Courier Font

Indicates the use of code such as tags or attributes, scripting language code such as statements, operators, or functions, and code such as objects, methods, or properties.

Bold

Indicates information that you must type.

Italics

Indicates a new term.

Apply It

An Apply It section takes the code from the preceding task one step further. Apply It sections allow you to take full advantage of XML code.

Extra

An Extra section provides additional information about the preceding task. Extra sections contain the inside information to make working with XML easier and more efficient.

What's on the Web Site

The accompanying Web site contains the sample files for the book *XML: Your visual blueprint for building expert Web sites with XML, CSS, XHTML, and XSLT*.

Introducing XML

F ew inventions have revolutionized the way the world thinks and acts faster than the World Wide Web. Two decades ago, it did not exist, whereas today, there are few companies or individuals who have not been affected by it. Most Web pages are written in the Hypertext Markup Language, or HTML, which is an easy-to-use and easy-to-learn language used to describe the structure and formatting of a document. However, HTML does not give authors a way to describe the actual content of their pages. Often, this is not terribly important, but it can pose problems. Search engines, for example, do not know how to differentiate between the uses of common words on Web pages.

A Google search for the word *serenity* will bring up a mixture of results that include pages that discuss the 2005 movie of that name, sites that discuss products that happen to be called *Serenity*, and pages that just happen to use that word.

XML was created to help solve this issue. XML stands for *Extensible Markup Language*. Although XML looks and feels very much like HTML, it has a very different purpose. XML describes the data of a document instead of its visual appearance. Therefore, a Web page about movies written in XML can let search engines or other computers know that its use of *Serenity* is a reference to a film title.

XML Versus HTML

There is a common misconception that XML was invented to replace HTML. In fact, both languages were created from the same parent language, SGML, or *Standard Generalized Markup Language*. Neither is intended to replace the other. HTML, and its latest incarnation, XHTML, are still appropriate for most Web pages because they do not need to describe the data. XML is useful when the data on a site is more important than the appearance. Although many Web sites would benefit from being converted or rewritten as XML, the vast majority are better off as HTML.

It Is Just Text

XML files are plain text. This is one of the great things about XML. No special or expensive software is required to create or maintain XML files. The free text editor included with every operating system will work fine as an XML editor.

It is also important to understand that, as text files, XML cannot "do" anything. A lot of beginning developers expect their XML files to be able to perform advanced programming procedures and are disappointed when they find that they cannot. XML is used to describe the data in the document — and nothing more.

Extensibility

The "extensible" part of XML's name is perhaps the most important. In HTML, there is a predefined set of tags to use. Unless you want to develop your own browser, you are limited to that set of tags. With XML, there is no predefined tag set. Instead, you, the developer, invent the tags that you want to use as you go along. Whatever tags work for your application are the ones that you can use.

XML documents are often compared to database tables. Although you have to be careful not to take the analogy too far, it is helpful to think of creating a database table when you create an XML file. Just as there is no book or Web site that sets out exactly what you can and cannot call the fields in a database, there is nothing that forces you to use any particular term or set of terms in your XML. This is why XML is sometimes referred to as a *meta language* — a language used to define other languages.

Introducing XSLT

One of the most important aspects of XML documents is that they maintain an absolute separation between the data and the display of that data. HTML is a presentational language, so experienced Web designers are used to thinking of what their page says and what it looks like at the same time; this separation of presentation and content can be difficult to grasp at first.

There are many advantages to separating content and presentation. The biggest of these is that by having the content described in one place and the presentation described elsewhere, developers can very easily repurpose existing documents. Take a situation where you have one set of data that needs to be displayed on the Web and in print. By separating the data from the presentation, one set of presentational rules can be applied for the Web and another for print, without having to update the underlying data at all.

XSLT, or Extensible Style sheet Language Transformations, was developed as a way to give developers a language to use to control the presentation of XML documents.

Advantages of XSLT

XSLT is very powerful. It has the ability to describe many programming concepts with which developers may be experienced, including looping and string matching.

XSLT is flexible. It can be used to generate XML, HTML, or plain-text documents from a single source XML file.

XSLT is XML-based, so it uses the same syntax as the source XML file.

XSLT files are plain text, so they can be created in the same editor being used for XML. Although there are fancy, expensive XSLT editors available, they are not required for development.

Disadvantages of XSLT

Like many powerful languages, XSLT can be difficult to learn at first.

Not all parsers support all aspects of XSLT, so there may be times when your document needs to be modified, possibly even including using nonstandard elements. This is particularly true with legacy systems.

Like XML, XSLT documents are ultimately plain-text files. Although you can build many advanced features into XSLT, you need some separate program to actually interpret the XSLT and do something with it.

Separate Content from Presentation

The concept in XML of separating the content of a document from the presentation is one of the most difficult concepts for modern developers to grasp. The computers we use today provide us with a rich visual environment in which to work. Older developers can recall the days of black screens filled with lines of green text, but few recall those days with anything approaching fondness, and younger developers have no more experience with it than they do driving a Model T.

Given that we are so used to creating documents in word-processing programs that show us exactly what the document will look like when printed, it is not surprising that most of us want our documents to look "pretty" from the very beginning. However, developing XML requires that the developer be more patient and develop the content of the document in a strict code view, while worrying about its visual presentation later.

Advantages of Separation

Keeping the content and presentation separate has many advantages. First, and most important, it allows the document to be easily repurposed. XML documents are designed to hold data. By keeping the presentation separate, you do not tie that data to one specific type of presentation. Therefore, a single XML document can be formatted to display in a word processor, on the Web, in a cell phone, or in a database application, all without needing to change the underlying XML code at all. Second, by keeping any presentational code out of the XML document, that document stays small. Smaller documents are easier to maintain and faster and easier to send electronically, either over the Web or via email.

Introducing XHTML

ven experienced Web designers are often afraid of XHTML, thinking that it is some new incarnation that will require hours of additional learning time. In fact, XHTML is nothing more than a newer version of HTML.

In creating XHTML documents, you use the exact same set of tags that you have always used in HTML 4.01. The only important difference is that XHTML uses a much stronger syntax than its predecessor did.

XHTML Syntax Rules

XHTML uses the XML syntax for writing Web pages. Most HTML 4.01 documents can be converted to XHTML with a few minor modifications.

Use Lowercase for All Tags

In XHTML, all tags must be written in all lowercase letters. This will possibly require the most work to convert a document from HTML 4.01 if that document used uppercase or mixed case for its tags. Care must be taken to ensure that all tags, both opening and closing, are converted to lowercase to create a valid XHTML document.

All Tags Must Be Properly Nested

Although never a specific requirement, it has always been a good idea to properly nest tags in HTML, so this should not be a problem now that it is actually required. Proper nesting simply means that closing tags must be presented in the opposite order from the opening tags, so you can use a "first in, last out" methodology.

All Attributes Must Have a Value, and the Value Must Be Quoted

There are a few attributes in HTML 4.01 that do not have a value but are instead a single word. An example is the `checked` attribute for the `input` tag in forms when creating check boxes and radio buttons. In XHTML, you must have a value, so instead of simply saying `checked` as the attribute, you now use `checked="checked"`. All attribute values must always be surrounded by quotation marks in XHTML, although you can use either single or double quotation marks.

All Tags Must Be Closed

This rule is the one that causes XHTML to look the most different from HTML 4.01 documents. In HTML 4.01, there are some elements, such as `hr`, `br`, `meta`, and `img`, that do not contain content and will thus have no corresponding closing tags. In XHTML, closing tags are required for all elements. Empty elements, such as those listed previously, can be expressly closed with a traditional closing tag, or you can use a shorthand syntax by adding a slash to the end of the tag: `<hr />`, `<br />`, `<meta />`, `<img />`.

You Must Provide a Valid DOCTYPE Declaration

The `DOCTYPE` declaration points to the DTD, or Document Type Definition, that defines the XHMTL tag set. There are three `DOCTYPE`s for XHTML: *transitional,* which enables you to use any tag from the HTML tag set; *frameset,* which enables you to use HTML frames and their assorted tags; and *strict,* which requires that you only use structure tags and attributes, keeping all your presentational code in cascading style sheets.

Introducing CSS

The Web was invented as a way for scientists to share information. Although scientific papers are of course very important, their writers focus primarily on the content of the page and do not generally worry so much about the visual appearance of the document. The original versions of HTML therefore contained little or no presentational markup. However, as soon as the Web became more generally popular, companies started wanting to present their content in a much more visually rich way. Because HTML did not provide for the ability to set things like colors and background images, early developers simply added their own HTML tags to achieve these looks. Over time, the language became a horrible mishmash of logical and presentational markup, much of it specific to one browser or another. There was a period of time in the mid-1990s where many Web designers would build two different versions of their page, so one would work correctly in Internet Explorer and the other in Netscape.

Cascading style sheets (CSS) were developed to solve these problems. By removing all the presentational code from HTML and replacing it with a language designed specifically for presentation, Web designers are now able to create much smaller and simpler Web pages that can work across many different browsers and operating systems. Their Web pages also load faster and can easily be adapted to work in other media, such as on cell phones and PDAs. They are also much more accessible to people with disabilities.

CSS Syntax

CSS uses a different syntax from HTML or XML. It is not tag-based. Instead, it consists of rules, which are made up of a selector and a declaration. The selector is the tag to which the rule should be applied. The declaration is made up of property/value pairs, with each property and value separated by a colon, and each pair separated by a semicolon. The entire declaration is enclosed within curly braces — for example:

```
p {color:#FF0000; font-size:95%; font-family:Arial,
Helvetica, sans-serif;}
```

CSS Versions

Currently, CSS exists in two widely supported versions. Version 1 provides for font properties such as font face, size, and emphasis; colors of text and backgrounds; text attributes, including word and line spacing; alignment of elements; margins, padding, and borders; and ID and class selectors. Version 2 added support for positioning of elements in a variety of ways; several new, but not widely supported, font properties such as shadows; and the support for different media types such as printers and projectors. A third version of CSS that will include many more powerful ways to specify selectors and several new features, such as transparency, has been in the works for nearly a decade.

Browser Support

Support for CSS in the browsers has long been a thorn in the side of developers. The good news is that most of the modern browsers come very close to fully supporting CSS1, and almost all of them support the most common features of CSS2. Mozilla's Firefox browser is perhaps the most standards-compliant browser currently available and supports almost all of CSS1 and CSS2 — and even a few scattered CSS3 properties. In late 2006, Microsoft released Internet Explorer 7, which has the best implementation of CSS of any browser ever released by that company. Although IE7 still has some odd quirks and bugs in its CSS support, it is far, far better than its predecessor. Apple's Safari, the third most commonly used browser, is also very good at supporting CSS1 and CSS2, although it too has some odd bugs here and there.

View XML in a Browser

Most modern Web browsers have the ability to parse XML, but only at a basic level. They will read the XML document and ensure that it is well-formed. If the document is not well-formed, the browsers will return an error, which specifies exactly what is wrong in the document and on which line the error occurred, although the line and actual error may not always be precisely accurate. If there are no errors, the browsers will display the document.

Because browsers are designed primarily for XHTML display, they will examine the XML document for a reference to a style sheet. If one is present, they will use it. Currently, modern browsers support CSS versions 1 and 2 and XSLT version 1. Older browsers, such as

Internet Explorer 5 and 6, may be buggy in their display of the page when using CSS. There are even a few examples in which the browser will correctly display certain CSS properties when applied to XHTML but not when the same properties are applied to XML.

If the document is not attached to a style sheet, the browser will use its own internal XSLT style sheet to display the XML's document tree, a view that closely resembles the plain code view from the original editor. Both Mozilla Firefox and Microsoft Internet Explorer add extra functionality via DHTML to the view of XML, enabling you to expand and collapse tags to hide child tags, thus making browsing through documents much easier.

View XML in a Browser

IN INTERNET EXPLORER

① Click File → Open.

The Open dialog box appears.

② Click Browse.

③ Navigate to and click the XML file that you want to open.

● You need to set the Files of Type drop-down list to All Files.

④ Click Open.

All files in the directory are displayed.

⑤ Click OK.

The file opens in the browser, displaying the document tree.

⑥ Click the minus sign next to a tag to collapse it or the plus sign to expand it.

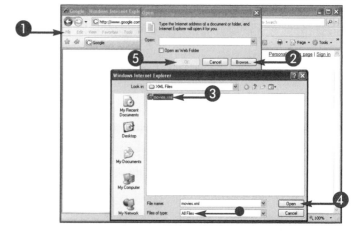

IN FIREFOX

1 Click File → Open File.

The Open File dialog box appears.

2 Navigate to and click the XML file that you want to open.

3 Click Open.

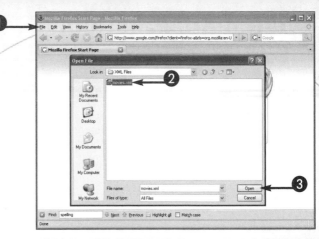

The file opens in the browser, displaying the document tree.

Extra

If a style sheet is provided, the browsers will render the XML document according to the style sheet. If you used CSS to style the XML, you will get a page that looks very much like a traditional Web page. If you used XSLT to transform the document to XHTML, you will see the resulting XHTML; if you transformed to XML, you will get the newly created XML document tree.

Neither Internet Explorer nor Firefox will validate the XML by itself. It is possible to download an extension to Internet Explorer, called the Internet Explorer Tools for Validating XML and Viewing XSLT Output. This free download, available from Microsoft's Web site, adds the ability to right-click an XML document and have Internet Explorer validate it against a schema or DTD. As of this writing, no similar extension exists for Firefox. There are several XML validators available for Firefox, but none are as simple to use as Microsoft's is for Internet Explorer. The same holds true for Safari and other browsers for the Macintosh.

Introducing the Anatomy of an XML Document

A ll XML documents follow the same basic structure. All well-formed XML documents are made up of an XML prolog, a series of optional parsing instructions, and the document itself. The document is made up of a series of nested tags.

Because all documents have this identical structure, any parser can correctly interpret the XML, even if the actual document contents vary greatly. This is a big part of what makes XML such a versatile and powerful language.

The XML Prolog

The XML prolog is a declaration that lets the parser know that this is an XML document, which version of XML is being used, and which character encoding set should be applied to the document. The XML prolog is not a tag, but rather a special instruction to the parser. Therefore, it has a slightly different syntax from the tags:

```
<?xml version="1.0" encoding="UTF-8" ?>
```

The question marks at the beginning and end of the prolog are what designates it as a parsing instruction instead of a tag.

Although there is currently only one version of XML in widespread use, by identifying it in all documents, you ensure that your XML 1 document will continue to be correctly parsed in the future, even if later versions of the language change radically. The encoding is the character set to be used on the document. UTF-8, the most common encoding set, has become a de facto standard for XML, HTML, email, and many other uses, as it allows your document to correctly display a wide variety of characters and symbols. XML supports other encoding standards as well.

Parsing Instructions

Following the XML prolog, you can optionally provide one or more parsing instructions. The most common parsing instruction is a link to a style sheet that uses either CSS or XSLT:

```
<?xml-stylesheet type="text/xsl" href="moviestyles.xsl" ?>
```

Like the prolog, this is not an XML tag, so we use the question marks at the beginning and end to designate it as a parsing instruction. The type attribute provides the MIME type

encoding, which tells the parser what kind of document it should expect to see. In the case of both CSS and XSLT, you are using text documents, with the appropriate subtype. The href attribute provides the path to the style sheet. This can be either relative or absolute, and if absolute, can be given either as a full file path on a local machine or shared server or as a URL for a remote resource.

The Document

The document itself is the XML data that you plan to add. This can be just a few lines or many hundreds or even thousands of lines. The document will consist of nested XML tags. You must provide one root element whose tag wraps around every other element, so its closing tag will be the very last line of the

document. Within the root, you can have as many parent/child relationships as you need for your document. Remember, with XML you get to make up the information as you go. There is no limit as to how many elements you can use or how complex the structure of your document should be.

Choose a Good Text Editor

XML documents are plain text, so they can be created in almost any program. However, there are many applications on the market that are better for editing XML than others.

Ultimately, the decision as to which editor you use will be based on personal choice; important factors include price and operating system availability.

Altova XMLSpy

XMLSpy from Altova is a full-featured commercial application. It is extremely powerful, especially when combined with the other products in the Altova XML suite, which include a program to visually create XSL documents and a program to help visually create schemas. XMLSpy can import XML data from a wide variety of external sources, can correctly read and interpret XSL and schema documents, and provides many other advanced features. It also includes a built-in browser, based on the Internet Explorer engine, for viewing XML documents.

XMLSpy's nicest feature, however, is perhaps its code editor. XMLSpy will automatically create closing tags, and if you attach the XML document to a schema, it will even provide code hinting as to the appropriate tags and attributes to use in your document. It provides for code coloring to help you know when you have made a mistake and line numbers to help find errors.

The biggest downside to XMLSpy is its cost. It is perhaps the most expensive XML editor on the market and can be almost cost-prohibitive in its Enterprise version. Altova does provide for a free 30-day trial of the product.

Microsoft XML Notepad 2007

Microsoft released this free application early in 2007 to provide developers with a simple, friendly method of creating XML. Whereas its small size makes for a quick download and it is certainly easy to use, it lacks a code view editor, instead forcing developers to create their XML in a visual environment.

Eclipse

Eclipse is an open-source Java editor. Its open architecture has allowed it to be reconfigured to serve other purposes, including an XML plug-in that gives it many advanced XML features. The main program and the XML plug-in are available for free and work on practically any platform. In fact, the program does not even need to be installed; it can be run directly off a flash drive. Although the plug-in lacks many features, it is under constant development, with new features and editions being released regularly.

Exchanger

The Exchanger XML editor is a cross-platform, feature-rich editor. There is a free version available for noncommercial use and a professional edition available for purchase. Some of its key features include support for XML schemas, DTDs, and RELAX NG editing, the ability to search on XPath and regular expression strings, a visual data-grid view, and a powerful XSLT debugger.

Adobe Dreamweaver CS3

Adobe Dreamweaver CS3, available for both Windows and Macintosh systems, is not, strictly speaking, an XML editor, but it has a fantastic code editor that includes many of the same features as XMLSpy, such as code coloring, tag completion, and line numbers. In its Design view, Dreamweaver also enables developers to visually create styles, using either CSS or XSL. However, because its focus is on Web design, you can only create XSL documents that transform to XHTML. Also, Dreamweaver has no support for schemas at all.

Oxygen

Oxygen is an XML and XSLT editor available for both Windows and Macintosh systems and is very affordable. Its editor supports XML, XSLT, XML schemas, and RELAX NG. It includes an XSLT debugger and also contains a Subversion client to assist in version control and tracking when working in a group setting.

Notepad

Although not technically an XML editor, Notepad, the free text editor available on all copies of Microsoft Windows, will work for creating XML because it does not attempt to add any of its own markup. Notepad does not provide any additional tools, so you are completely on your own to type everything. It also cannot parse the document, so you will need to use a browser or other parser to check your documents for well-formedness.

Create Your First XML Document

All XML documents need to follow the syntax rules of XML. Documents that follow these rules are said to be *well-formed*. XML parsers will display an error message anytime your document breaks one of these syntax rules.

A well-formed XML document must be case-sensitive. It does not matter whether you use lowercase, uppercase, or mixed case, but you must be consistent. If attributes are provided for tags, they must have a value, and that value must be enclosed within quotation marks. All tags must be closed, and tags must always be properly nested. Element names cannot contain spaces or other special characters, and they must begin with a letter or underscore character.

XML documents must follow these rules to be well-formed so that XML parsers can read them, but your documents should also be human-readable, so use longer, descriptive names for your elements and attributes.

XML documents must begin with an XML declaration, which lets the parser know that this is an XML page, which version of XML you are using, and the encoding type of the page. The XML declaration should look like this:

```
<?xml version="1.0" encoding="UTF-8" ?>
```

After the declaration, you will insert your XML root element, followed by the remainder of your page. Each tag will look like an HTML tag, but you can determine the elements to use based on the needs of the document. The root element will contain all other elements on the page, so the very last line of the code will be the closing tag of the root element.

Create Your First XML Document

1 Open your XML editor to a new page.

● If you are using Altova XMLSpy, click the New button, choose xml Extensible Markup Language, and click OK.

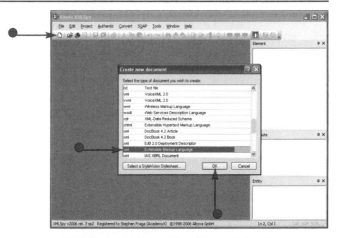

2 Type **<?xml version="1.0" encoding="UTF-8" ?>**.

Note: *Some editors such as XMLSpy will add this automatically.*

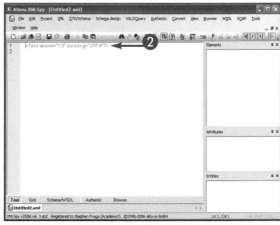

③ Type the root element of your document, surrounded by angle brackets.

④ Close the root element by repeating the opening element in a tag and adding a slash before the element name.

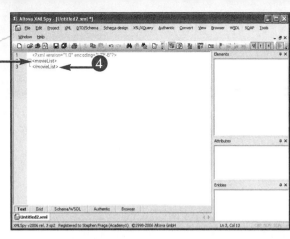

⑤ Click the Check Well-Formedness button to make sure that the document is well-formed.

● The Validation area appears, stating whether your document is well-formed.

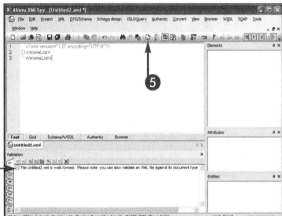

Extra

The encoding value in the XML declaration essentially tells the parser which set of characters to use for the document. UTF-8 is the Western Latin encoding set, which includes characters from the western European languages. Therefore, any document in English, French, German, or even Russian or Greek can use this character set. You will often see encoding set to **ISO-8859-1**, which is the same set as UTF-8.

An important aspect of writing any program is commenting your code, and XML is no different. XML comments use the same syntax as HTML comments. They begin with a less-than symbol, followed by an exclamation mark and two dashes. The comment ends with two dashes and the greater-than symbol:

```
<!-- Comment goes here -->
```

Any text between the opening and closing comment delimiters will be ignored by the XML parser. The more you comment your code, the easier it will be for others to read and interpret what you are trying to do in your document. It is practically impossible to overcomment code.

Add Child Elements and Data to Your Document

Your XML document can be made up of as many or as few levels of elements as you need. Although many levels of nesting are sometimes necessary for the document structure you are creating, simpler documents are easier to read, easier to maintain, and more uniformly supported by parsers. For example, Microsoft Excel cannot properly interpret XML documents with more than a single level of child elements.

All elements in your document can contain other elements, or they can contain the actual data of your document, or both.

Child elements must be properly nested within parent elements, so this is legal:

`<parent><child>Data</child></parent>`

whereas this is not:

`<parent><child>Data</parent></child>`

In the second example, the closing `child` tag is after the closing `parent` tag, resulting in improper nesting. Your XML parser would throw an error in the second example.

Most of your elements will contain data. This can be just about any block of text or numbers or both. There are a few special characters that are not allowed, but for the most part you can insert whatever information you need to store in the document. Ideally, the information within each element should be about one thing, just as in standard database design. For example, depending on how the data is going to be used, it is generally better to use separate elements for first and last name, rather than one combined name element.

Add Child Elements and Data to Your Document

① Open an XML document that contains a root element.

② After the opening root element, type a child element's opening and closing tags.

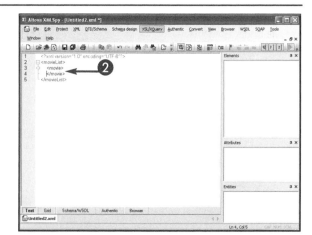

③ After the opening child tag, type another child element's opening and closing tags.

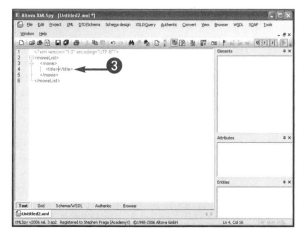

4 After the child's opening tag, add some text as data.

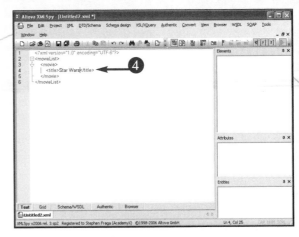

5 Click the Check Well-Formedness button to make sure that the document is well-formed.

● The Validation area opens to show if there are errors or no errors in the document.

6 Click File → Save.

The file is saved.

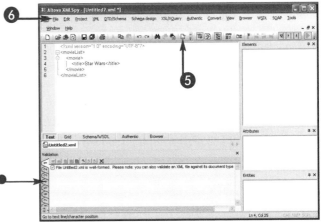

Extra

Although XML does not require that elements be presented in a particular case, it is important to remember that the language is case-sensitive, so you must always code opening and closing tags using the same case and always use the same case every time you code an element.

You should be consistent throughout your document on casing. If you use a mixed-case name for the root element, you should use mixed-case names for the elements throughout the document. Although the parsers will not enforce this, maintaining consistency will reduce the chances that you will enter an element in the wrong case.

XML is not whitespace-sensitive. It is recommended that you place each element on its own line and indent child tags. However, the parser will read and interpret the code in the same way if you write your code on one line. The disadvantage to doing this is that the code is far less readable for you and other developers. Although adding whitespace does increase the file size, most developers agree that the time saved in writing and editing easy-to-read code far outweighs potential costs of distributing marginally larger files.

Add Attributes

ttributes can be used to further define XML elements. An attribute appears within the opening tag of an element. It must consist of a name and a value, separated by an equals sign. The value must be enclosed in quotation marks, although you can use either single or double quotation marks for this purpose. The name of the attribute cannot contain spaces or other characters except letters, numbers, and the underscore. Like elements, attribute names are case-sensitive. You should maintain the same casing as you are using for your elements to make your document easier to maintain. Properly formed attributes look like this:

```
<element attribute="value">Data</element>
```

Like element data, attribute values can be anything — single words, multiple words, or numbers. They should be used to further describe the element in question.

One of the most difficult aspects of developing your XML document is deciding when you should use an attribute and when you should use a child element. Elements are more flexible and usable. Attributes should be used for information that merely expands on the element, whereas elements should be used to contain the important data of the document. Parsers in general provide powerful tools for manipulating element data, while many will partially or completely ignore attributes and their values. HTML provides many good examples of this. For instance, the `table` tag is important — it defines a table. The `width` attribute of that tag is less important — it merely adds information about the table.

Add Attributes

① Open an XML document that contains a root element and at least one child element.

② In the child element, add an attribute, an equals sign, and two quotation marks.

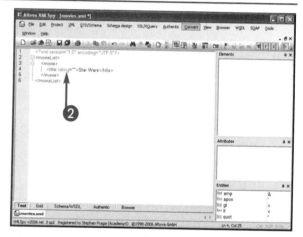

③ Between the quotation marks, give the attribute a value.

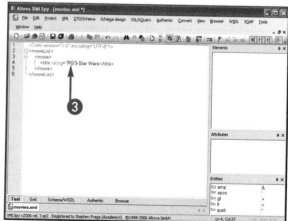

④ After the closing tag of the child element, add a new element with the same attribute but a different value.

⑤ Add data to the new child element.

⑥ Close the new child element.

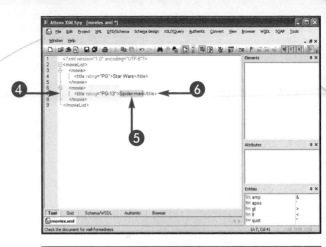

⑦ Click the Check Well-Formedness button to make sure that the document is well-formed.

● The Validation area opens to show if there are any errors.

⑧ Click File → Save.

The document is saved.

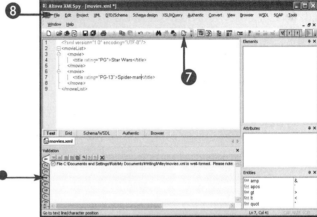

Extra

XML elements can contain more than one attribute. In fact, they can contain as many attributes as you think they need. Multiple attributes are listed in name=value pairs, separated by one or more spaces. All attributes must be within the opening tag and are never repeated in the closing tag:

```
<element attribute1="value" attribute2="value">
```

A single attribute may never be repeated in an element. However, attribute values may contain any characters, so if you needed to provide more than one value for a particular attribute, you could use a space-separated or comma-separated list as the attribute's value.

When an element has more than one attribute, the order in which those attributes are listed is irrelevant, so the example above could be rewritten to reverse the attributes without causing problems.

```
<element attribute2="value" attribute1="value">
```

Add Entities
and CDATA

There are times when the data of your document may contain characters that may confuse the XML parser into thinking that they are XML rather than data. Perhaps the most obvious of these characters are the greater-than and less-than characters, which denote the beginning and end of a tag, but other characters, such as single or double quotation marks and the ampersand, can cause similar problems.

Entities are a code-based representation of these problematic characters. All entities begin with an ampersand, which is followed by the code for the character, and then a semicolon. XML has five of these entities built into the language: > — the greater-than symbol; < — the less-than symbol; & — the ampersand; " — the double quotation mark; and ' — the single quotation mark.

Using a long string of entities in text can become cumbersome to write and difficult to read. When you have situations that may require many instances of illegal characters, you can use a CDATA block. All text within CDATA is rendered by the parser as plain text instead of XML.

A CDATA block begins with a less-than symbol, an exclamation mark, an opening square bracket, the letters CDATA, and another opening square bracket. The block ends with two closing square brackets and a greater-than symbol:

```
<![CDATA[ Potentially problematic text ]]>
```

CDATA sections are particularly useful if you need to include XML in the data of your document that you want to store as plain text rather than be parsed.

Add Entities and CDATA

① Open an XML document that contains at least one element.

② Add a child element to your document.

③ Add data to the document that requires the use of an entity, such as an ampersand or quotation marks.

④ Click the Save button.

The document is saved.

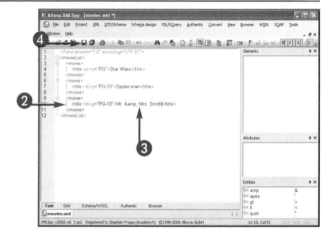

⑤ Open the document in a Web browser.

● The document appears in the browser with the entity code replaced by the correct character.

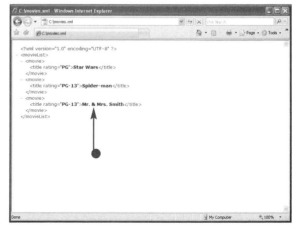

6 After the first child element, add another child element, including both the opening and closing tags.

7 Add a CDATA section between the opening and closing tags of the new element: **<![CDATA[** .

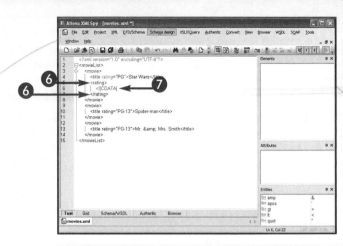

8 Add a short block of text to the element's data.

9 Close the CDATA section: **]]>**.

When viewed in a browser, the data will be displayed as plain, unparsed text.

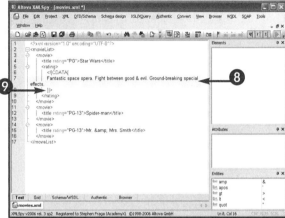

Extra

One particularly useful application of CDATA is its capability to store XML documents within other XML documents, while preventing the internal XML from being parsed and possibly generating errors or confusion.

Many complicated Web applications use XML as a data store due to its light weight and open availability. Using a CDATA section, a set of XML-formatted text can be stored within another XML document. Although this could be done using character entities, it would be much more difficult to read.

Using CDATA,

```
<movieInfo>&lt;actorName&gt;Harrison Ford&lt;\&gt;</movieInfo>
```

could be replaced by this:

```
<movieInfo><![CDATA[<actorName>Harrison Ford</actorName>]]></movieInfo>
```

This way, you can retain the readability of the internal data, but because it is contained with CDATA, it will not be parsed.

Because XML authors can invent their own tags, the possibility exists that two XML documents could use the same element names for different purposes. If these two documents need to be combined, this duplication will cause problems. A namespace nicely solves this issue. When you declare a namespace, you can give the elements being imported a unique identifier, letting the parser know that these tags are from the other document. This is particularly important when you begin validating your XML.

For example, you may have developed an XML document describing your movie collection in which you used an element called `rating` to reference the formal rating from the Motion Picture Association of America. Another developer may be creating an XML document who has chosen to use a `rating` element to denote his or her own personal opinion of the film. If these documents needed

to be combined into a single XML file, a namespace would be required to denote the difference in the logic of the two `rating` elements.

To define a namespace, you need to add an `xmlns` attribute to the root element of your document. This attribute is used to create the unique identifier for the namespace. The value of the attribute points to a URL or local directory that defines the elements from the namespace. This attribute will only appear in the root element of your document. It is possible to use more than one namespace by simply providing additional `xmlns` attributes with different prefixes.

In the document itself, you need to add the prefix defined in the `xmlns` attribute to each element that comes from the external namespace. Make sure to include the attribute on both the opening and closing elements.

Using a Namespace

1 Open an XML document with an element and child elements.

2 In the root element, add the namespace attribute.

3 Add the prefix for the namespace.

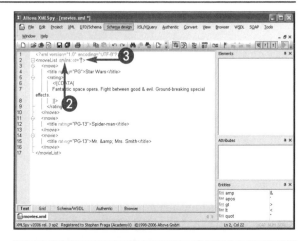

4 Set its value to a fictitious address, such as **<movieList xmlns:ot= "http://www.othertitles.com">** in this example.

5 Add a set of tags from the namespace language.

Note: *Be sure to use the namespace prefix on each tag.*

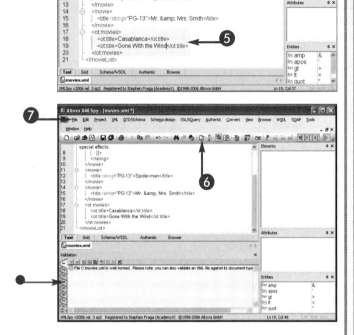

6 Click the Check Well-Formedness button.

● The Validation area opens to show if there are any errors.

7 Click File → Save.

The file is saved.

Extra

Some XML languages can be used to work with other markup languages and will therefore require the use of a namespace to distinguish between the two (or more) languages being used in the document. One example of this is a language called *MXML*. MXML was developed by Macromedia (now owned by Adobe) for developing rich applications using a program called *Flex*. MXML documents are merely XML that use the special mx namespace developed for Flex. XSLT, the language for transforming XML documents, and XSD, the language for defining schemas for XML, also rely on a similar use of namespaces.

However, not all languages built on XML require a namespace. RSS, or Really Simple Syndication, is a common example of this. In general, languages that require a namespace will be more flexible than those that do not, as the namespace enables you to embed other markup languages within the larger document.

Introducing
Schemas

A s an XML developer, you can create any tags that you want for your document. However, in order for other developers or parsers to understand your document, you need to provide instructions as to how the document should be structured. You need to specify what elements will be used in the document, in what order they should appear, whether they are optional or required, and what, if any, attributes they will contain.

W3C XML Schema

The World Wide Web Consortium, or W3C, is the body that developed XML and its associated technologies. Recognizing the need to provide a method of defining XML, they created an XML Schema language which has become the standard for defining valid XML. The W3C Schema is an XML-based language that, while extremely complex, is also extremely powerful.

The word *schema* comes from the Greek word for shape or plan. Thus, you use your schema to provide a plan for your document. Schemas are sometimes referred to as the "grammar" of an XML document.

Schema of Schemas

The concept of the W3C Schema being itself an XML document creates something of a chicken-and-egg paradox. If schemas are used to define XML, but the schema is an XML document, then what is being used to define it? The answer is what is called the "schema of schemas," a master document maintained by the W3C from which all other schemas are defined. Therefore, unlike when you create a traditional XML document, when creating a schema, you will be using a predefined set of tags, which are defined in this schema of schemas.

Microsoft XML Data-Reduced Schema

The W3C often works very slowly, taking input from many developers around the world, discussing problems, and then issuing recommendations that in turn must be thoroughly discussed. In the late 1990s, Microsoft was preparing to release a series of products that would rely on XML and needed a schema on which to base them. Because the W3C's schema was not yet ready, Microsoft developed one of its own, which unfortunately was fundamentally different from the one eventually developed by the W3C. However, Microsoft, which is in fact a member of the W3C, agreed that after the group was done developing their schema, the company would abandon its schema, which it did. There are still remnants of the Microsoft schema in existence, as it was made publically available, and some XML development was done based on it. If you encounter documents that were created based on the Microsoft schema, it is probably worth the time to rewrite the schema using the W3C standard because future support for the Microsoft method is not assured.

What a Schema Defines

You will use your schema to provide a plan, or roadmap, for XML documents created from it. Although many beginning developers tend to think of XML documents as standalone entities, in many cases you will actually need to create many different XML documents that follow the same basic structure. For example, if you are developing a Web site, you may decide to put the data for each page into an XML document. Although the individual documents will have different data, they would all probably follow the same structure, which is what the schema defines.

What a Schema Defines *(continued)*

In your schema, you specify the following:

- The name and capitalization of the root element

- The names and capitalization of the elements that will be nested directly under the root

- The names and capitalization of elements nested below them, and so forth

- Which elements will contain other elements and which will contain data

- For elements that contain data, the type of data that they will contain, such as text or numbers

- Whether or not elements are required and whether or not they can be repeated within a document

- Which elements can contain attributes, what those attributes are, whether or not they are required, and what kinds of information they can contain

- The order in which elements can appear

Creating Your Schema

Because schemas are nothing more than XML documents, you can create them in the same editor that you use to create your regular XML. If you have the data that you plan to use in another program and use that program to export the XML, it will most likely be able to export a schema for you as well. Many advanced XML editors, such as Altova XMLSpy, can automatically generate schemas from a sample XML file. There are also dedicated schema-creation tools available to use.

Which Comes First?

Logically, you cannot create an XML document until you have some idea of the structure that you plan to follow, so the argument can be made that the schema should be created before any XML documents based on it. In practice, however, most developers actually formulate a general idea of what they want in their heads and then begin by creating a sample XML document. From that, they create their schema. Often, they will think of things as they create the schema that require minor tweaks in the XML. Then they can create any additional XML documents that they need, using the schema as their guide.

Publishing Your Schema

You can create a schema that is specific to the needs of the XML document that you are creating, or you may find that your schema is of general enough interest that others may want to build XML documents off it as well. By placing your schema on a publically accessible Web site, you can make it available to anyone else who wants to use it. Several very popular new technologies, such as RSS, were started in this way.

Using an Existing Schema

Many organizations and corporations have published standardized schemas for their industries, so before you spend a lot of time developing your own, you may want to see if one already exists that will suit your needs. You can use a traditional search engine to find schemas or contact organizations or companies within your industry directly.

Using the Schema Namespace

Schemas are XML documents modeled after the schema of schemas. As such, they have a predefined set of elements that must be used. However, to enable developers to expand on the schema concept, the W3C created these schema elements in a namespace. When you create a schema, all the elements you use will be in this namespace, so you will begin every element in the document with the namespace prefix. Although this can be a bit tedious, it is necessary to keep XML as flexible as possible. Note that most professional-level XML editors will handle some of this for you, particularly by automatically adding closing tags with the proper prefix on the element.

As with other namespaces, the schema namespace is defined in the root element of the document. You need to reference the schema of schemas in the namespace definition, which is located at http://www.w3.org/2001/XMLSchema. You will commonly use the xs prefix for the namespace. Thus, your root element will look like the following:

```
<xs:schema xmlns:xs="http://www.w3.org/
2001/XMLSchema">
```

Notice that you are using the namespace for this element. A common beginner's mistake is to forget to put the namespace prefix on this root element.

All tags from the schema use a mixed-casing syntax. They always begin with a lowercase letter. If the name of the element is made up of more than one word, the first letter of each additional word will need to be capitalized. The schema namespace follows these rules for its attribute names and values as well.

Using the Schema Namespace

1 Open your XML editor to a new page.

- To do so in Altova XMLSpy, you click the New Document button, choose Extensible Markup Language as the type of document, and click OK.

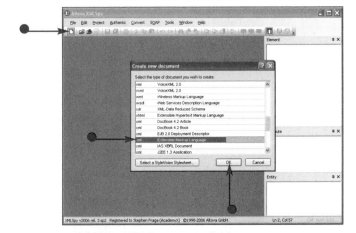

2 Add the XML prolog.

3 Add the schema root element.

4 Create a reference to the xs namespace.

5 Add the closing schema root element.

6 Click the Check Well-Formedness button to confirm that the document is well-formed.

● The Validation area opens to show if there are errors or no errors in the document.

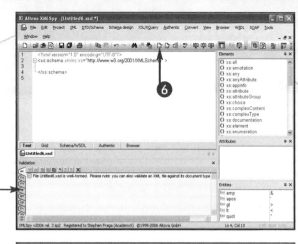

7 Click the Check Validity button to confirm that the document is valid.

● The Validation area confirms the validity of the document or states that it is not valid.

8 Save the document with an .xsd file extension.

The file is saved.

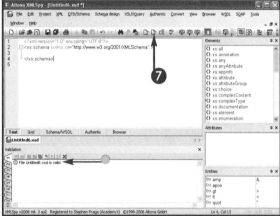

Extra

Technically, the namespace prefix used in your schema document can be anything. You actually define it in the `xmlns` attribute in the root element, so you can make it anything you want. The following is valid:

```
<myschema:schema xmlns:myschema="http://www.w3.org/2001/XMLSchema">
```

However, you will need to append the namespace prefix onto every element in the schema document and onto both the opening and closing tags. Therefore, you do not want the prefix to be more than a couple letters. The `xs` prefix used here and throughout the rest of the book has become the adopted standard prefix for schemas, and it is considered a best practice to stick with it.

The World Wide Web Consortium uses UNIX-based servers for its Web sites. Although the server being used rarely matters to most casual Web users, there is one very important difference between UNIX-based servers and Windows-based servers that can cause errors, and that is that UNIX is a case-sensitive file system. Because it is considered a best practice to make all Web page filenames lowercase, this difference is rarely apparent. However, the W3C does not always follow practices adopted by the rest of the Web community, and they frequently utilize mixed-case filenames. The location of their schema document is no different, and it must be typed using the correct case, or your schema document itself will not be validated.

Add Complex Type Elements

I n XML, there are two types of elements: complex and simple. Simple elements are those that contain nothing but data and do not have attributes. Because most elements on the page need to either contain other elements or have attributes or both, most elements in your document need to be defined as a complex type.

Complex type elements are defined with the `xs:element` element, in which you provide the name of the element. You then nest an `xs:complexType` tag within the `xs:element`. You define the parameters of the complex type using one of several child elements of `xs:complexType`. If the element is going to contain only other elements, as will almost certainly be the case with your root element, you use the `xs:sequence` element to declare that this will contain other elements. Within the `xs:sequence`, you define one or more elements using the `xs:element` element. Note that these child

`xs:element` elements merely state that the complex type contains the element and does not define it.

You will use `xs:sequence` when you want to specify an exact sequence of child elements. If you want to give your XML authors a choice as to which elements they can use, you use `xs:choice` instead. Note that you use `xs:sequence` even if you only have one child element.

```
<xs:element name="movieList">

<xs:complexType>

    <xs:sequence>

        <xs:element name="movie" />

    </xs:sequence>

</xs:complexType>

</xs:element>
```

Add Complex Type Elements

1 Open an XML Schema document.

2 Add an opening `<xs:element>` tag.

3 Set the `name` attribute to the name of the root element of the XML document.

4 Add an opening `<xs:complexType>` tag.

5 Add an opening `<xs:sequence>` tag.

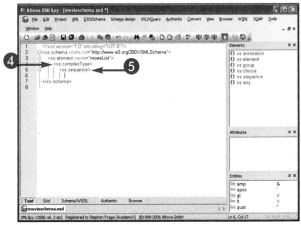

⑥ Add an opening `<xs:element>` tag.

⑦ Add a `name` attribute to the `<xs:element>` tag.

⑧ Set the value equal to the name of the child element.

⑨ Make the `<xs:element>` tag self-closing by adding a slash before the closing angle bracket.

⑩ Close the `<xs:sequence>` tag.

⑪ Close the `<xs:complexType>` tag.

⑫ Close the `<xs:element>` tag.

⑬ Click the Check Well-Formedness button to confirm that the document is well-formed.

The Validation area opens to show if there are errors or no errors in the document.

⑭ Click the Check Validity button to confirm that the document is valid.

● The Validation area confirms the validity of the document or states that it is not valid.

⑮ Click the Save button.

Note: *The document must be saved with an .xsd file extension.*

The file is saved.

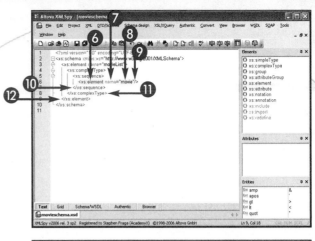

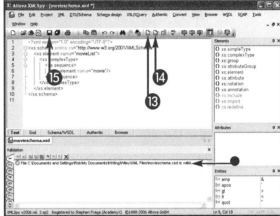

Apply It

You can create a sequence of nested child elements by supplying a series of `xs:element` tags in the order in which the children should appear in the XML:

```
<xs:element name="movie">
            <xs:complexType name="movie">
                <xs:sequence>
                    <xs:element name="title" />
                    <xs:element name="review" />
                </xs:sequence>
            </xs:complexType>
</xs:element>
```

Add Data
Types

A primary feature of database applications and programming languages is the capability to define and enforce data types. That is, you can define a particular field in a database or variable in a program and say that it can only contain a certain kind of information, be that a string of text, or a type of number, or a date. XML schemas give you the ability to define data types for XML elements. There are a wide variety of data types available in schemas, but the most common are `string` for plain text, `int` for integers, `decimal` for numbers that contain decimal points, and `boolean` for true/false values.

After you have defined a data type for a particular element, the XML will not pass a validation test if the data in that element does not match the data type. It is a good idea to put a comment in the schema document

noting the data type to help you remember; however, if you plan to have others use the schema, it is perhaps best to create separate documentation that in part notes the required data type.

Data types are added to your schema through the `type` attribute. For complex type elements that contain a sequence or choice of nested elements, the `type` attribute is added to the innermost `xs:element` tag to define the data type of the children. Complex type elements that contain only simple content, and are thus only complex due to the presence of an attribute, use the `xs:extension` element with a `type` attribute to define the data type. Because the allowable values of the `type` attribute are actually specified in the schema of schemas, you must append the namespace prefix to the data type.

Add Data Types

① Open an XML Schema document.

② Add an opening `<xs:element>` tag.

③ Add an opening `<xs:complexType>` tag.

④ Add an opening `<xs:sequence>` or `<xs:choice>` tag.

⑤ Add one or more opening `<xs:element>` tags with appropriate names.

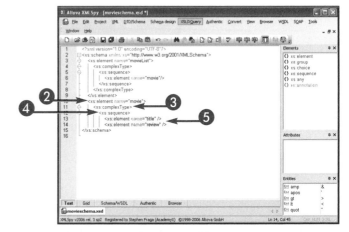

⑥ Add the `type` attribute to these tags.

⑦ Add the appropriate data type.

⑧ Close all open tags.

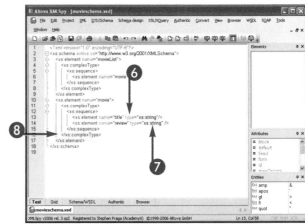

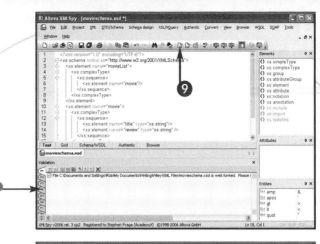

⑨ Click the Check Well-Formedness button to confirm that the document is well-formed.

● The Validation area opens to show if there are errors or no errors in the document.

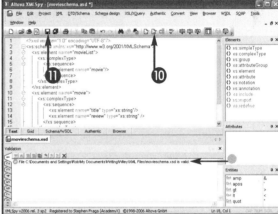

⑩ Click the Check Validity button to confirm that the document is valid.

● The Validation area confirms the validity of the document or states that it is not valid.

⑪ Click the Save button.

The file is saved.

Extra

Take care to ensure that you use the proper data type. One very common mistake is to use a numeric data type for elements such as phone numbers, zip codes, Social Security numbers, and other similar types of information. Although all of these do in fact contain numbers, most also use nonnumeric characters such as dashes that would not be valid in a numeric data typed field. As a general rule, only data that would be used for mathematical calculations, such as the price of an item or the quantity in stock, should be represented with numerical data types. Additionally, the W3C Schema provides for a wide variety of numerical data types, enabling you to specify the range of possible numbers, whether or not a decimal is allowed, and if so, the number of possible digits after the decimal point.

You will want to periodically check your schema document for both well-formedness and validity. Unlike regular XML documents, which should reference a schema but do not always need to, the schemas always reference the schema of schemas, so everything you do in this document should be validated. Many XML editors, including Altova XMLSpy, have a built-in validity checker, which greatly simplifies this process.

Add Attributes

Many of your elements will need attributes to further describe their content. Attributes are defined in the schema within a complex type element definition. If the element in question will only contain data, it is defined within the complex type using `xs:simpleContent`; if the element will contain other elements, it is defined with `xs:complexContent`. Within this element, you need to add an `xs:extension` element, wherein you will use the `base` attribute to set the data type of the value of the attribute, which will most often be either `xs:string` for text or `xs:int` for whole numbers.

Finally, within the `xs:extension` element, you use the `xs:attribute` element to define a name for the attribute. You can also add the `use` attribute to `xs:attribute`, which allows you to set the attribute to either `required`, `optional`, or `prohibited`.

At first, all of these nested tags can be overwhelming, but after you grow more accustomed to their use, things really will start making sense. In this case, I am saying that you will have a complex element that will contain simple contents, whose data type will be extended by an attribute whose value will be of a certain type. Past XML data definition languages lacked the verbose nature of schemas and were certainly easier to type, but they also lacked the flexibility provided by schemas.

It is necessary to add the data type through the `xs:extension` element when using attributes because the simple type definition does not allow it. In this case, you are actually extending the string data type to allow for the attribute, not the element itself. This is one of those highly technical details that can make truly understanding schemas extremely difficult.

Add Attributes

① Open an XML Schema document.

② Add a new `<xs:element>` tag.

③ Set `name` equal to the name of an element that contains an attribute.

④ Add a new `<xs:complexType>` tag.

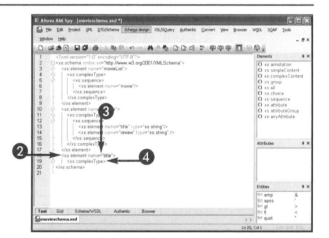

⑤ Add an `<xs:simpleContent>` tag.

⑥ Add an `<xs:extension>` element.

⑦ Set the `base` attribute of the `<xs:extension>` to an appropriate data type.

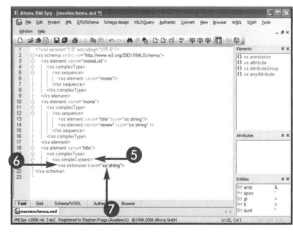

28

8. Add an `<xs:attribute>` element.

9. Set `name` to the name of the attribute.

10. Set `use` to the appropriate value.

11. Make the `<xs:attribute>` element self-closing by adding a slash before the closing angle bracket.

12. Close the `<xs:extension>` element.

13. Close the `<xs:simpleContent>` element.

14. Close the `<xs:complexType>` element.

15. Close the `<xs:element>` element.

16. Click the Check Well-Formedness button to confirm that the document is well-formed.

    The Validation area opens to show if there are errors or no errors in the document.

17. Click the Check Validity button to confirm that the document is valid.

● The Validation area confirms the validity of the document or states that it is not valid.

18. Click the Save button.

    The file is saved.

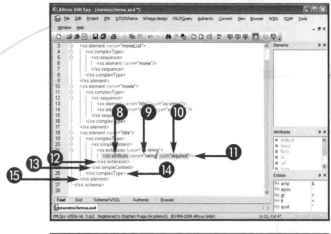

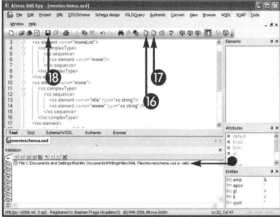

Apply It

It is possible to create attributes as a global declaration at the top of the schema, which can then be referenced throughout the document, by using the `xs:attributeGroup` tag:

```
<xs:attributeGroup name="fileattrs">
<xs:attribute name="path" type="xs:string" />
</xs:attributeGroup>
<xs:element name="filename">
                <xs:simpleContent>
                    <xs:extension base="xs:string">
                        <xs:attributeGroup ref="fileattrs" />
                    </xs:extension>
                </xs:simpleContent>
</xs:element>
```

Add Simple Elements

A t least some of the elements in your document are going to be simple elements. A simple element is one that does not have attributes and will only contain data. Simple elements are not nearly as common as they would seem, as you will find many more cases for elements to need either child elements or attributes or both to adequately describe them. However, when you do encounter an element that will only contain data, it is very easy to define in your XML schema, as follows:

```
<xs:element name="reviewAuthor"
type="xs:string" />
```

The `element` element used in this manner is always presented as an empty tag, so it is important to remember the trailing slash at the end.

The only thing that you must provide for a simple element is the `name`. The `type` attribute is optional. However, it does provide important additional data and will most likely always be present. You may also choose to provide `minOccurs` and `maxOccurs` attributes to set the minimum and maximum number of allowed occurrences of the element.

Except when being defined within a sequence element, the exact order in which elements are defined in the schema is unimportant. Some developers define the elements in the order in which they will appear in the XML, whereas others prefer to define all the complex type elements first, followed by the simple type elements. You should use whichever method will make the most sense to you.

Add Simple Elements

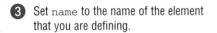

1 Open an XML Schema document.

2 Add another element directly nested under `<xs:schema>`.

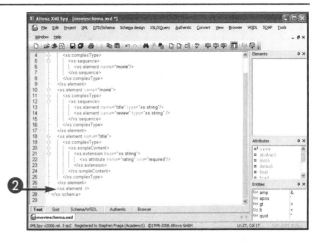

3 Set `name` to the name of the element that you are defining.

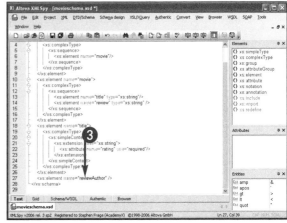

④ Add a `type` attribute, setting it to an appropriate value.

⑤ Click the Check Well-Formedness button to confirm that the document is well-formed.

● The Validation area opens to show if there are errors or no errors in the document.

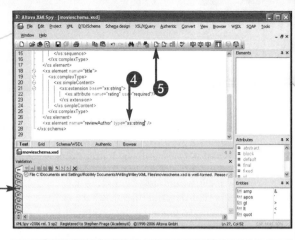

⑥ Click the Check Validity button to confirm that the document is valid.

● The Validation area confirms the validity of the document or states that it is not valid.

⑦ Click the Save button.

The file is saved.

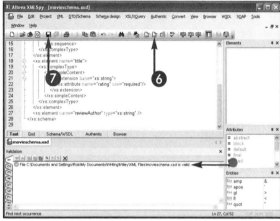

Extra

You can further restrict the use of data in your XML by using facets, which extend the built-in data types. There are eight facets built in to the schema, but the most useful are those that restrict the lengths of strings, provide for a set of default values, and restrict ranges of numbers. All these facets are defined using the `xs:restriction` element.

`xs:maxLength` and `xs:minLength` can be used on the string data type to set maximum and minimum lengths for that string. One or more `xs:enumeration` elements can be used to provide set choices from which the value can be selected. Finally, the `xs:minInclusive`, `xs:maxInclusive`, `xs:minExclusive`, and `xs:maxExclusive` elements allow you to set ranges in which numeric data must lie.

```
<xs:element name="password">
<xs:simpleType>
                <xs:restriction base="xs:string">
                    <xs:minLength value="8" />
                    <xs:maxLength value="16" />
                </xs:restriction>
</xs:simpleType>
</xs:element>
```

Add Mixed Elements

Complex type elements are those that contain other elements instead of data. There is, however, a subclass of complex type elements, known as mixed elements, that can contain both data and other elements. Consider an example of a movie review. Although the review itself would just be text, it may contain other elements that describe the structure of the review, such as something to denote a paragraph or a heading within the review, or elements that reference other data, such as marking the title of the film in some way when used within the review, such as the following:

```
<review><para><title>Serenity</title> is the continuation of the canceled TV show <title>Firefly</title>.</para></review>
```

In this example, the review element contains another element, para. The para element, however, contains both another element, title, as well as otherwise

unmarked text. This element would need to be defined in the schema as a mixed type element.

Mixed type elements are still defined as complex type but then further described as a mixed type. The mixed type will usually contain a choice of other elements, as well as a definition of the type of data it can contain:

```
<xs:element name="para">

    <xs:complexType mixed="true">

        <xs:choice>

            <xs:element name="title" />

        </xs:choice>

    </xs:complexType>

</xs:element>
```

Add Mixed Elements

① Open an XML Schema document.

② Add an opening `<xs:element>` tag.

③ Set the name of the element.

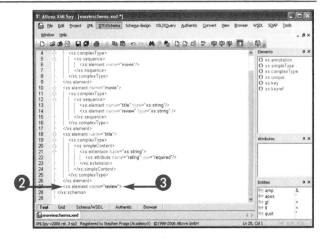

④ Add an opening `<xs:complexType>` tag.

⑤ Add the `mixed="true"` attribute.

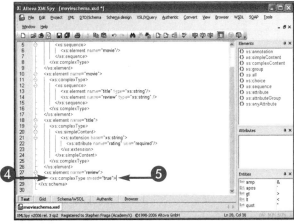

6 Add an opening `<xs:choice>` tag.

7 Add two or more `<xs:element>` elements for the child tags.

8 Close the `<xs:choice>` element.

9 Close the `<xs:complexType>` element.

10 Close the `<xs:element>` element.

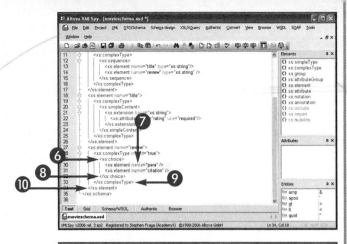

11 Click the Check Well-Formedness button to confirm that the document is well-formed.

The Validation area opens to show if there are errors or no errors in the document.

12 Click the Check Validity button to confirm that the document is valid.

● The Validation area confirms the validity of the document or states that it is not valid.

13 Click the Save button.

The file is saved.

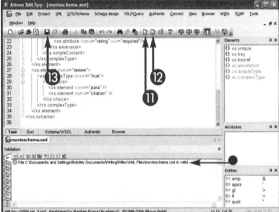

Extra

In addition to giving a choice of elements through `xs:choice`, you can also use `xs:sequence` or `xs:all`. The first tag, `xs:choice`, provides a list of mutually exclusive elements, one of which must be provided. `xs:sequence` specifies that each of the elements must be given, in the exact order as they are listed in the schema. `xs:all`, on the other hand, states that each of the elements listed must appear once, and only once, but they can appear in any order. If you use `xs:all`, it must be defined at the top of the schema document and is most often used within the root element's definition.

Each of these selectors are commonly found on mixed element declarations, but they need not be. They can and often are used on complex type definitions that will contain only other elements, such as the root. The only thing that creates a mixed content element is the presence of the mixed attribute of the `xs:complexType` element. It is up to the schema developer to determine which is the most appropriate for the element in question.

Restrict the Recurrence of Elements

Often, you will want to give those who are creating documents from your schema the flexibility to use child elements as often as they want to. Sometimes, however, you may have to limit the number of times an element can be used. For example, if you were storing the roster of a major league baseball team in XML, you would need to limit the number of players listed to 25.

In XML schemas, you have the ability to set both a minimum and a maximum number of occurrences of an element. In the case of the baseball roster example, it would not be enough to set a maximum for the players to 25 because that number is also the minimum number of players allowed. In the `xs:element` element, you can use the `minOccurs` and `maxOccurs` attributes to enforce these limits.

If you want to make a child element optional, you should set `minOccurs` to a value of zero. If you want to allow the developer to use as many occurrences of an element as they want to, you should set `maxOccurs` to a value of `unbounded`. You can also set either or both of them to a specific number. It is legal to set them to the same number to set an exact number of occurrences. The default value for both attributes is one, so if you do not specify these, the element will be required, with a minimum occurrence of one, and will not be repeatable, with a maximum of one. By definition, the root element of the document is required and cannot be repeated, so these attributes are not allowed when defining the root. They can be used on any other element declaration in the document, however.

Restrict the Recurrence of Elements

① Open an XML Schema document.

② Add an opening `<xs:element>` tag or use an existing opening `<xs:element>` tag.

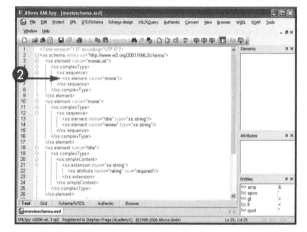

③ Add a `minOccurs` attribute.

④ Set the value of `minOccurs` to either 0 to make the element optional or a number to set the minimum number of times the element can occur.

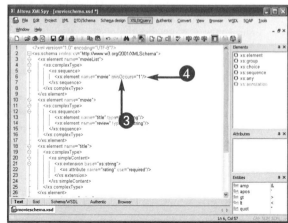

⑤ Add a maxOccurs attribute.

⑥ Set the value of maxOccurs to either "unbounded" or a number.

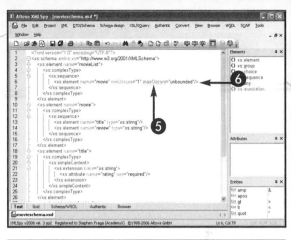

⑦ Click the Check Well-Formedness button to confirm that the document is well-formed.

The Validation area opens to show if there are errors or no errors in the document.

⑧ Click the Check Validity button to confirm that the document is valid.

● The Validation area confirms the validity of the document or states that it is not valid.

⑨ Save the document with an .xsd file extension.

The file is saved.

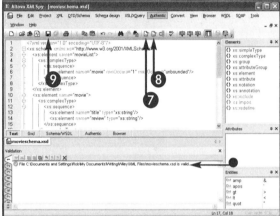

Extra

Careful planning is the key to creating a successful schema. XML documents are case-sensitive, and although your schema document has a special file extension, it is still XML. Whatever casing you use in your schema must be used throughout all XML documents created from it. Therefore, it is absolutely critical that you devise one method of capitalization and stick to it throughout the document. You should also decide from the very beginning whether you want to use dashes or underscores to separate the words in multiword element names, or mixed casing, or some other naming scheme. Then be sure to be consistent throughout the schema. Otherwise, the documents you create based on this schema will be extremely difficult to code.

You must also carefully plan out the use of minOccurs and maxOccurs. Consider any special cases that may arise in which it would be legal to have more or fewer of a particular element than would be considered "normal." You want to be sure that you do not force your into a "hack" to get around an overly tight restriction in the schema. At the same time, however, you need to make sure that the schema is sufficiently restrictive to give you the best possible guarantee of good data.

Link Your XML to Your Schema

After you have created your schema, you need to link your XML documents to it, so the validator knows where to look for the schema. Any number of XML documents can be linked to a single schema.

To point the parser at the proper schema document, you need to add an attribute to the root element of your XML. Generally, this will be the noNamespaceSchemaLocation attribute. However, by adding this attribute to your root element, you would in effect be making the document invalid, as this attribute would not be defined in the schema itself. This problem is easily rectified by declaring the noNamespaceSchemaLocation attribute as being part of its own namespace; namely, the W3C XMLSchema-instance namespace, which exists primarily to give developers access to this attribute.

Therefore, in order to properly "attach" an XML document to a schema, you first need to declare the schema instance namespace, which is usually defined with the xsi prefix. Then you can use the noNamespaceSchemaLocation attribute from that namespace to provide the path to your schema document.

The actual path used to point to the schema can be document-relative or an absolute path. If you are using the Web, you can also provide a site-root relative path.

Here is an example of a properly formed root element pointing to a schema in the same directory:

```
<myRoot xmlns:xsi="http://www.w3.org/2001/
XMLSchema-instance"
xsi:noNamespaceSchemaLocation=
"mySchema.xsd" >
```

Link Your XML to Your Schema

① Open an XML document that will be based on a schema.

② In the root element, add the xmlns attribute.

③ Add the xsi prefix.

④ Set the value of the attribute to the path **http://www.w3.org/2001/ XMLSchema-instance**.

Note: *Pay close attention to the casing of this path.*

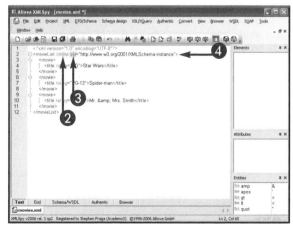

⑤ Add the `xsi:noNamespaceSchemaLocation` attribute.

Note: *Again, watch the case of this attribute.*

⑥ Set the value of the attribute to the path to the schema's .xsd document.

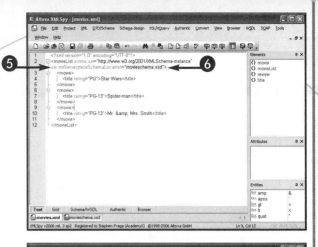

⑦ Click the Check Well-Formedness button to confirm that the document is well-formed.

The Validation area opens to show if there are errors or no errors in the document.

⑧ Click the Check Validity button to confirm that the document is valid.

● The Validation area confirms the validity of the document or states that it is not valid.

⑨ Save the document with an .xsd file extension.

The file is saved.

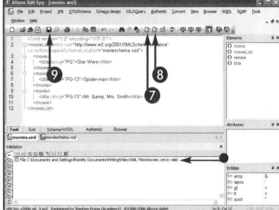

Apply It

If your document uses elements from another namespace, you will need to reference the schema for that namespace by using the `xsi:schemaLocation` attribute instead of, or in addition to, the `xsi:noNamespaceSchemaLocation` attribute.

```
<movieList xmlns:xsi="http://www.w3.org/2001/XMLSchema-instance"
xsi:noNamespaceSchemaLocation="movieListSchema.xsd"
xsi:schemaLocation="http://www.someothersite.com/a-schema.xsd" >
```

Check the Validity of the Document

It is very important to remember that although all parsers check for a document's well-formedness by default, few will automatically validate the document, even when an explicit link to a schema is provided.

Every parser has a slightly different method for validating documents. XMLSpy has a toolbar button to check the validity, but it also validates the document whenever you save and will display a warning message if you attempt to save a document that is not valid. Although the message provides for the option to save anyway, it is recommended that you fix any errors immediately so that they do not get forgotten and cause other issues later. Neither Microsoft Internet Explorer nor Mozilla Firefox have built-in validators, but both have free extensions available for download that add

validation capabilities. Other parsers, such as Microsoft Office products, generally allow you to begin working with the XML but will later decide on the need to validate and return errors if such validation fails.

Although parsers usually ignore validation issues initially, invalid documents will fail to work or be interpreted correctly, so processes such as transforming XML using XSLT will fail or produce unexpected results. Therefore, it is extremely important that you always check the validity of every XML document before attempting to use it and immediately fix any validation issues. The exact method of handling a validation error will vary greatly from parser to parser. Some will treat the error as little more than an informational warning, whereas others will consider it a fatal error and refuse to proceed until the document is fixed.

Check the Validity of the Document

CHECK VALIDITY IN XMLSPY

1. If necessary, declare the `XMLSchema-instance` namespace.

2. If necessary, use the `xsi:noNamespaceSchema Location` attribute to add a reference to a schema.

3. Click the Check Well-Formedness button.

   The Validation area opens to show if there are errors or no errors in the document.

4. Click the Check Validity button.

- The Validation area confirms the validity of the document or states that it is not valid.

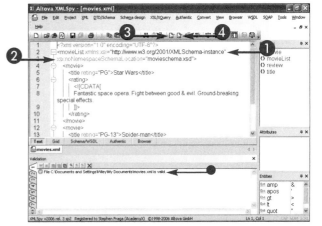

CHECK VALIDITY IN INTERNET EXPLORER

1. Download and install the Internet Explorer Tools for Validating XML and Viewing XSLT Output from www.microsoft.com/downloads/details.aspx?Family Id=D23C1D2C-1571-4D61-BDA8-ADF9F6849DF9&displaylang=en.

2. Open an XML document that contains a reference to a schema in the browser.

3. Right-click the document.

4. Click Validate XML.

   A message appears, stating if there are errors or no errors in the document.

CHECK VALIDITY IN MOZILLA FIREFOX

1. Download and install the Firefox XML validator from https://addons.mozilla.org/en-US/firefox/addon/2897.

2. Click Validation.

3. Click Validation.

   The DecisionSoft XML Schema Validator window opens.

4. Click Browse.

5. Navigate to and click the schema document.

6. Click Open.

7. Click Browse.

8. Repeat steps **5** and **6** for the XML document.

9. Click Validate.

   The Schema Validator window updates.

10. Click Click Here.

    The validation results are shown.

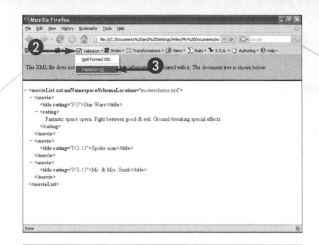

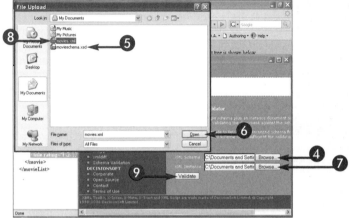

Extra

Many other validation tools for Internet Explorer and Firefox, and for other browsers such as Apple's Safari or the Opera browser, are also available. Note that most validators are only capable of comparing the document to a W3C Schema or a DTD. If you are using some other schema such as RELAX NG, you will need to find a validator that is appropriate to that language.

SorceForge.net, a Web site devoted to making open-source software available, has many alternative validators available. In addition, there are many more editors and parsers available, written in a wide variety of languages and serving many different purposes, from SourceForge.net. Although a selection of commercial software can be found there, most of the selections available from the site are completely free. The SourceForge Web site's built-in search engine includes a ranking system to give you an idea of how likely the result is to match your search. Although some SourceForge.net software can be difficult to install and configure, it has a very active developer's forum to give you assistance.

Build a Schema Visually Using XMLSpy

Altova XMLSpy is an extremely powerful application that can dramatically reduce the time required to create XML documents, XSL style sheets, and schemas. When you open a schema in XMLSpy, the program defaults to a Schema Design view that allows you to build the schema visually while XMLSpy writes the necessary code for you. Features like this are a large part of the reason why many professional XML developers rely on XMLSpy for their daily workflow.

The Schema Design view has two modes: the Schema overview and the Content Model view. The Schema overview is itself divided into sections, with the top half of the main window showing a list of all the elements defined in the schema, and the bottom showing any attributes or constraints applied to the selected element. A group of panels on the right side of the screen enables you to

browse through the elements in the schema, provides details of the elements, and lists any facets applied.

The Schema Design view includes many other features to simplify the process of creating schemas, including the ability to reorder the elements in the schema through drag and drop and right-click contextual menus for copying and pasting elements in the schema or from other schema documents.

The Content Model view provides a simple diagram view showing the relationships between the elements in the schema, which can greatly facilitate understanding complex schemas. This view enables you to navigate visually through your schema from one node to the next. You can drag and drop within this view to rearrange the nodes relationship to one another, and the view itself is easily configurable.

Build a Schema Visually Using XMLSpy

① In Altova XMLSpy, click File → New.

The Create New Document dialog box opens.

② From the list of file types, scroll to the bottom and click xsd W3C XML Schema.

③ Click OK.

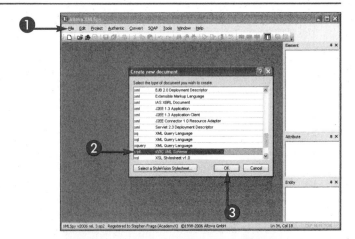

A new schema document is created.

④ Replace the text ENTER_NAME _OF_ROOT_ELEMENT_HERE with the name of your root element.

⑤ Click the Content Model View icon.

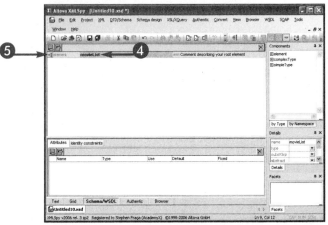

The Content Model view is displayed.

6 Right-click in the window.

7 Click Add Child.

8 Click Sequence.

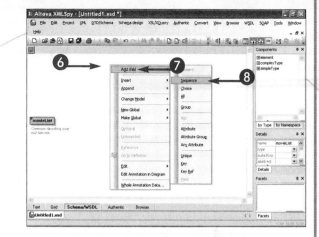

• A sequence compositor is added.

9 Right-click in the window.

10 Click Add Child.

11 Click Element.

A new element is added.

12 Enter the name of the child element.

13 Right-click the child element.

14 Click Unbounded.

• The view updates to show that the element can have an infinite number of occurrences.

15 Click the Show Globals icon.

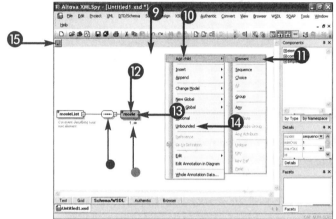

Extra

You will notice that XMLSpy adds `xs:annotation` and `xs:documentation` elements to the schema. These elements are not used by the parser to validate XML; instead, they provide you with a way to embed notes about your schema and XML directly into the schema file itself.

Using the annotation and documentation elements is safer than embedding this information into the schema with XML comments because although comments are allowed, some parsers may choose to remove them at runtime. Having them embedded with actual markup guarantees that they will remain intact and further gives you the opportunity to use the markup to generate self-documenting applications.

Almost any schema element can take the annotation element as a child, and it in turn supports the documentation child element. The text in the documentation element should be a human-readable block of information that adequately describes the element in question, including details such as optional and required attributes, data type, and repeatability.

continued

T
he Schema overview mode of the Schema Design view enables you to select globally defined elements and attributes from a simple list. The program will display any attributes or identity constraints for the selected item in helper windows below the list, making it very easy to set data types, usage constraints, and default or fixed values for those attributes. You can insert, append, or delete global elements and complex types by simply adding them to the table in the top section of the Schema overview mode. By selecting a global or complex type, you can add or modify its parameters from the helper window.

The Content Model view also provides helper windows for selected elements, allowing you to modify its properties. Although only one global or complex type can be displayed at a time, you can easily jump from one to another. It supports cut or copy and paste to add or move objects, and a rich context menu makes it easy to work in the mode.

Creating complex type elements with restrictions can often be difficult in a pure-code view, as it is easy to forget or become confused about the restrictions. XMLSpy's visual editor makes this process much simpler, providing tools that allow you to visualize the restrictions, as well as giving you hints on possible restrictions to add.

The application also enables you to customize the display of the schema, choosing which parameters should be displayed, so you can hide the display of items that you know you will not use. It also allows you to import definitions from other namespaces and globally redefine components of the schema. It will also automatically generate a schema from a DTD, another schema, or relational databases.

Build a Schema Visually Using XMLSpy *(continued)*

The Schema Design view is displayed.

16 Click the Insert icon.

17 Click Element.

A new element is added.

18 Type in the name of the child element that you added in step **12**.

19 Click this icon next to the new element.

The Content Model view is displayed.

20 Right-click in the window.

21 Click Add Child.

22 Click Sequence.

● A sequence compositor is added.

23 Right-click in the window.

24 Click Add Child.

25 Click Element to add a new element.

26 Enter the name of the child element.

27 Right-click the child element.

28 Click Unbounded.

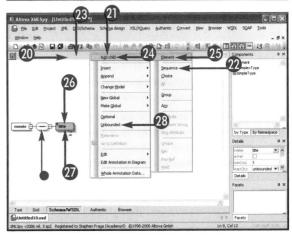

The view updates to show that the element can have an infinite number of occurrences.

㉙ In the Details entry helper, click the `type` down arrow and select `xs:string`.

㉚ Right-click the sequence compositor.

㉛ Click Add Child.

㉜ Click Element.

A new element is added.

㉝ Enter the name of the child element.

㉞ Click the Text tab.

The text view of the schema is displayed.

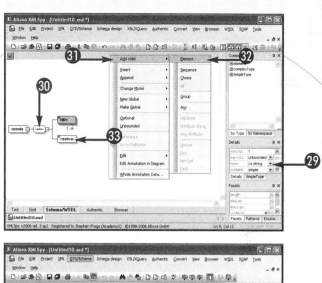

Extra

Although the `xs:annotation` and `xs:documentation` elements added by XMLSpy help others use your schema, it is often necessary to create separate, detailed documentation. Separate documentation is helpful in almost any case, but it is particularly necessary if you plan to publish your schema for general public use.

XMLSpy contains an automatic documentation generator. By filling out a simple dialog box, you can have the application create a detailed document that explains everything users will need in order to create valid XML from your schema. You can choose to include or exclude global and local elements, groups, complex and simple types, and attributes. For each of these, you can have the application generate a graphical diagram similar to its Content Model view, including the node's properties, namespace, children, type, attributes, and many more details. You can also include the actual source code of the relevant portion of the schema. This documentation can be generated as either HTML or a Microsoft Word document.

Introducing DTDs

Before the World Wide Consortium finished developing the XML Schema language, developers needed a way to define XML documents. Although many standards were proposed, most developers relied on an older method known as Document Type Definitions, or DTDs. DTDs and schemas serve the exact same purpose: They both allow you to prescribe the rules for creating XML documents by setting which elements will be included in your document, in what order those elements should appear, and what attributes, if any, they should contain. However, DTDs and schemas vary greatly in their syntax and flexibility.

One of the more challenging aspects of creating a DTD is that it will be written in a non-XML format originally inherited from the Standard Generalized Markup Language (SGML) on which XML is based. Therefore, to create an XML document that validates against a DTD, you must learn and write in two entirely different languages. However, DTDs will tend to be considerably less verbose than XML schemas, and thus you will be able to develop them much more rapidly.

Although most developers agree that it is far better to use the more powerful and robust XML Schema language, it is nonetheless important to understand DTDs because you are likely to encounter them in legacy documents.

Schemas versus DTDs

In addition to the issue of DTDs using a different syntax from schemas, the latter has several advantages over DTDs:

- Schemas allow developers to specify the exact number of occurrences of an element. DTDs only allow you to say that a item is repeatable or not.

- Schemas allow for data typing, which is simply not supported in DTDs.

- Schemas support namespaces, which DTDs do not, enabling you to easily build off of other existing schemas instead of having to create everything from scratch.

- Schemas support embedded documentation, which DTDs do not.

Existing DTDs

Many Web developers are actually already familiar with DTDs, even if they have never encountered the term before, because HTML and XHTML are in fact defined by DTDs. Both HTML 4.01 and XHTML 1 have three DTDs from which you can work: Transitional, Strict, and Frameset. There are now many Web sites that will validate your Web page against the appropriate DTD, and some Web design tools, such as Adobe Dreamweaver CS3, have validators built in to the software.

DTD Support

DTDs are more widely supported than schemas, which remains the best reason to learn them. Any XML-aware application is going to support DTDs, whereas only newer parsers are likely to correctly implement schemas. The first versions of Microsoft Office that were XML-aware, for example, could only validate XML against a DTD.

General DTD Syntax

The general syntax for DTDs relies on three primary declarations: one for elements, one for attributes, and one for entities. A simple DTD may look like this:

```
<!ELEMENT movieList (movie+)>
<!ELEMENT movie (title, review)>
<!ELEMENT title(#PCDATA)>
<!ATTLIST title rating #CDATA #REQUIRED>
```

Note that all keywords from the DTD syntax are capitalized.

DTD Location

DTDs are usually stored in a file separate from the XML, which facilitates reusing the same DTD on many pages. It is possible, however, to create an embedded DTD, whereby all the DTD information is stored in the same file as the XML. This obviously limits the DTD's usefulness but can often be helpful in initial development, as you only need to work with a single document.

If you use an external DTD, it is an accepted practice to save the file with a .dtd extension. Although the XML specification does not actually require this, most editors will not properly recognize the DTD if it does not have this extension. The file may be stored anywhere, as you can provide a relative, local, or remote address to it.

Whitespace in DTDs

DTDs are completely whitespace insensitive, so your only consideration is readability. Although it is generally considered best to place each declaration on its own line, this is not required. Longer declarations can be written to span multiple lines if it improves the readability of the document. Whitespace can be added within the declaration as well, and some developers prefer to tab between the element name and the data in the parentheses, thus nicely lining up all the parenthetical data. This is again purely a matter of personal style and taste.

Referencing External DTDs on XML Pages

You use the DOCTYPE declaration on XML pages to reference a particular DTD. The syntax for the DTD is as follows:

```
<!DOCTYPE root_element LOCATION "path_to_DTD">
```

The !DOCTYPE is simply the declaration's identifier. Following this is a case-sensitive reference to the XML file's root element. Next, there is a keyword identifying the location of the DTD, which can be either SYSTEM if the DTD file is on the same local system as the XML file or PUBLIC if on a remote Web server. Finally, a path to the DTD file is provided.

Embedded DTDs

Should you decide to create an embedded DTD, you follow the same general syntax for the element, attribute, and entity declarations. However, you will wrap all the declarations within the DOCTYPE's declaration:

```
<!DOCTYPE root_element [
<!ELEMENT element_name (children)>
<!--etc-->
]>
<!--XML document -->
```

Embedded DTDs follow the same rules in regards to whitespace as with external DTDs, so the preceding declaration could be written in a single line if you preferred, although again, readability should be a primary consideration.

Comments in DTDs

DTDs allow for the same commenting syntax as normal XML, so you can begin the comment with the left-angle bracket, followed by an exclamation point and two dashes, and end the comment with two dashes and the right-angle bracket. Comments can span as many lines as needed. It is recommended that you place a comment towards the top of the DTD with general information such as the purpose and author of the DTD and then comment any relevant lines that would not be clear by themselves.

Create a Simple DTD

DTDs are made up of a series of declarations. The order in which the declarations are written is irrelevant to their function. Some developers prefer to list all elements first, in the order they would likely appear in the XML document, and then any attributes, and finally any entities, whereas others prefer to list elements and their attributes together.

Elements are declared with the !ELEMENT declaration. You provide the name of the element in question, followed by the element's contents in parentheses. If the element will contain other elements, you provide either a comma-separated list of those in the order they must appear or a choice of elements separated by the pipe character. If the element will contain string data, you use the #PCDATA keyword, which stands for *parsed character data* and represents any string of letters, numbers, whitespace, and entities.

You can also specify whether child elements are required or optional, and repeatable or not, through a series of special delimiters. Listing the child with no delimiter means that the child is both required and not repeatable; a plus sign states that the child is required and may be repeated; a question mark denotes that the child is optional and cannot be repeated; and an asterisk marks the child as optional and repeatable. If you use either the plus or the asterisk, you cannot restrict the exact number of possible repetitions — DTDs allow for one or more, or zero or more, but nothing more specific than that.

Create a Simple DTD

① Open your XML editor to a new page.

● To do so in Altova XMLSpy, you click the New Document button, choose Extensible Markup Language as the type of document, and click OK.

② Type the XML prolog.

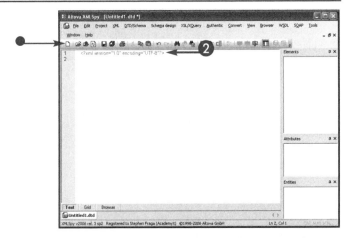

③ Type an !ELEMENT declaration.

④ Add the name of an element that will contain child elements.

⑤ Add a set of parentheses.

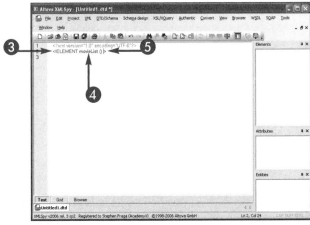

6 Inside the parentheses, add a comma-separated list of child elements.

7 Add a delimiter to denote whether each child is optional or required and repeatable or not.

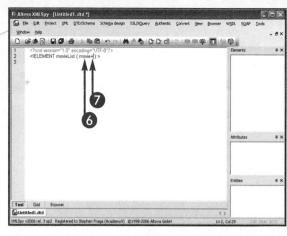

8 Add another `!ELEMENT` declaration for each child element defined in step **6**.

9 Add either lists of the child's children or `#PCDATA` designations.

10 Click File → Save.

Note: *Make sure that you save the document with a .dtd extension.*

The file is saved.

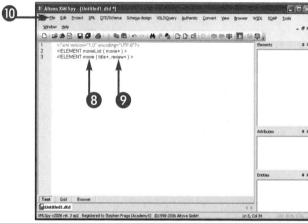

Extra

It is possible to designate elements as containing mixed data, or both child elements and content, by using the choice syntax:

```
<!ELEMENT review (#PCDATA | title*)>
```

This example states that the review element can contain either parsed character data or zero or more child `title` elements.

You can also nest choices of elements by providing nested parentheses:

```
<!ELEMENT address (street, city, (state | province))
```

In this case, the `address` element has a single required `street` element, followed by a single required `city` element, followed by either a single `state` element or a single `province` element. Be careful to close all open parentheses when performing nested operations like this.

Add Attributes

Attributes for elements can be created in DTDs by using the !ATTLIST declaration, in which you provide the name of the element that will contain the attribute, followed by the name of the attribute, followed by a statement as to the kind of information that the attribute will contain. DTDs support ten types of attribute values: CDATA, NMTOKEN, NMTOKENS, enumeration, ENTITY, ENTITIES, ID, IDREF, IDREFS, and NOTATION. In practice, only CDATA, NMTOKEN, and enumeration are commonly used. CDATA states that the value of the attribute will be a string of text, possibly containing whitespace characters. NMTOKEN states that the value will be a single word, with no whitespace. Enumeration enables you as the DTD developer to provide a list of possible values for the attribute, with each possible value separated by a pipe character.

After stating the attribute type, you need an additional keyword to set the attribute default. The three possible keywords are #REQUIRED, in which case the attribute must always be present, but no exact default value is given; #IMPLIED, which makes the attribute optional and again does not provide a default value; #FIXED, in which the attribute always has exactly one value, whether it is expressed present in the XML or not; or a quoted literal string.

A full attribute declaration might look like this:

```
<!ATTLIST title rating (G | PG | PG-13 | R | NR) #REQUIRED >
```

An attribute with a fixed value would look like this:

```
<!ATTLIST document initialVersion CDATA #FIXED "1.0">
```

Add Attributes

1. Open a DTD document.

2. Add an ATTLIST declaration.

3. Specify the name of the element that will contain the attribute.

4. Specify the name of the attribute.

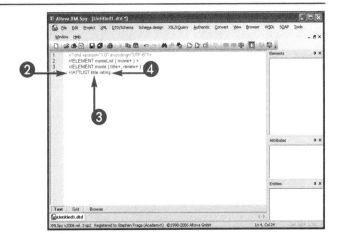

5. Set the attribute type.

6. Set the attribute default.

7. Click File → Save.

The document is saved.

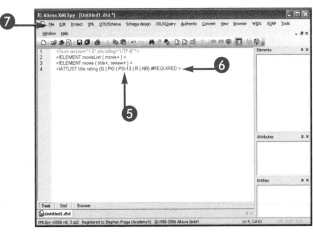

Add Entities

When creating longer XML documents, it is reasonable to assume that there will be a certain amount of repetition within the data. You may have a list of employees' addresses, and because most of your employees are likely to live in a few cities and are likely to all live in the same state, you will need to enter that data over and over.

DTDs enable you to define your own general entities to use as shortcuts in your XML. You use the !ENTITY declaration to create a custom entity and provide the code for the entity, followed by its literal equivalent. Then the XML can reference the entity by preceding the code with the ampersand character and suffixing it with a semicolon.

So, the entity declaration in the DTD

`<!ENTITY company "The ACME Corporation">`

would allow for this code in the XML:

`<ourWork>&company;</ourWork>`

Parsers would correctly interpret the entity and replace &company; with The ACME Corporation. Some visually based parsers, such as Web browsers, will display the entity's replacement directly.

XML has five built-in entities, for the right and left angle brackets, the ampersand, the double-quotation mark, and the apostrophe. It is not necessary to declare any of them in your DTD.

Entities can be used in the value of an attribute, as long as the attribute type allows for the characters from the entity, such as CDATA.

Add Entities

① Open a DTD document.

② Add an !ENTITY declaration.

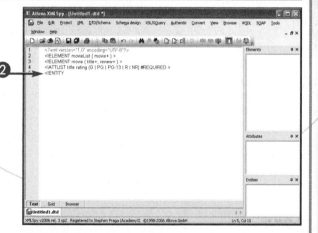

③ Add the name of the entity.

④ Add the replacement string for the entity.

⑤ Click File → Save.

The document is saved.

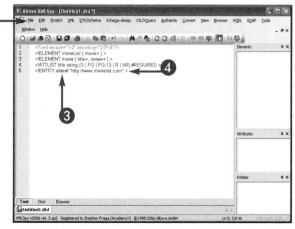

Using Parameter Entities

General entities provide shortcuts within your XML document itself, but you will just as often encounter the need to use shortcuts with your DTD. For example, you may have one attribute that can be used in many elements. XHTML provides many examples of this: The `class`, `id`, `style`, and `title` attributes are valid in almost every XHTML element. Rather than redefining the attribute for each element, you can create a parameter entity to represent the attribute to simplify defining it. More common is the situation in which you have an element that can be the child of many other elements. Again, XHTML is full of examples of this. Almost every element that is a valid child of the body element is also a valid child of the `div`, `td`, `form`, and many other elements. Instead of having to list that element over and over as a child, you can reference a parameter entity instead.

In addition to saving initial development time, parameter entities make your code easier to update: If you need to change the name of an attribute or element, you can do so in one place, and that change will affect every element that uses the attribute. Also, using a parameter entity reduces the likelihood of errors that may be introduced by having to retype the actual attribute or element name over and over.

The syntax for creating a parameter entity is the same as that for creating general entities, except that you use a percent sign before the code for the entity and repeat the use of the percent sign in referencing the entity. The code for the parameter can be any characters that would be legal in whatever context it is used. A comma-separated list can be provided to give a series of possible values, any of which could be used in place of the entity. Parameter entities should be created at the top of the DTD, before any declarations.

Using Parameter Entities

1 Open a DTD document.

2 Near the top of the document, add an entity declaration.

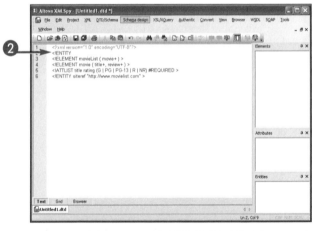

3 Add a percent sign.

4 Add the entity name that the parameter will reference.

5 Add the code for the parameter.

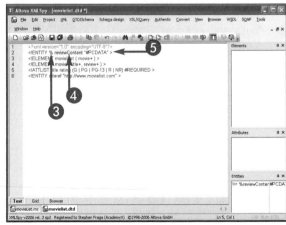

6 Create a new element declaration.

7 Reference the entity as a child of the new element.

8 Click File → Save.

The document is saved.

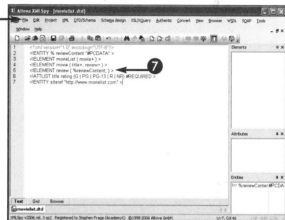

Apply It

You can add entities for special characters, similar to what you find in XHTML, but providing the ACSII numerical code equivalent for the character as the replacement string in your DTD, as in the following:

```
<!ENTITY nbsp    " ">
<!ENTITY copy    "&#169;">
<!ENTITY reg     "&#174;">
<!ENTITY trade   "&#8482;">
<!ENTITY frac14  "&#188;">
<!ENTITY frac12  "&#189;">
```

These can be used in either parameter or general entities.

Introducing RELAX NG

While the W3C was working on their specification for schemas, several other organizations developed alternatives. Although most of those alternatives, such as Microsoft's XML-Data Reduced, have been abandoned by both their developers and the community, several have survived and continued to thrive. RELAX NG, which stands for Regular Language for XML Next Generation, is one of those. It has been adopted by many document-centric XML developers, such as those behind the OpenDocument project.

As compared to the W3C Schema, RELAX NG has several advantages. It is a much simpler language and thus much easier to learn. It has an XML-based syntax and a condensed non-XML syntax. It fully supports many of the advanced features of the W3C Schema, including namespaces, data types, and complex definition references.

However, RELAX NG is still not as widely adopted as the W3C Schema, and many parsers and editors do not recognize it, so care should be taken to ensure full software support before developing applications that rely on RELAX NG.

The Simple Approach to Validation

A common criticism of the W3C Schema language is that it is too complex and tries to do too many things. DTDs are strictly about defining the structure of an XML document. Schemas define the structure, but at the same time they enable developers to put limits on what kinds of information can exist in tags, check the integrity of Internet references, bind XML documents to complex objects, and model complex ideas. Although this makes schemas very powerful, it is a big part of the reason for their complexity. The developers of RELAX NG wanted to merely update the ideals behind the DTD and kept the focus of the language strictly on validation. Therefore, you will not find many of the more complex features of the W3C model in RELAX NG. Whether this is a good or bad thing depends on whom you ask, but in general, if you are looking for a straightforward way to define the structure of your XML, and nothing more, then RELAX NG will work for you. If the complexity of the W3C Schema is needed, it is available to be used.

RELAX NG XML Syntax

The XML-based syntax of RELAX NG offers a so-called "Russian doll" version and a condensed version. The "Russian doll" version enables the developer to define the XML's root element and then define each nested element within it, with those nested elements containing other nested elements. Although this syntax can become difficult to manage, particularly with large documents, it does closely resemble the structure of the actual XML file.

The condensed version allows for easier definitions of recursive elements, and more closely resembles the structure of W3C Schema documents, in which child elements are defined separately from the parent elements.

RELAX NG Compact Syntax

The compact syntax, which does not use XML, more closely resembled the syntax used by DTDs. Although it is every bit as powerful of the XML syntax, some developers may find its considerably less verbose structure easier to work with.

RELAX NG File Extensions

RELAX NG files should end with .rng if they use the XML-based regular syntax or .rnc if they use the compact syntax. Although neither of these is required, parsers that are compliant with RELAX NG may not properly recognize the document if these extensions are not used.

Editors and Validators

Most mainstream XML editors and validators only recognize the official W3C formats. However, many open-source projects have adopted RELAX NG and created their own tools for its use. Most of the validators available are built on Java; many only work on Linux systems. Almost all are available under various open-source licenses. There are a handful of editors available as well, including the open-source, Java-based xmloperator, and commercial products from Topologi Collaborative Markup Editor and oXygen. The RELAX NG home page at www.relaxng.org has links to these and other tools for using the language.

Namespaces

RELAX NG treats namespaces in essentially the same way as XML does. In particular, XML documents do not assume that the namespace actually exists or points to anything. In the W3C Schema, however, any declared namespace must be "real." RELAX NG takes the XML approach and treats namespace-denoted elements as somehow unique, but they do not have to be attached to an actual namespace.

It is possible to define all the RELAX NG elements as coming from a namespace. The root element of the document will contain an xmlns attribute referencing the RELAX NG definition document, so this could have a namespace prefix attached to it, and then that prefix can be used on each element. This can be particularly important if your XML document may contain elements with the same names as RELAX NG elements, such as text or data.

Key RELAX NG Elements

There are several elements in RELAX NG that are worth noting.

\<grammar\>	**\<element\>**
The grammar element is frequently used as the root element of a RELAX NG document. If used, it will have an xmlns attribute pointing to the main RELAX NG schema at http://relaxng.org/ns/structure/1.0.	Sometimes used as the root element of a document, this key element is used to provide the names for elements in the XML and will generally be used as a container to further describe the element.
\<start\>	**\<oneOrMore\> and \<zeroOrMore\>**
If using the grammar element as the root, the start element will immediately follow grammar, with the element definitions nested within it.	Child elements of the element element, oneOrMore and zeroOrMore enable the developer to specify the frequency of the children of the element being defined.
	\<text\>
	An element that represents textual data to be placed within an element.

Create a RELAX NG Document in XML

RELAX NG supports the use of a "regular" syntax, which uses XML. This in turn has a structured "Russian doll" syntax and a compact syntax. The "Russian doll" syntax looks something like this:

```
<grammar xmlns="http://relaxng.org/ns/
structure/1.0">

<start>

<element name="movieList"><oneOrMore>

<element name="movie"><oneOrMore>

<element name="title"><text /></element>

</oneOrMore></element>

</oneOrMore></element>

</start>

</grammar>
```

The condensed syntax is not any shorter but makes it easier to define recursive elements:

```
<grammar xmlns="http://relaxng.org/ns/
structure/1.0">

<start>

<element name="movieList"><oneOrMore><ref
name="movie" /></oneOrMore></element>

</start>

<define name="movie">

<element name="movie"><oneOrMore><ref
name="title" /></oneOrMore></element>

</define>

</grammar>
```

Create a RELAX NG Document in XML

1 Open a new XML document in your editor.

● If using Altova XMLSpy, click File → New, select xml, and click OK.

Note: *Because most editors do not expressly support RELAX NG, you will most likely need to create a normal XML document.*

2 Add an opening grammar root element.

3 Add the xmlns attribute.

4 Set the value of xmlns to **"http://relaxng.org/ns/structure/1.0"**.

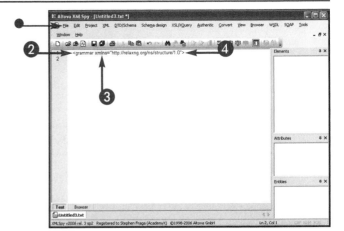

5 Add an opening start element.

6 Add an opening element element.

7 Add the name attribute and set it to the name of the root element of your XML.

8 Add an opening oneOrMore element.

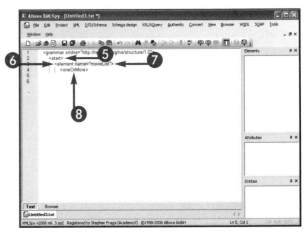

⑨ Add an opening `element` element.

⑩ Add the `name` attribute and set it to the name of the first child of the root element.

⑪ Add a `text` element.

⑫ Make this tag self-closing by putting the trailing slash before the angle bracket.

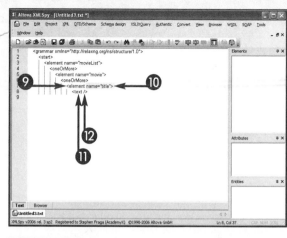

⑬ Close the second `element` element.

⑭ Close the `oneOrMore` element.

⑮ Close the first `element` element.

⑯ Close the `start` element.

⑰ Close the `grammar` element.

⑱ Click File → Save.

Note: *You will most likely need to manually add the .rng extension to the file.*

The file is saved.

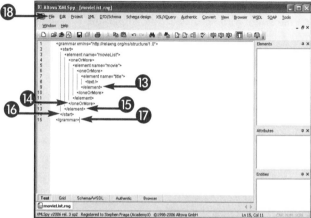

Extra

There are no hard-and-fast rules as to when it is proper to use an attribute and when it is better to use an element. Therefore, unlike the W3C Schema, RELAX NG treats attributes very much like elements. So when you create RELAX NG documents, you define attributes in essentially the same way you define elements.

There was perhaps no greater need in the development community than for data types when you could use nothing but DTDs, so the only successful replacements were those languages that supported them. RELAX NG's developers decided it was easier to simply implement the W3C Schema's data types rather than create their own set that they knew would end up being essentially the same. There are several other open libraries of data types that can be implemented into RELAX NG parsers, but the W3C's is the most commonly used.

In DTDs, mixed content is represented by the use of #PCDATA, which it inherited directly from SGML. In W3C Schemas, mixed content is not directly dealt with; it is rather implied through the use of the mixed attribute of the `complexType` element. In RELAX NG, there exists a `text` element which replaces #PCDATA but serves essentially the same purpose.

Using the RELAX NG Compact Syntax

Although most developers would prefer to learn one language syntax and stick to it, RELAX NG provides the option of using a non-XML syntax. The differences between the regular XML and the compact syntax are purely syntactical — in the end, they do the exact same thing and support the exact same features.

XML documents are by design verbose and human-readable. Although this is not always considered a bad thing, one of the leading RELAX NG developers, James Clark, designed the compact syntax to directly mimic the XML-based language with less code. You should be aware that not all RELAX NG parsers implement the compact syntax; however, many translators exist that will convert it to the XML syntax.

The non-XML syntax is a combination of Java declarations, including the use of curly braces; DTD notations; and several other programming concepts.

When defining elements, you use the `element` keyword, followed by the name of the element, and then curly braces to denote what the element will contain:

```
element movieList {movie+}
```

Use the `text` keyword to denote an element whose contents will be data:

```
element review { text }
```

Attributes are defined as being part of the contents of an element:

```
element title { attribute rating {text},
text }
```

As with regular XML, whitespace is unimportant in using this syntax.

Using the RELAX NG Compact Syntax

① Open a new plain-text document in your editor.

● If using Altova XMLSpy, click File ➜ New, select xml, and click OK.

Note: *Because most editors do not expressly support RELAX NG, you will most likely need to create a normal XML document.*

A new file opens.

② Add an `element` declaration.

③ Add the name of the element.

④ Add a pair of curly braces.

⑤ Between the curly braces, add the name of a child element.

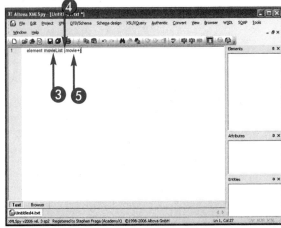

6 Add a new `element` declaration.

7 Add the name of another element.

8 Add another pair of curly braces.

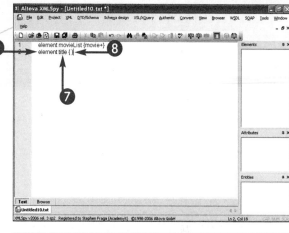

9 Add an `attribute` declaration.

10 Add a content declaration for the element.

11 Click File → Save.

Note: *You will probably have to manually add the .rnc file extension.*

The file is saved.

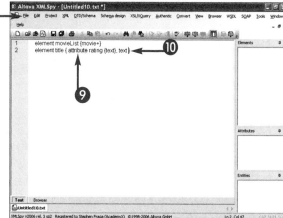

Apply It

You can use the DTD notations in RELAX NG to denote the number of occurrences of a child element.

```
element addressCard { name+ }
element name { firstName, lastName, address }
element firstName { text }
element lastName { text }
element address { street1, street2?, city, state, zip }
```

Using Microsoft Access 2003 to Generate XML

Most companies rely on computerized databases to store most if not all of their important data. Many smaller organizations use Microsoft Access for this purpose. Access is Microsoft's desktop relational database system, designed for individual users to store and easily access large amounts of data.

Microsoft was one of the early adopters of XML, seeing it as a lightweight, universal file format from which all their key products could work and share information. The Microsoft Office products, including Access, got their first taste of XML in the versions released in 2000. The two versions that followed, XP and 2003, greatly enhanced the XML capabilities.

Many developers see XML as a sort of plain-text database file. Although this dramatically overestimates what XML can do and dramatically underestimates the power and flexibility of modern database systems, some comparisons between the two are appropriate. Database systems such as Access store their information in tables, with columns or fields denoting the kind of information and rows of the data itself. XML has its elements to define the kinds of information and the data within the element for that information. The W3C Schema enables developers to set information on the recurrence of elements and data types, very much like you can do in the Table Design view in Access.

Access 2003 provides the ability for designers to export any table or query to XML. The program will generate an XML document of the data, and if needed, a schema document as well. In addition, other views such as reports can be exported as XML, schemas, and XSLT.

Using Microsoft Access 2003 to Generate XML

① In Microsoft Access 2003, click File → Open.

The Open dialog box appears.

② Browse to a database file.

③ Click Open.

The database file opens, and the Database window appears.

④ If necessary, click Tables to go to the Tables object.

⑤ Right-click the table to be exported.

⑥ Click Export.

The Export Table dialog box opens.

⑦ Click the Save As Type down arrow and select XML.

⑧ Type a name for the file.

⑨ Click Export.

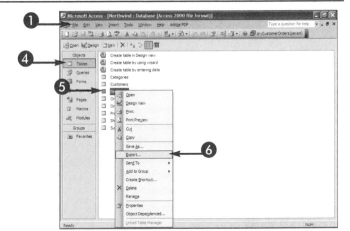

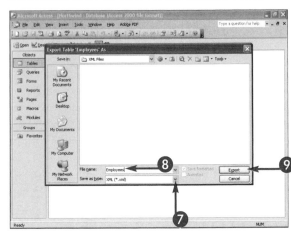

The Export XML dialog box opens.

🔟 Make sure that both Data (XML) and Schema of the Data (XSD) are selected.

⑪ Click OK.

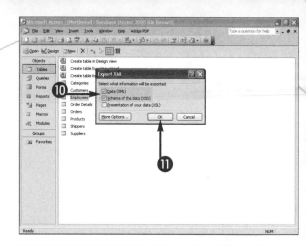

⑫ Open your XML editor.

⑬ Click File → Open.

The Open dialog box appears.

⑭ Browse to the XML file that you exported from Access and click it.

⑮ Click Open.

The XML file opens.

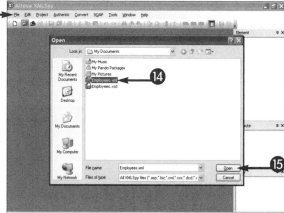

Extra

Microsoft Access is a relational database system, meaning that all the information is stored in a series of tables that are related to one another. Database designers go through a process called *normalization* to create well-structured tables with a minimum of repetitive data. In a well-designed database system, no one table is likely to contain all the information needed.

XML, as a text-based file, does not support complex joining methodologies like relationships. XML files need to have repetitive data because they really exist alone. They are not normalized in the way that database tables are. Therefore, each individual table in your Access database would need to be exported as a separate XML document, and each is likely to have its own schema.

If you need the information from several related tables to be exported to a single XML document, you should create a query in Access that joins the information together. That query could then be exported as XML, giving you the single file that you want.

Using Microsoft Access 2007 to Generate XML

I n early 2007, Microsoft released a new version of its Office system. In what was perhaps the biggest redesign of the software in its history, all four of the core Office products — Word, Excel, PowerPoint, and Access — underwent a major facelift. Although the cosmetic changes are the most readily apparent to users, the programs likewise underwent major changes in the core ways in which they operated and saved documents.

Most importantly, all the Office programs went from being merely XML-aware to being truly XML-based. Each got a new default file extension; in the case of Access, files are now saved as .accdb. There are many advantages to using the new file formats, but one of the nicest is that they are actually XML-based. With Access files, you cannot view or alter the underlying XML, but

the fact that the database is actually storing its information as XML opens a lot of opportunities for it to more easily communicate with other systems.

However, it is still possible to have Access generate a separate XML file of the data in a table. Just as in prior versions, Access 2007 can export the information from a table and include the table's data as XML and the design and structure of the table as a schema. Access 2007 provides a brief wizard to step you through the process of exporting the data to XML by prompting you for a file location and then asking if you want just the XML, the schema, the XSLT, or all of these. The wizard also enables you to save your choices and rerun them again later without having to step through the wizard.

Using Microsoft Access 2007 to Generate XML

① In Access 2007, click the Office button and select Open.

② In the Open dialog box, select a database file to open.

The database opens.

③ From the Navigation pane menu, click Object Type.

The Navigation pane updates.

④ Click Tables.

A list of the tables in the database appears.

⑤ Right-click the table that you want to export.

⑥ Click Export ➜ XML File.

The Export – XML File Wizard opens.

⑦ If necessary, correct the filename and path for the XML file.

⑧ Click OK.

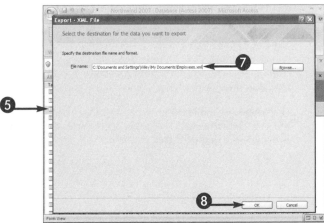

The Export XML dialog box opens.

9 Make sure that both Data (XML) and Schema of the Data (XSD) are checked.

10 Click OK.

The Export – XML File Wizard reappears.

11 Click Close.

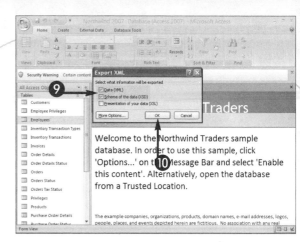

12 Open your XML editor.

13 Click File → Open.

The Open dialog box appears.

14 Browse to the exported file's location and click it.

15 Click Open.

The XML file opens.

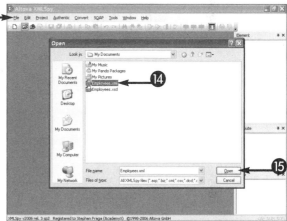

Extra

XML element names cannot contain spaces or other special characters. Unfortunately, Access is much more forgiving, allowing almost any character to appear in the name of a database field. Although most database designers agree that having spaces in field names is a bad practice, there are plenty of databases in existence that use spaces in the filename.

The Access XML Export feature handles this problem by replacing spaces in the field name with an escape sequence made up of an underscore, the hexadecimal equivalent of a space, which is x0020, and another underscore. It replaces slashes with _x002F_ and any other illegal character with its hexadecimal equivalent. Although this certainly reduces the readability of the file, it is nice that Access handles this issue gracefully.

The schema document that Access produces uses a Microsoft-specific namespace, od, which references the officedata schema. This allows Access to reference its native data types, formatting, and indexing features in the schema that it creates.

Using Microsoft Excel 2003 to Generate XML

Although Microsoft Excel was never intended to be a database application, its layout of rows and columns leads many users to treat it as such. Although it lacks the ability to create complex relationships such as you can in Access or other true database applications, in many ways this is an advantage when exporting to XML, as Excel does not support those complexities either. In fact, in many ways viewing data in Excel can be seen as a table-based representation of the XML.

Like Access, Excel 2003 is very XML-aware. If you already have your data in the program, you can easily export it to XML. However, because Excel lacks the ability to truly define its data in any meaningful way, it cannot create a meaningful schema, either. Excel, for example,

understands data typing in limited ways — you can define the format of a cell to hold text or numbers or currency, for instance — but many Excel developers will not necessarily perform the steps needed for this data typing.

A much bigger limitation in using Excel is its inability to support more than one level of nesting. Although an XML file can in theory have as many parent-child relationships as you need, there is no way for Excel to represent this. Excel data has one set of fields or columns and one set of rows. When exporting data from Excel, this tends to not be a big issue because it is simply impossible to create complex data structures like that in the program. However, care must be taken if you are importing complex XML into Excel, as you may get somewhat unexpected results.

Using Microsoft Excel 2003 to Generate XML

① In Excel 2003, click File → Open.

The Open dialog box appears.

② Browse to the Excel file that you want to export and click it.

③ Click Open.

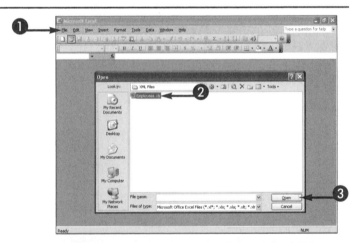

The file opens.

④ Click File → Save As.

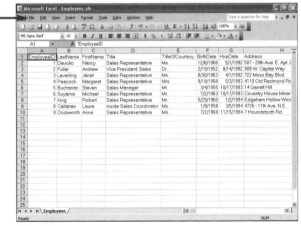

The Save As dialog box opens.

5 Click the Save As Type down arrow and select XML Spreadsheet.

6 Click Save.

The file is exported.

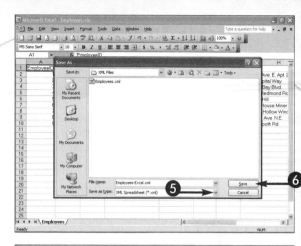

7 Open your XML Editor.

8 Click File → Open.

The Open dialog box appears.

9 Browse to the file that you exported from Excel and click it.

10 Click Open.

The file opens.

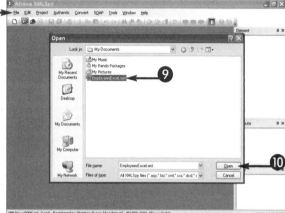

Apply It

If you have a pre-existing schema, you can map the schema to Excel columns and then export an XML file that is valid to the schema.

In Excel, click Data → XML → XML Source to select your schema document. Click and drag the appropriate element from the XML Source task pane to the column heading to which it corresponds. Then you will be able to select XML Data as the file format when exporting.

Using Microsoft Excel 2007 to Generate XML

Like the other Office products, Excel underwent a major overhaul with its 2007 release. Gone are all the menus and toolbars, replaced with something that Microsoft calls *the Ribbon,* which is essentially a toolbar, menu, and panel set all rolled into one.

One of the more interesting things in the Office 2007 products is their total reliance on XML for their data. In fact, all the Office 2007 products use XML as their default file format. It does not look like it; Excel files are saved with an .xlsx extension. However, this is in reality a compressed file format. You can even go into Windows, change that extension to .zip, and uncompress it. Inside, you will find a series of files, any of which can be opened to view the raw data, be it from the styles of the document or the information contained within the cells. All of this is possible because that raw data is in fact XML, so these files will open not in Excel, but rather whatever XML editor you use. The file violates a key concept of XML — that the files be human-readable — but it is impressive nonetheless that you can dig down to this level and view the data.

Because Excel is basically running on XML now, it of course is quite intelligent when it comes to exporting XML. Just as in older versions, the nature of Excel means that you cannot represent complex nested structures of data, but you can easily take the data and export it to an XML file directly within the Excel window.

Using Microsoft Excel 2007 to Generate XML

1 In Microsoft Excel 2007, click the Office button → Open.

The Open dialog box appears.

2 Browse to an Excel 2007 file and click it.

3 Click Open.

The file opens.

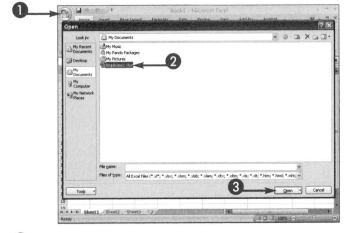

4 Click the Office button → Save As → Other Formats.

The Save As dialog appears.

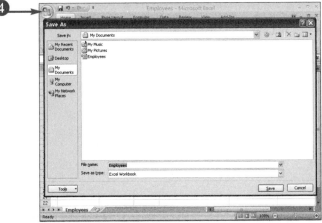

5 Click the Save As Type down arrow and select XML Spreadsheet 2003.

6 Click Save.

The document is saved.

7 Click the Office button ➔ Close.

Excel closes.

8 Open your XML editor.

9 Click File ➔ Open.

The Open dialog box appears.

10 Browse to the file created by Excel and click it.

11 Click Open.

The file opens.

Apply It

You can work more closely with XML in Excel 2007 through the Developer tab of the Ribbon. This tab does not appear by default but can be easily added by clicking the Office button ➔ Excel Options. Then in the Popular section, check the Show the Developer Tab in the Ribbon box. Click OK, and the new tab will be added to the Ribbon.

The Developer tab has a section devoted to XML tools, allowing you to set a source, import and export XML, map properties, and more.

Introducing XHTML

Many Web developers seem reluctant to learn XHTML. They think that they have finally gotten the hang of HTML, and along comes this new language — and if HTML is serving their purposes just fine, why should they take the time to learn something new? Fortunately, it turns out that they do not need to learn anything new because XHTML is not a new language at all. It is in fact just HTML, with all the exact same tags and attributes with which HTML developers are already familiar. The only difference between HTML and XHTML is that the latter requires that you write better code.

HTML Equals Sloppy Code

HTML has always allowed you to write very sloppy code. There are not too many syntax rules in the language, and from the beginning, browsers were designed to let you violate those rules. It is impossible to get a Web browser to actually throw a runtime error on HTML. Anytime your code has something that a browser does not recognize, it will simply ignore it. If there is something that is not quite right, the browser generally guesses at what was meant and moves on. Although this approach is nice for beginners, experienced programmers know that it is always far better to have a program throw an error when something is wrong. Errors are easy to fix: The program says you did something wrong on line 4, so you go fix it. Anyone who has done advanced Web design knows that the browsers' insistence on not throwing errors actually makes things harder, not easier, because when you look at a page and it is just not displaying "right," you have to do a lot of work to try to figure out what exactly is wrong.

XHTML Equals Good Code

XHTML requires that you write the same HTML as you have been, but write it better. Specifically, XHTML requires that you follow the XML syntax rules for writing your HTML:

- All elements are case-sensitive and must be typed using lowercase letters.

- All elements must be properly nested.

- All attributes must have a value, and that value must be enclosed in quotation marks.

- All elements must be closed.

The first of these two rules should not have a big impact on your code. Hopefully, you are already writing code using a consistent case, and because it is simply easier to write in all lowercase letters, most developers do that anyway. Also, you are hopefully already properly nesting tags.

The last two rules are what make XHTML documents look a little bit different from regular HTML. Although most HTML attributes have values, there are a scattered few that do not. For example, this is a valid HTML check box form field, with an attribute to precheck the box:

```
<input type="checkbox" name="subscribe" value="true"
checked>
```

To be valid XHTML, the checked attribute needs a value. In developing XHTML, the W3C decided to simply repeat the name of the attribute as its value for any attribute that did not previously have a value, so the input box would now be written:

```
<input type="checkbox" name="subscribe" value="true"
checked="checked" />
```

The final rule is the one that tends to get most beginners' attention. In HTML, there are container elements — elements for which there is both an opening and a closing tag — and there are empty elements, which do not have a companion closing tag because they have no content. Some of the most common empty elements are img, br, hr, meta, link, and input, but there are others. Because XHTML follows the XML syntax, and XML requires closing tags, XHTML does as well. Any of the empty elements can be written by either providing a closing tag:

```
<br></br>
```

Or, more commonly, by using the self-closing shortcut from XML:

```
<br />
```

The XHTML DOCTYPEs

XHTML is an XML language based on a DTD developed and maintained by the W3C. In fact, there are three slightly different DTDs from which you can choose to write your code: Transitional, Strict, and Frameset.

XHTML Transitional allows you to use the exact same code you used in HTML 4.01 but simply write it using the XML syntax rules. Presentational tags such as `font`, presentational attributes such as `align`, and using tables for layout are all okay under XHTML Transitional.

XHTML Strict requires that you limit yourself to purely structural tags and use cascading style sheets for all of your presentation. In addition, any special characters, such as ampersands and angle brackets, must be escaped by using the appropriate character entity. XHTML Frameset allows you to use the frame and frameset tags to create frames-based pages. Note that you would only use the Frameset `DOCTYPE` on the frames page itself, whereas the pages that are being displayed within the frames would use either the Transitional or Strict `DOCTYPES`.

The three `DOCTYPES`, which must be present as the first line of code of your document, are as follows:

XHTML Transitional:

```
<!DOCTYPE html PUBLIC "-//W3C//DTD XHTML 1.0
Transitional//EN" "http://www.w3.org/TR/xhtml1/
DTD/xhtml1-transitional.dtd">
```

XHTML Strict:

```
<!DOCTYPE html PUBLIC "-//W3C//DTD XHTML 1.0 Strict
//EN" "http://www.w3.org/TR/xhtml1/DTD/xhtml1-
strict.dtd">
```

XHTML Frameset:

```
<!DOCTYPE html PUBLIC "-//W3C//DTD XHTML 1.0
Frameset//EN" "http://www.w3.org/TR/xhtml1/DTD/
xhtml1-frameset.dtd">
```

Regardless of which `DOCTYPE` you use, you should also provide an `xmlns` namespace designation in the root `html` element, pointing to the appropriate namespace, which is the same for all three `DOCTYPES`: http://www.w3.org/1999/xhtml. Technically, you should also begin your document with the XML prolog, but in practice, most modern browsers will render your page incorrectly if you do this.

XHMTL Versions

The most common version of XHTML being used is XHTML 1. XHTML 1.1 does exist and is supported by many major browsers. It drops the three "flavors" of XHTML 1 and only supports the Strict. To use XHTML 1.1, use the following `DOCTYPE`:

```
<!DOCTYPE html PUBLIC "-//W3C//DTD XHTML 1.1//EN"
"http://www.w3.org/TR/xhtml11/DTD/xhtml11.dtd">
```

In addition, you must provide the `xmlns` attribute on the `html` tag, pointing to the XHTML 1.1 namespace at http://www.w3.org/1999/xhtml, and you must begin the document with the XML prolog.

XHTML 2 is still under development. As of April, 2007, the W3C has announced that it expects to have the XHTML 2 specification completed by June 2008. XHTML 2 will introduce several new concepts into the language, including support for XForms, a vastly improved Web form interface; support for XFrames to replace HTML frames; the introduction of an `nl` tag to specifically designate a navigation list; the ability for any element to act as a hyperlink; the removal of `alt` text as an attribute of an image, instead replacing it with text between the opening and closing `img` tags; and the final removal of the few remaining presentation-only elements.

Unfortunately, although the W3C may officially release XHTML 2 in 2008, Web developers can expect to have to wait several more years after that before the browsers fully support it.

Validating XHTML

Even if you use XHTML, the browsers will not automatically validate your document, just as they do not automatically validate any XML. However, several online tools exist to validate your XHTML, which will display specific errors in your code. The W3C hosts a free online validator at http://validator.w3.org that enables you to check online documents or upload files from your computer. Some Web design tools such as Adobe Dreamweaver also include built-in XHTML validation tools.

XHTML Transitional requires several basic components to be present on every page. First, you need to add the proper DOCTYPE:

```
<!DOCTYPE html PUBLIC "-//W3C//DTD XHTML
1.0 Transitional//EN" "http://www.w3.org/
TR/xhtml1/DTD/xhtml1-transitional.dtd">
```

As with any XML DOCTYPE, this line identifies the root element of the document — html. Then it states that the DOCTYPE is on a publically available server with the PUBLIC keyword. Next, it provides a local identifier for the DTD, which most browsers should be able to call internally. If they cannot, a URL to the Web server that hosts the DOCTYPE is provided as a backup.

Following the DOCTYPE, you need to provide the root element of the document, html. Within the root, you

should provide an xmlns attribute to establish the namespace from which the XHTML elements will come:

```
<html xmlns="http://www.w3.org/1999/xhtml">
```

Within the html element, there are two required elements: head and body. The head provides information about the document that is used by the browser and some search engines. It contains one required element, title.

The body contains all the information that will appear visually in the browser window.

No elements can appear outside of either head or body except html, and the closing html tag must be the very last line of code on the page.

Create a Basic XHTML Transitional Page

① Open a new text document in your editor.

● In Notepad, click File ➔ New.

A new file opens.

② Type the XHTML Transitional DOCTYPE.

③ Type an opening html tag.

④ Type the xmlns attribute.

⑤ Type **http://www.w3.org/1999/xhtml** as the value for the attribute.

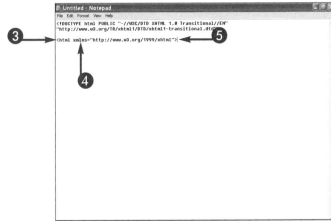

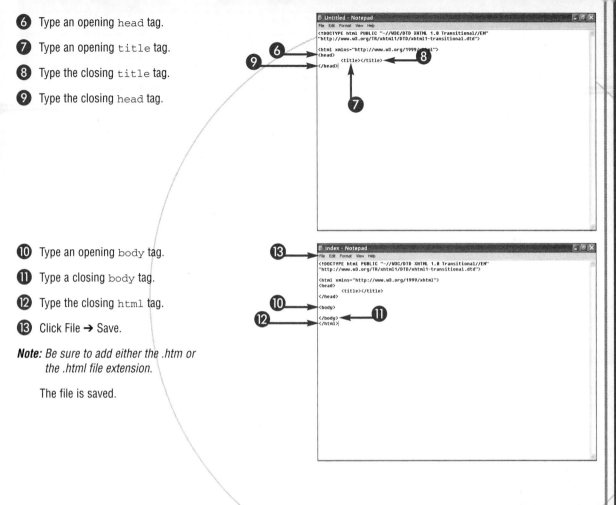

6 Type an opening head tag.

7 Type an opening title tag.

8 Type the closing title tag.

9 Type the closing head tag.

10 Type an opening body tag.

11 Type a closing body tag.

12 Type the closing html tag.

13 Click File → Save.

Note: *Be sure to add either the .htm or the .html file extension.*

The file is saved.

Extra

The code presented here would be identical if you wanted to use XHTML Strict. Under XHTML Frameset, you cannot have a body tag. Instead, you provide a frameset element, with a set of nested frame tags or nested frameset tags with their own frame tags. Each frameset element has either row or col attributes to describe the dimensions of each frame within it. Each frame element must include a reference to the page that will be loaded within it and should include a name attribute to uniquely identify the frame. Note that there are many disadvantages to using frames, including that search engines frequently give lower rankings to frames-based pages and that frames pages are generally less accessible to persons with disabilities.

Most visual Web editors will automatically add these basic structure tags to every new document. Care must be taken, however, to ensure that the editor is inserting valid XHTML elements. Older editors in particular are not likely to add either the DOCTYPE or the xmlns attribute, or they may insert an incorrect DOCTYPE. Many also add a series of meta tags in the head; although this is not incorrect, you need to check to be sure that they are properly closed.

Add a Title

E very XHTML document must have a title. The `title` is the only element in the head of the document that displays its contents to the user. It is not displayed in the browser window but rather on the browser's title bar. The title is also used as the default text for the name of the favorite or bookmark if your user decides to save a reference to your page, and most search engines use it as part of the cataloging process. For these reasons, care should be taken to ensure that each page has a meaningful title.

Always include your company or organization name in the title of every document. Ideally, the title should always begin with the name of the company or organization. Because this is used by search engines, do not use an abbreviation for the company name, unless

that is what the company is commonly called. After the company or organization name, provide a few words that describe the page in question, such as "Home Page" or "Products in Our Catalog."

You cannot include any other XHTML tags within the title, nor can you format the title in any way. If you do place other tags within the title, they will be displayed on the browser's title bar as straight text.

A good way to determine a good title is to imagine that a user adds your page to their favorites and accepts the default name for the favorite — your title. Six months later, that user should be able to look at her list of favorites and see your title as descriptive enough for her to be able to tell what the page is and why she wanted to save it.

Add a Title

ADD A TITLE

① Open an XHTML document in your editor.

● In Notepad, click File ➔ Open.

The file opens.

② Between the opening and closing title elements, add a descriptive title.

③ Click File ➔ Save.

The file is saved.

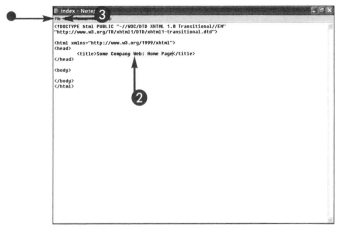

VIEW THE TITLE

① Open a Web browser.

② In Microsoft Internet Explorer, click File ➔ Open.

In Mozilla Firefox, click File ➔ Open File.

The Open dialog box appears.

③ Click Browse.

The Browse dialog box appears.

4 Navigate to the page that you created and click it.

5 Click Open.

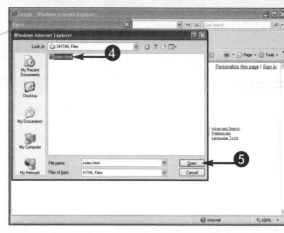

The page opens.

6 Notice the title on the browser's title bar.

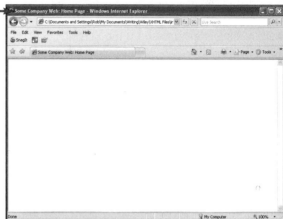

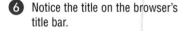

Extra

It is very easy to get into a rhythm when creating pages, especially in visual design tools such as Microsoft Expression Web Designer or Adobe Dreamweaver, and forget to set good titles on pages. A simple Google search for "untitled documents" brings up millions of pages where the designer forgot to title the document or was using a tool such as Dreamweaver and forgot to change it from the default. Get in the habit early of making setting the title the first thing that you do on a page.

Technically, the title can be of any length. Practically, however, you should keep it short. A browser has only so much space that it will use to display the title, and it needs to include the name of the browser, so if necessary, it will truncate the title on the title bar. The exact amount of space allowed varies based on the browser and the screen resolution of the user's computer. Likewise, there is a limit as to how much of a title will be displayed by the browser when the user looks at her favorites, which again varies depending on the browser. In general, keeping your title to 5-10 words and under roughly 50 characters is a good idea.

Add Headings

One of the goals of the development of XHTML is to get designers to use proper structural, or *semantic,* markup. Over the years as HTML evolved, many designers started using improper HTML elements for items on their pages such as headings because they thought a different element might look better than the proper one. Modern Web designers have a powerful presentational language in cascading style sheets that can make any XHTML element look however they want, so there is no good reason anymore to not use proper markup.

The first step in using proper markup is the XHTML heading tags. XHTML defines six headings to mark up logical sections of your page. Good graphical designers have been using this structure for centuries. They place a headline of some sort at the top of the page that describes at a glance the main point of the page. Below that, they have secondary headings to mark off subsections of the page. The six XHTML heading tags serve this same purpose. The h1 element is used to provide a headline for the page. Logically, it should be at the top of the document, and although nothing in the language requires it, an argument can be made that each page should be "about" only one thing and should only have one h1. After the h1, each section of your page should be marked with an h2, then sections within the sections with h3, and on down through h6 if necessary. Although every page should have an h1, not all pages will need the other levels of headings. But you should never skip a level, so you should not have an h3 without an h2.

Add Headings

ADD HEADINGS

① Open an XHTML document in your editor.

● In Notepad, click File ➜ Open.

The file opens.

② Within the body tags, add an h1 tag.

③ Type the text of heading.

④ Close the h1 tag.

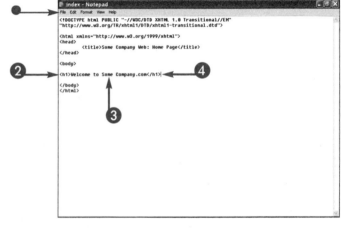

⑤ Type an h2 tag.

⑥ Type the text of the heading.

⑦ Close the h2 tag.

⑧ Click File ➜ Save.

The file is saved.

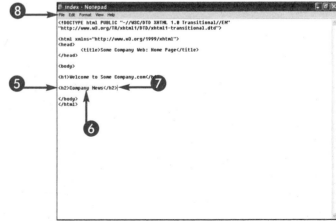

VIEW THE HEADINGS

1 Open a Web browser.

2 In Microsoft Internet Explorer, click File ➔ Open.

In Mozilla Firefox, click File ➔ Open File.

The Open dialog box appears.

3 Click Browse.

4 Navigate to the page that you created and click it.

5 Click Open.

Your headings appear on the page.

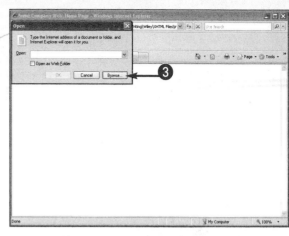

Extra

Search engines rely on headings when cataloging your site. They give more weight to text within an h1 tag than any other text on the page. However, do not try to "cheat" by placing all your text within h1 tags and then using style sheets to make it look normal. Search engines' technology will catch this and give you a lower ranking — or possibly even blacklist your page.

Properly using headings also increases the accessibility of your document. Screen readers for the blind and other assistive technologies let the user know how many headings are on a page and allow them to scan through those headings to find the information they need, just as sighted users scan pages based on headings. A page that "fakes" headings through visual styles may still be usable to sighted visitors who would not be able to tell the difference, but it becomes unusable to blind visitors. It does not take any extra work to use the headings properly, so the rewards of getting better search results and not needlessly turning away potential customers who happen to be disabled should make it worthwhile.

E very Web designer wants to get good search engine results. An entire industry has arisen around "search engine optimization" (SEO). Although SEO companies can often be helpful, many Web designers focus far too much on things such as descriptive meta tags, which most modern search engines ignore, and on trying to figure out ways to trick search engines while ignoring the single best thing you can do to improve your search results: have well-written, meaningful content on your page. It is not enough to have the number one ranking on Google if no one who clicks the link to your page actually stays and buys your product.

In XHTML, you cannot have text directly in the body element itself. It must be enclosed within some block

element, and the most obvious and most useful block element for your text is the paragraph, p. Any amount of text can be placed within the p element, and any inline elements, such as images and anchors for hyperlinks, can be placed within it as well.

The p element, as a block-level element, creates its own space on the page, with margins above and below. Another trap many designers fall into is in deciding that they do not like the space above and below the paragraph, so they once again try to "fake it" by using the break element, br, instead. Because cascading style sheets can easily reduce or remove the space, there is no valid reason to not use the proper element. You will find that using the paragraph element properly greatly enhances the flexibility of your design.

Add Text

ADD TEXT

1 Open an XHTML document in your editor.

● In Notepad, click File → Open.

The file opens.

2 Within the body, type an opening paragraph tag.

3 Type in a paragraph of text.

4 Type the closing paragraph tag.

5 Type another paragraph tag.

6 Type more text.

7 Type a closing paragraph tag.

8 Click File → Save.

The file is saved.

VIEW THE TEXT

1 Open a Web browser.

2 In Microsoft Internet Explorer, click File ➜ Open.

In Mozilla Firefox, click File ➜ Open File.

The Open dialog box appears.

3 Click Browse.

4 Navigate to the page that you created and click it.

5 Click Open.

Your text appears on the page.

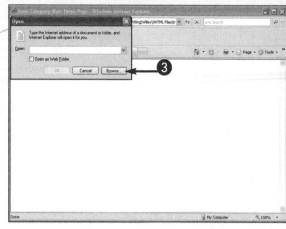

Apply It

If you work in a team environment, you may find that you need to create the layout of a page before the content is developed. You can use dummy text to fill your pages while you wait for the actual text. A common set of dummy text is "Lorem ipsum," which is fake Latin, and can be obtained from www.lipsum.com.

```
<p>Lorem ipsum dolor sit amet, consectetuer adipiscing elit. Pellentesque vitae justo nec
lorem mollis bibendum. Duis placerat, libero sed aliquam fringilla, ligula orci euismod nisl,
sed pretium purus lectus sed nulla. Sed elementum commodo ipsum. Quisque sollicitudin metus
quis nisl. Sed aliquet mi eu nisl. Morbi sed neque. Vivamus ipsum. Etiam iaculis commodo nisl.
Nunc pretium ipsum sed justo. Duis faucibus, augue id rhoncus vestibulum, nulla ipsum luctus
nunc, eget facilisis nibh elit eu pede. Donec mi est, lacinia quis, nonummy vel, pharetra sed,
mi.</p>
```

Using Entities

General entities are used exclusively to add special characters to your page. General entities supported in XHTML fall into three categories. There is an entity to represent whitespace, which would be otherwise ignored by the browser. Then there is a set of entities to represent characters that have special meaning to XHTML and would confuse the browser. Finally, the largest group of entities represents characters that simply cannot be entered directly from a normal keyboard.

All entities follow the same syntax. They begin with an ampersand, are followed by a word or abbreviation that represents the entity, and end with a semicolon, such as ©.

The whitespace entity is , which stands for "nonbreaking space." Browsers ignore consecutive spaces in code, allowing designers to create whitespace in their code for readability, but this does not allow you to present extra space on the page, except with this entity.

The entities that represent characters that would confuse the browser because they have special meaning in XHTML are < for the right angle bracket, > for the left angle bracket, & for the ampersand, " for the double quotation mark, and ' for the apostrophe. In practice, the only one of these symbols that must always use the entity is < because the browser will always interpret this as the beginning of a tag. Rarely will an unescaped ampersand or quotation mark confuse the browser. However, proper XHTML suggests that these should always be used, and they are required in XHTML Strict and XHTML 1.1.

The final group of entities represents characters such as the copyright and trademark symbols, foreign characters such as ç and ñ, and monetary symbols.

There are a total of 252 character entities in XHTML.

Using Entities

ADD A SPECIAL CHARACTER

1 Open an XHTML document in your editor.

● In Notepad, click File → Open.

The file opens.

2 Type an opening paragraph element.

3 Enter text that would require the use of an entity.

4 Replace the character with the required entity.

5 Close the paragraph element.

6 Click File → Save.

The file is saved.

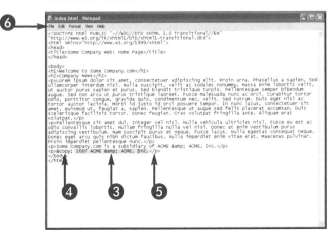

VIEW THE CHARACTER

1 Open a Web browser.

2 In Microsoft Internet Explorer, click File ➔ Open.

In Mozilla Firefox, click File ➔ Open File.

The Open dialog box appears.

3 Click Browse.

4 Navigate to the page that you created and click it.

5 Click Open.

● The special character appears on the page.

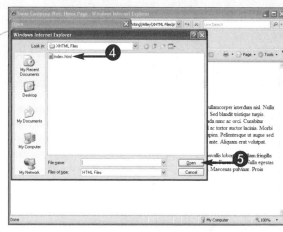

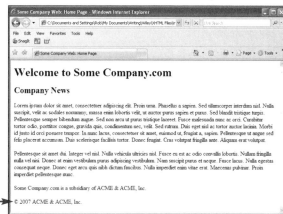

Extra

Entities are allowed and must also be used within the values of attributes if you want those values to contain characters represented by the entities. For example, hyperlinks to pages deep within sites will often contain ampersands:

```
<a href="http://www.somepage.com/catalog.htm?productID=1234&categoryID=5678">
```

To make this code valid, you must use the ampersand's character entity:

```
<a href="http://www.somepage.com/catalog.htm?productID=1234&amp;categoryID=5678">
```

Unfortunately, this may not always be possible, particularly if the target of the link is being generated automatically by a content management system or some other server-side application. In that case, you need to make your page XHTML Transitional, which suggests, but does not require, that all characters be escaped.

One of the primary purposes of the creation of the original version of HTML is hyperlinking, which provides the ability to link related information in documents. Hyperlinks are an essential feature of any Web site. Text and images on a page can be linked to any other resource, whether it be another document within the same Web site or a document on an entirely different Web site. The resource to which you link can be of any format. Although Web pages most commonly link to other Web pages, you can also create links to PDF (Portable Document Format) files, or directly to images, or to Microsoft Word or Excel files, or even music and video files. If the resource exists on a Web server, a link can be created to it.

XHTML uses the anchor tag, `<a>`, to create a hyperlink. This tag has a single required attribute, `href`, which takes a value equal to the path to the resource to which you are linking. This path can be expressed as either a document-relative or an absolute path. Document-relative paths provide the location of the resource relative to the location of the current file. If they exist in the same directory on the server, it is only necessary to give the filename and extension. If the resource to which you are linking exists in another directory, but that directory is in the same directory as the file on which the link exists, then you provide the name of the directory, a slash, and then the filename and extension. Absolute paths include a complete URL, including the http://, and must always be used when linking to resources on other Web sites.

Add a Link

ADD A LINK

① Open an XHTML document in your editor.

- In Notepad, click File ➔ Open.

  The file opens.

② Type an opening paragraph element.

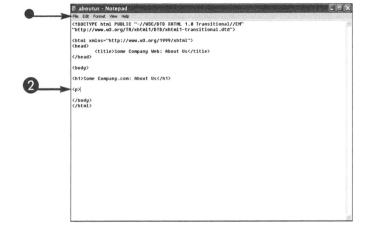

③ Type an opening anchor element.

④ Type an `href` attribute.

⑤ Type the value of the `href` attribute, using either a relative path to another XHTML document or an absolute path to another Web site.

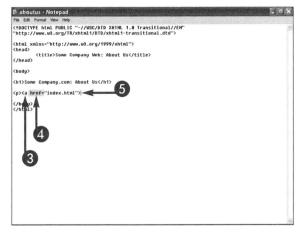

6 Type the text to describe the link.

7 Close the anchor tag.

8 Close the paragraph tag.

9 Click File → Save.

The file is saved.

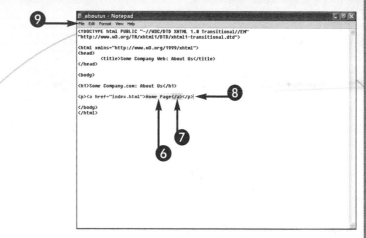

VIEW THE LINK

1 Open a Web browser.

2 Open the file that you created.

In Microsoft Internet Explorer, click File → Open.

In Mozilla Firefox, click File → Open File.

Your link appears on the page.

3 Click the link.

The file to which you linked opens.

Extra

Here are a few best practices to consider when adding hyperlinks to your pages:

● Always clearly identify the resource to which you are linking. This is especially true for links to non-XHTML information, such as PDF or music or video files that may be large files that will be slow to download.

● Do not use "Click here." It is generally easy to reword the link text and avoid it. For example, instead of saying, "Click here to see our contact information," it is less wordy and less clichéd to say, "Our contact information can be found here."

● Be sure that all links are clearly identified. A growing trend on the Web, particularly on blog sites, is to have links in the text of the blog be identified by nothing other than a slight color change, say from black to dark gray. It is difficult for many users to identify such a subtle color change, and color-blind users are unlikely to see it at all. Your users should not feel as though they are on a treasure hunt to find the links on your page.

● If your hyperlink is going to do something unusual, such as open the target resource in a new window, then be sure to clearly identify this behavior to your user in advance.

Add an Image

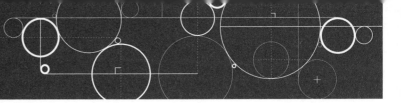

The Web is a rich visual medium, and images play an important role in the appearance of any Web page. The current generation of Web browsers support three image formats: .gif, .jpg, and .png. GIF images, sometimes referred to as CompuServe GIFS after the company that originally created them, use a limited palette of up to 256 colors and thus are ideal for buttons, logos, and line art. They can have a transparent background and can be animated. A JPG, or JPEG, which stands for Joint Photographic Experts Group, can contain up to 16.7 million colors and is used throughout the Web for photographs. Most modern digital cameras save files as .jpg by default. The PNG format was created as an alternative to GIFs and supports a wider JPG palette, while also supporting GIF-specific features such as transparency. Almost any modern graphics program can save to any of these formats.

Images are placed on XHTML pages through the `<img>` tag. There are two required attributes to the tag: `src` and `alt`. The `src` attribute takes as its value a relative or absolute path to the image itself. The `alt` attribute enables the designer to add a text description of the image, which is used by screen readers and other devices that visually impaired users rely on to navigate the Web and by search engines in cataloging the pages.

Optionally, you can add width and height attributes to the tag, which should specify the exact dimensions of the image. Although not required, these attributes can speed the rendering of the page, as the browser will know how much space it needs to leave for the image when it first lays out the text.

`img` is an empty element and thus must be self-closing by placing a slash immediately before the end angle bracket.

Add an Image

ADD AN IMAGE

1. Open an XHTML document in your editor.

● In Notepad, click File ➔ Open.

   The file opens.

2. Type an opening paragraph element.

3. Type an image element.

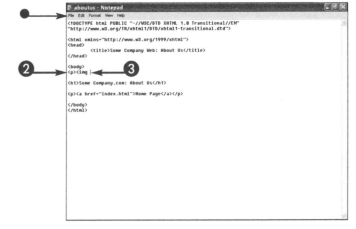

4. Type an `src` attribute.

5. Type the value of the attribute, providing a path to an image file.

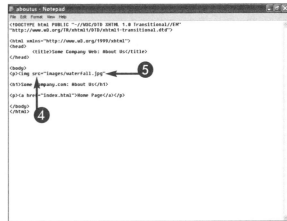

6 Type an `alt` attribute.

7 Type a description of the image as the attribute value.

8 Type a closing slash and the closing angle bracket.

9 Click File → Save.

The file is saved.

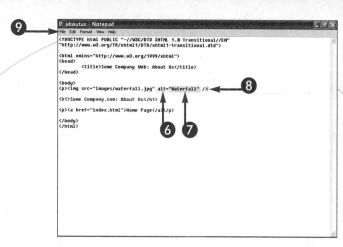

VIEW THE IMAGE

1 Open a Web browser.

2 Open the file.

In Microsoft Internet Explorer, click File → Open.

In Mozilla Firefox, click File → Open File.

● The image appears on the Web page.

Extra

You can use an image as a hyperlink by wrapping the anchor tag around the image tag:

```
<a href="contactus.html"><img src="contacticon.gif" alt="Contact Us" border="0" /></a>
```

When used as a hyperlink, images will by default display a border, but this can be easily removed by setting the image tag's border attribute to a value of zero.

The `alt` attribute's value will appear as a ToolTip when a user moves his or her mouse over an image in Internet Explorer. Firefox and most other browsers do not exhibit this behavior, which is technically not a part of the specifications for how browsers should act. If you would like a ToolTip to appear on mouse-over on images that serve as links, you can add the `title` attribute to the anchor tag. Most modern browsers will display the text in a `title` attribute as a ToolTip.

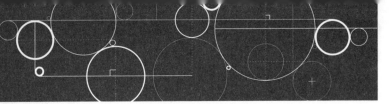

Add a Table

Many Web sites find the need to present tables of information, whether they be a company directory, or a comparison of product features, or a set of scientific data. XHTML provides a rich set of elements to mark up tables.

All table markup must be enclosed within the `<table>` tag. Following that, you can have an unlimited number of table rows, designated by the `<tr>` tag. Within each `<tr>`, you present one or more `<td>` elements. The `td` element stands for "table data" and is used to denote the content of the individual table cell. Any markup that can be legally placed within the body of an XHTML document can be placed within a `td`, so your table cells can have headings, paragraphs, or lists, just to name a few.

```
<table>
      <tr>
```

```
      <td>Name</td>
      <td>Phone</td>
   </tr>
   <tr>
      <td>Bill</td>
      <td>555-1212</td>
   </tr>
</table>
```

Table markup can become quite verbose, so it is strongly recommended that you add plenty of whitespace within the markup to make it easier to read. Put each table row and table cell on its own line and indent the markup for the cells below the rows to make it clear which row contains which cells.

Add a Table

ADD A TABLE

1 Open an XHTML document in your editor.

● In Notepad, click File → Open.

The file opens.

2 Type an opening table element.

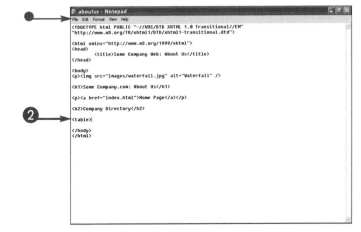

3 Type an opening table row element.

4 Type an opening table data element.

5 Type content for the table cell.

6 Close the table data tag.

7 Type as many opening table data elements, their contents, and their closing tags as you need.

8 Type a closing table row tag.

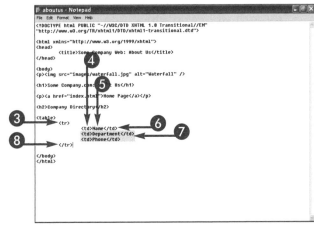

9 Repeat steps **3** to **8** for the remaining rows of the table.

10 Type a closing table tag.

11 Click File → Save.

The file is saved.

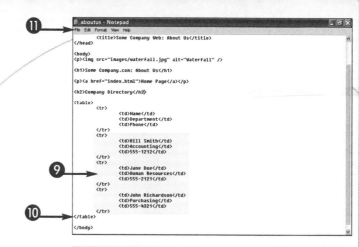

```
            <title>Some Company Web: About Us</title>
</head>

<body>
<p><img src="images/waterfall.jpg" alt="Waterfall" /></p>

<h1>Some Company.com: About Us</h1>

<p><a href="index.html">Home Page</a></p>

<h2>Company Directory</h2>

<table>
        <tr>
                <td>Name</td>
                <td>Department</td>
                <td>Phone</td>
        </tr>
        <tr>
                <td>Bill Smith</td>
                <td>Accounting</td>
                <td>555-1212</td>
        </tr>
        <tr>
                <td>Jane Doe</td>
                <td>Human Resources</td>
                <td>555-2121</td>
        </tr>
        <tr>
                <td>John Richardson</td>
                <td>Purchasing</td>
                <td>555-4321</td>
        </tr>
</table>

</body>
```

VIEW THE TABLE

1 Open a Web browser.

2 Open the file that you created.

In Microsoft Internet Explorer, click File → Open.

In Mozilla Firefox, click File → Open File.

● The table appears on the Web page.

Extra

Tables can be made easier to read and more accessible by the addition of a few extra elements. The header row or column of your table should use <th> tags instead of <td>. By default, text within the <th> is displayed as bold and centered. The optional <caption> tag, which if used must appear immediately after the opening <table> tag, places text above, but just outside, the table. XHTML tables are marked up by row rather than by column, but styles such as background colors and widths can be applied to columns using the <col> tag, which needs to come immediately after the <caption>. You should provide one <col> tag for each column in the table, and any styles applied to the <col> tag apply to any cells within that column.

Visually impaired users can find using tables particularly difficult. To assist them, make sure that you always have a header row, properly marked up with the <th> tag. You should also add a summary attribute to the table tag itself, in which you provide a brief synopsis of the table's content and structure. Screen readers, software used by visually impaired visitors to your site, will read the summary and provide the visitors with an idea as to what the table looks like.

Create Lists

Almost every Web site contains at least one list. Lists are frequently used for products offered by the site, or members currently on the site, or form controls. All navigation on the Web can be argued to be a list; after all, navigation is really nothing more than a list of links to the other pages on the site.

XHTML supports two types of lists: ordered and unordered. Ordered lists are displayed as a series of consecutively numbered items and use the `<ol>` tag. An unordered list is displayed using bullets and relies on the `<ul>` tag for its markup. Although each has a unique container element, both use the same XHTML element to

denote the items in the list: `<li>`. Here is the basic setup of an unordered list:

```
<ul>
        <li>List Item</li>
        <li>List Item</li>
</ul>
```

Lists can contain any number of items, and the actual contents of a list item can be just about anything. You will find that lists, and in particular unordered lists, are one of the most versatile sets of tags in XHTML.

Create Lists

CREATE A LIST

① Open an XHTML document in your editor.

● In Notepad, click File → Open.

The file opens.

② Type an opening unordered list element.

③ Type an opening list item element.

④ Type the list item.

⑤ Close the list item element.

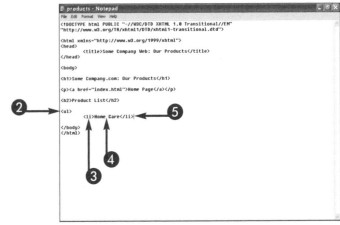

6 Repeat steps **3** to **5** for each additional list item.

7 Close the unordered list element.

8 Click File ➜ Save.

The file is saved.

```
 products - Notepad
File  Edit  Format  View  Help
<!DOCTYPE html PUBLIC "-//W3C//DTD XHTML 1.0 Transitional//EN"
"http://www.w3.org/TR/xhtml1/DTD/xhtml1-transitional.dtd">

<html xmlns="http://www.w3.org/1999/xhtml">
<head>
        <title>Some Company Web: Our Products</title>
</head>

<body>

<h1>Some Company.com: Our Products</h1>

<p><a href="index.html">Home Page</a></p>

<h2>Product List</h2>

<ul>
        <li>Home Care</li>
        <li>Garden Care</li>
        <li>Car Care</li>
        <li>Pet Care</li>
</ul>

</body>
</html>
```

VIEW THE LIST

1 Open a Web browser.

2 Open the file that you created.

In Microsoft Internet Explorer, click File ➜ Open.

In Mozilla Firefox, click File ➜ Open File.

● The list appears on the Web page.

Some Company.com: Our Products

Home Page

Product List

- Home Care
- Garden Care
- Car Care
- Pet Care

Apply It

You can nest lists within other lists and can even mix list types, by including an ordered or unordered list tag within another list's list item tag:

```
<ul>
        <li>Unordered Item
            <ol>
                    <li>Ordered Item</li>
                    <li>Ordered Item</li>
            </ol>
        </li>
        <li>Unordered Item</li>
</ul>
```

Understanding XSLT

One of the most important concepts to keep in mind about XML is that the language maintains an absolute separation between content and presentation. Unlike XHTML, which is by design a presentational language that attempts to simultaneously define the content and how that content should be displayed, XML documents are solely about the content. Formatting of XML documents is done in a separate document, using the Extensible Style sheet Language, or XSL.

The XSL Building Blocks

There are basically three components of XSL. The first and most commonly used is Extensible Style sheet Language Transformations, or XSLT. XSLT enables developers to programmatically transform their XML documents to other formats, such as HTML or plain text. The second component of XSL is Extensible Style sheet Language Formatting Objects, or XSL-FO, which is used to define page layout and formatting instructions for printed documents, enabling developers to convert their XML to formats designed for printing, such as PDF and RTF. The final component is a companion language called *XPath*, which allows for the addressing of elements within XSL documents.

XSLT Editors

XSLT documents are written in XML, using a schema developed by the World Wide Web Consortium, or W3C, the body that is responsible for developing Web standards. Therefore, you can use the same editor for XSLT that you use for your regular XML documents. That said, there are several specialized editors for XSLT. Altova, the company that makes XMLSpy, also markets a product called *MapForce,* which allows for fairly easy creation of XSLT documents to transform XML to XML, and *StyleVision,* a product that provides a visual means of creating XSLT documents to transform XML to XHTML and text, as well as creating XSL-FO documents for conversion to PDF or RTF formats. Adobe Dreamweaver CS3 and its immediate predecessor, Macromedia Dreamweaver 8, provide tools to visually create XSLT documents for transforming XML to XHTML.

XSLT Documents

XSLT documents are maintained separately from the XML that they will transform. This keeps the content — the XML document — apart from the presentation — the XSLT. It also enables developers to create multiple XSLT documents to transform the same XML, so it is possible to repurpose an XML file to many different uses and formats.

The Power of XSLT

Many developers, even experienced ones, find XSLT intimidating. Although there are not that many elements in the language, it is extremely powerful and versatile. Just about everyone is surprised by just how much XSLT can actually do. For example, a partial list of its capabilities includes looping through an XML file and performing a particular function repeatedly on elements, sorting elements based on their data, generating new elements and attributes, including other style sheets at runtime, adding static text to the output, and defining and using variables.

Although the syntax of XSLT can be a bit unwieldy, its power and flexibility make it a language well worth learning.

XSLT Templates

XSLT performs its transformation tasks by creating one or more *templates,* or roadmaps of the eventual output, and then applying those templates to selected elements in the XML. Templates enable you to tell the parser what information to pull from the original XML and how to transform that to the new format.

The Parts of an XSLT Document

As an XML file, XSLT documents must be well-formed and follow the syntax rules of XML. An XSLT document consists of three different sections: the XML declaration, required on every XML document; the style sheet element, which is the root of the XSLT document and contains a namespace declaration for the XSLT; and one or more templates, which provide the instructions as to how the document will be transformed. In addition to these required sections, your XSLT document may also include comments to help explain the document and, possibly, other elements from the language for more complex transformations.

Attaching the XSLT Document to the XML

After you have built your XSLT, you will need to reference the style sheet in your XML so that the parser knows which style sheet to use. To do this, you need to add an `xml-stylesheet` parsing instruction to the XML document:

```
<?xml-stylesheet type="text/xsl"
href="path_to_xsl_document" ?>
```

As a parsing instruction, this line of code needs to appear at the top of the document, just below the XML declaration and before any XML elements. Also, it is not an element and thus has no corresponding closing tag. The path to the XSL document can be document- or site-root relative or absolute.

Running XSLT Transformations

Most XML parsers are capable of running XSLT transformations, provided that they support the format to which the XML is being transformed. Microsoft Word, for example, can apply XSLT transformations to text, and Web browsers support XSLT to XHTML. Many of these applications, however, make it difficult to save the resulting output. Altova's products are the exception here, as they not only make it easy to create the XSLT initially, but they also make applying the transformation and saving the output simple.

Most parsers apply transformations by default if an XML document with the appropriate `xml-stylesheet` parsing instruction is opened in the parser.

Planning Your Transformations

Spending the time to carefully plan your transformations before you write them will pay dividends in the long run. XSLT documents can quickly become fairly long, and trying to make wholesale changes to them later on can require a lot of work.

Before you sit down at an editor, think through how you want the output to appear. It can sometimes be helpful to create a rough sketch to help visualize the results. Although you may change your mind about certain aspects of the transformation as you write it, be sure to consider the impact of those changes on the overall document to help minimize the possibility of creating errors or undesired output along the way.

Whitespace

As with other XML documents, XSLT documents can contain as much whitespace as needed to ensure readability. However, your XSLT documents are likely to have more levels of nested elements than your regular XML, sometimes going as many as eight or ten levels deep. A document that contains a lot of whitespace and indented code will process in the same way as one that does not, and the former will be much easier to edit and maintain than the latter.

Understanding the XSLT Namespace

XSLT relies on its own namespace to expose the tags and attributes that it uses. As with other namespaces, you need to begin your document by declaring the namespace within the root element. By convention, the namespace uses the `xsl` prefix, although this is not actually required:

```
<xsl:stylesheet xmlns:xsl="http://
www.w3.org/1999/XSL/Transform">
```

The stylesheet Root Element

The root of the XSLT document is the `stylesheet` element. It always contains the namespace declaration, and it further has a required version attribute. The most widely accepted version is 1. XSLT version 2 was released in 2007 as an official recommendation, but parser support for version 2 is not yet widespread.

Some developers choose to use the `transform` element as the root of XSLT style sheets. This is a purely stylistic difference, as the language recognizes either. Some developers use `transform` instead of `stylesheet` to differentiate XSLT documents from XSL-FO documents, but the majority of XSLT developers seem to prefer using `stylesheet` as the root for either type.

The XSLT Top-Level Elements

XSLT documents may contain any one or more of the following elements directly under the root.

<xsl:output>

Use the `output` element to specify the type of document to which you want to transform your XML, the version of that document type, and the encoding character set.

<xsl:template>

The majority of your XSLT document will be made up of one or more `template` elements, in which you create the mapping of the original XML to the new format.

<xsl:import> and <xsl:include>

These two versatile elements enable you to import or include other style sheets. This modularization allows you to break overly long XSLT documents into smaller, more manageable pieces and to reuse existing style sheets.

<xsl:preserve-space> and <xsl:strip-space>

You can use these elements to tell the parser to either leave whitespace intact or to remove it from the resulting document. Documents with whitespace are easier to read, but the whitespace itself does add characters and thus file size to the documents.

<xsl:variable> and <xsl:param>

Used to declare variables and parameters in your XSLT, both of which allow you to dramatically reduce the overall size of the code by avoiding needless repetition.

Less Common Elements

A few other top-level elements that are only used in highly complex XSLT documents are `<xsl:attribute-set>`, which creates a set of named attributes for the resulting document; `<xsl:decimal-format>`, which sets a default format instruction for the document; `<xsl:key>`, which helps in linking XML documents; and `<xsl:namespace-alias>`, which enables you to map namespaces.

Template Child Elements

Child elements used within the <xsl:template> will make up the bulk of your document. They include the following:

<xsl:for-each>	Loops through the data
<xsl:value-of>	Returns the data within an element
<xsl:copy>	Copies an element from the original XML to the new document as is, including its values
<xsl:copy-of>	Similar to <xsl:copy> but also copies all children and attributes of the original
<xsl:element>	Creates a new element
<xsl:attribute>	Creates a new attribute
<xsl:apply-templates>	Applies a template to the XML node
<xsl:sort>	Sorts the data in the original XML. It cannot be used as a direct child of xsl:template and must instead appear as a child of either xsl:apply-templates or xsl:for-each.

XSLT Logical Elements

XSLT contains a set of logical elements that perform processing on the document, similar to the functionality in most programming languages. The key logical elements are

<xsl:if>	Performs conditional processing on a single condition
<xsl:choose>	Performs conditional processing on multiple conditions
<xsl:for-each>	Loops through the XML and performs the enclosed tasks once per iteration

Understanding XPath

In order to apply transformations to XML, XSLT needs some way of navigating through the document. Its companion language, XPath, provides this functionality. XPath is a somewhat odd creation, in that it is classified as an XML language even though it does not have tags and attributes or exist in a namespace, but is rather merely used as values in other XSLT and XSL-FO elements.

Path Expressions

The most common use of XPath is a path expression, which is made up of three parts: an axis, a node test, and a predicate. XPath expressions can be written in either an abbreviated format, which is by far the most common, or an expanded format that is far less readable but exposes many additional options to the developer.

Axis

The axis defines the relationship or position of a particular node that you are trying to find to the currently selected node. The axes available in XPath are `child`, `attribute`, `descendant`, `descendant-or-self`, `parent`, `ancestor`, `ancestor-or-self`, `following`, `preceding`, `following-sibling`, `preceding-sibling`, `self`, and `namespace`.

Node Test

The node test specifies the exact node for which you are searching, or a general expression.

Predicate

The predicate serves as a filter and is used if the axis and/or the node test returns more than the amount of information that you want.

Abbreviated Syntax

The XPath abbreviated syntax resembles the syntax used in most operating systems to designate the file structure. As an example, `/movieList/title/review` is the XPath abbreviated syntax to find the `review` element as a child of the `title` element, which is in turn a child of the `movieList` element. The `movieList` element here is specified as being the root of the document by the opening slash. A more complex example may be `movieList/*/[2]`, in which a node test and predicate are used to tell XPath to return the second child of any element that is a descendant of `movieList`.

Expanded Syntax

The expanded syntax of XPath requires that the axis always be specified. For example, `/child::movieList/child::title/child::review` finds the `review` element as the child of `title`, which is the child of the document root `movieList`. As another example, `child::movieList/child::*/child::[2]` finds the second child of any child element of `movieList`.

It is important to note that the following axes can only be used in the expanded syntax, as there is no equivalent in the abbreviated syntax: `descendant-or-self`, `ancestor`, `ancestor-or-self`, `following`, `following-sibling`, `preceding`, `preceding-sibling`, and `namespace`.

Finding the Current Node

The current node of the document is represented by a single dot in the abbreviated syntax in XPath. This is used within XSLT child elements to avoid needing to repeat XPath expressions from the parent element.

Finding Attributes

Attributes are designated in XPath with an @ symbol. So `/movieList/title/@rating` will find an attribute `rating` in an element title that is the child of the root element `movieList`.

Predicates

Predicates, or filters, are expressed in square brackets. `/movieList/title[@rating='PG']` finds any element `title` that has an attribute with a rating of PG that is also the child element of the root `movieList`.

XPath Functions

XPath contains many functions to help manipulate values. Their syntax is like the syntax used by most programming languages in which you have `functionname()`. The functions provide a powerful toolset for working in XPath. Many of the functions available are similar to those in other languages, such as `concat()`, `sum()`, `round()`, `string()`, and `boolean()`. Others are specific to XPath and are used for setting nodes, such as `position()`, or getting the properties of nodes, as in `name()` and `namespace-uri()`.

XPath 2

The most commonly available version of XPath is 1, but the W3C published the XPath 2 recommendation in January of 2007. XPath 2 recognizes many more data types than its predecessor and greatly expands on the number and capabilities of the built-in functions in the language. XSLT 2 relies on XPath 2, but neither are yet widely supported by parsers, so you need to check your parser's documentation to be sure either will work before attempting to implement them.

Specify an Output Format

The first important instruction in an XSLT style sheet after the root element is the output format. XSLT can output documents to XML, HTML, or plain text. Before it can effectively begin processing the file, it must know which format it is to use, which is done through the `<xsl:output>` tag:

```
<xsl:output method="xml" version="1.0"
encoding="UTF-8" />
```

or

```
<xsl:output method="html" version="4.01"
encoding="UTF-8" />
```

This empty element specifies the method of output, using either XML, HTML, or text as its value. Then it sets the

version of the outputted document, which will usually be 1 for XML and 4.01 for HTML. Finally, you are not required to but should specify an encoding type for the output. Assuming that you will be using a Western European language for the output, the encoding type will be UTF-8. This output element causes the parser to generate an appropriate XML declaration for XML output or root and meta element for HTML in the resulting document, either:

```
<?xml version="1.0" encoding="UTF-8" ?>
```

or

```
<html><head> <meta http-equiv="Content-
type" content="text/html; charset=UTF-8">
```

Specify an Output Format

① Open a new XSLT document in your editor.

In Altova XMLSpy:

● Click File ➔ New.

● Click XSLT Stylesheet v1.0.

● Click OK.

Choose Generic XSL/XSLT Transformation.

Click OK.

A new XSLT document appears.

② Type the `xsl:stylesheet` root element.

③ Type **version="1.0"**.

④ Type the `xsl` namespace declaration.

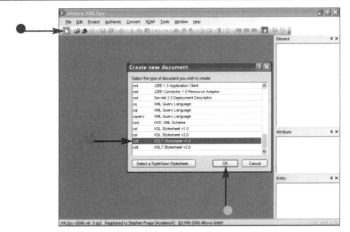

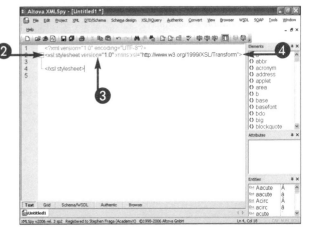

⑤ Type the `xsl:output` element.

⑥ Type **method="xml"**.

⑦ Type **version="1.0"**.

⑧ Type **encoding="UTF-8"**.

⑨ Type **indent="yes"**.

⑩ Type the closing slash and closing angle bracket.

⑪ Type the closing `xsl:stylesheet` tag.

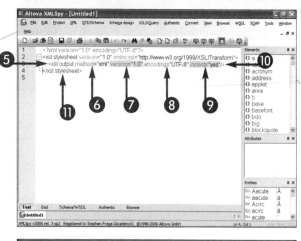

⑫ Click the Check Well-Formedness button to confirm that the document is well-formed.

● The Validation area opens to show if there are errors or no errors in the document.

⑬ Save the document with an .xsl file extension.

The file is saved.

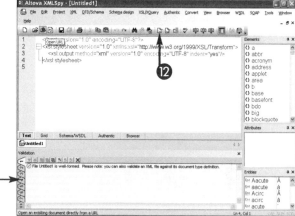

Extra

The default output for XSLT is XML, so not including an `<xsl:output>` tag is the same as including it and specifying a method of XML. Despite this, it is considered a best practice to always include it. Be sure that you include it as a top-level element in the document so that it is a child of the root `xsl:stylesheet` element and nothing else.

If you specify a method of HTML, the resulting document will be formatted according to the HTML 4.01 syntax rules. This can cause a certain amount of confusion because XML and thus XSLT treat empty elements differently from HTML 4.01. Therefore, when you write the HTML content in the XSLT document, you must follow the XML syntax rules for empty elements and ensure that they are always closed, either by explicitly closing them or by using the training slash shortcut. For example, the break element must be written as either `<br></br>` or `<br />`. Regardless of which technique you use to close the tag, however, the result will be an HTML empty element, `<br>`. If you want to transform your document to XHTML, you should use the default XML output type, as XHTML documents are technically XML.

Create an
XSLT Template

The most important and useful element within XSLT documents is `xsl:template`. The template provides the map that XSLT will use to convert elements from the original XML file to the new output file. For XML to XML conversion, the template will most likely contain a series of `<xsl:element>` and `<xsl:attribute>` elements, as well as `<xsl:value-of>` and `<xsl:text>` elements to construct the new document based on the contents of the original.

For XML to HTML, the template will most likely begin with the basic HTML structure tags, `<html>`, `<head>`, `<title>`, and `<body>`, and then contain additional HTML elements and `<xsl:value-of>` and `<xsl:text>` elements to convert the original document to the new format.

The `<xsl:template>` element will contain a match attribute that uses an XPath expression to map an initial location in the document. Often, the first `<xsl:template>` element in an XSLT document will have `match="/"`, representing the root element of the original XML file, although this is not always required. An example of a simple template is

```
<xsl:template match="/">

<!-- perform action on root element -->

</xsl:template>
```

XSLT documents can, and often will, contain multiple templates to perform different actions on different sections of the original XML document.

Create an XSLT Template

① Open an XSLT document that contains the root `stylesheet` element and the `output` element.

② Type an opening `xsl:template` element.

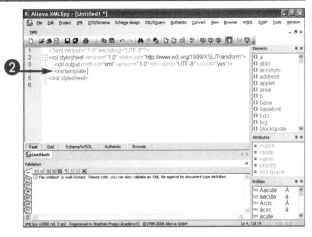

③ Type a `match` attribute.

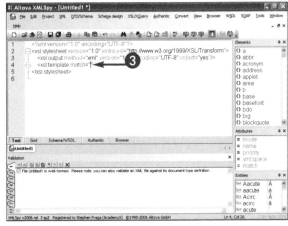

④ Use XPath to set the value of the
match attribute to an element in the
XML file that you plan to transform.

⑤ Type the closing xsl:template
tag.

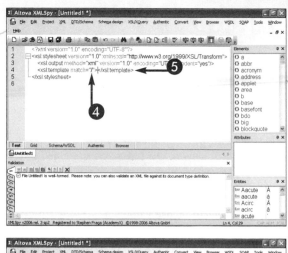

⑥ Click the Check Well-Formedness
button to confirm that the document
is well-formed.

● The Validation area shows if there
are errors or no errors in the
document.

⑦ Save the document with an .xsl file
extension.

The file is saved.

Apply It

You can create `<xsl:template>` elements that have a name attribute instead of a match attribute and
then use the `<xsl:call-template>` element to include the named template. This can be useful to include
repetitive content in a transformation:

```
<xsl:template name="credit">
                  This review written by John Smith
</xsl:template>
<xsl:template match="review">
                  <xsl:call-template name="credit">
</xsl:template>
```

Transform Element Values

Often, you will need to take the values of existing elements and apply them to the new document in your transformation. The `xsl:value-of` element serves this purpose.

The `xsl:value-of` element must appear within an `xsl:template` element. It takes one required attribute, `select`, which will have a value equal to an XPath expression for the element whose value you are selecting. XPath can use relative expressions, so if the `xsl:value-of`'s parent element used an XPath to reach the parent element of the one that you are trying to select, then the expression in the xsl:value-of would only need to reference from that point down — for example:

```
<xsl:template match="/movieList/title">
```

```
<xsl:value-of select="review" />
```

```
</xsl:template>
```

In this case, because the `xsl:template`'s XPath expression matched the `title` element within the `movieList` element, the `xsl:value-of`'s XPath expression, `review`, is selecting a child element of `title`. Although a complete XPath expression would have worked in the `xsl:value-of` element, there is no need for it.

When using `xsl:value-of`, if you select an element with child elements, only the parent's value, or the first child, will be selected. The values of any other child elements will not be returned — you would need to use separate `xsl:value-of` statements for them.

Transform Element Values

1. Open an XSLT document that contains the root `stylesheet` element and the `output` element.

2. Type an opening `xsl:template` element.

3. Type a `match` attribute.

4. Use XPath to set the value of the `match` attribute to an element in the XML file that you plan to transform.

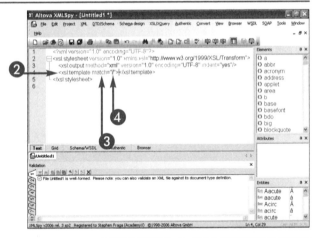

5. Type an `xsl:value-of` element.

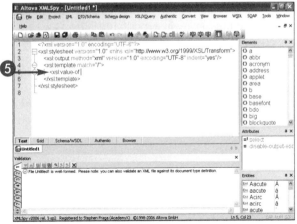

6 Type the `select` attribute.

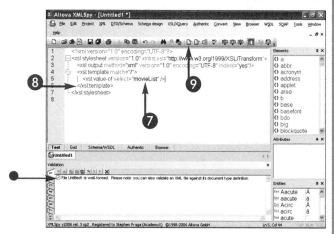

7 Set the value of the attribute to an XPath expression.

8 Type the closing `xsl:template` tag.

9 Click the Check Well-Formedness button to confirm that the document is well-formed.

● The Validation area shows if there are errors or no errors in the document.

10 Save the document with an .xsl file extension.

The file is saved.

Apply It

You can use `xsl:value-of` to select an attribute value and convert it to a string using the XPath @ attribute expression. This is particularly helpful when converting attributes to elements:

```
<xsl:template match="/movieList/title">
                <xsl:element name="rating">
                <xsl:value-of select="@rating" />
                </xsl:element>
</xsl:template>
```

In this case, the value of the attribute, such as `"PG"`, would be returned by the parser and then used as the value of the new `review` element. You will often find this necessary, especially when converting one XML document structure into a new structure.

Add Text to the Transformation

Sometimes, it will be necessary to output literal strings of text within the transformation. When transforming to HTML, for instance, you need to add the HTML structure elements to the output. You may also want to add static text for the page title, headings, copyright notices, and so forth. Any of this type of text can be typed directly into the XSLT document, and, as long as it does not violate any XML syntax rules, it will be output directly.

One special case, however, is whitespace. Parsers are unfortunately not completely consistent on how they deal with whitespace, particularly when it comes to multiple consecutive spaces and carriage returns. Fortunately, XSLT provides for an element to add literal text, including whitespace, to the output: `xsl:text`. Anything within the `xsl:text` element is output as literal text, including

whitespace. To force multiple consecutive spaces in the output, type an opening `xsl:text` element and then key in the number of spaces that you want to have and a closing `xsl:text` element. To force a carriage return, simply place a carriage return between the opening and closing `xsl:text` elements by pressing the Enter key between them. Experience and testing will reveal when you need to use `xsl:text` and when you achieve the results that you want without it.

```
<xsl:template match="/">

    <xsl:value-of select="firstname" />

    <xsl:text> </xsl:text>

    <xsl:value-of select="lastname" />

</xsl:template>
```

Add Text to the Transformation

① Open an XSLT document that contains the root `stylesheet` element and the `output` element.

② Type an opening `xsl:template` element.

③ Type a `match` attribute.

④ Use XPath to set the value of the `match` attribute to an element in the XML file that you plan to transform.

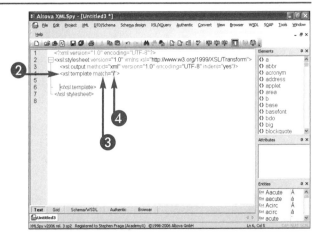

⑤ Type an `xsl:value-of` element.

⑥ Type the `select` attribute.

⑦ Set the value of the attribute to an XPath expression.

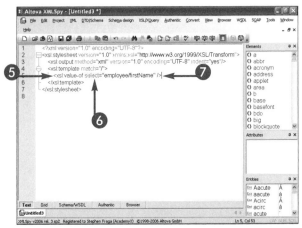

8 Type an `xsl:text` tag.

9 Enter the text you want or one or more spaces.

10 Type the closing `xsl:text` tag.

11 Type the closing `xsl:template` tag.

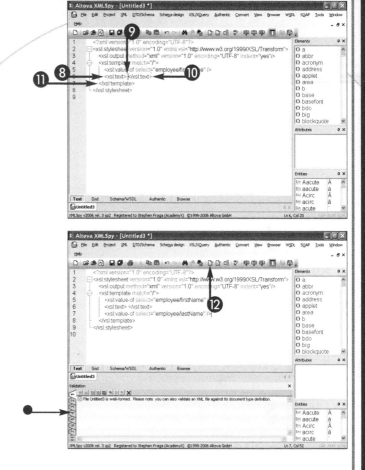

12 Click the Check Well-Formedness button to confirm that the document is well-formed.

● The Validation area opens to show if there are errors or no errors in the document.

13 Save the document with an .xsl file extension.

The file is saved.

Extra

To ensure that the result of the transformation is well-formed XML, parsers will by default convert angle brackets, quotation marks, apostrophes, and ampersands with their equivalent entities if any of those characters appear within an `xsl:text` block. This ensures that the output of `xsl:text` is literal text, so `<xsl:text><h1></xs:text>` would generate `&lt;h1&gt;`.

However, the `xsl:text` element has an optional attribute, `disable-output-escaping`, with possible values of `yes` and `no`. If `yes`, characters within the text block will not be escaped. Care should be taken if using this attribute to ensure that non-escaped characters will not appear within the `xsl:text` block.

This escaping or non-escaping of characters applies when using an output method of either XML or HTML; when outputting to text, no escaping occurs as the resulting document does not need to follow any well-formedness rules. The attribute also exists, and may be used in the same manner, for the `xsl:value-of` element. XSLT processors are not required to support this attribute, and if the use of the attribute generates an error by creating XML that is not well-formed, some processors will generate errors, whereas others may choose to ignore the attribute and simply escape the characters — so be sure to test its use on your processor before relying on it.

Simple XSLT documents require a single `xsl:template` block. Sometimes, however, you need to have an instruction that applies a template from one part of the XSLT to another. This is the role of `xsl:apply-templates`. The `xsl:apply-templates` element does not, as its name would seem to imply, actually generate output. Instead, it tells the parser which template rule should be applied in a particular context.

The `xsl:apply-templates` rule has an optional `select` attribute that can be used to provide an XPath expression for a particular element. If you do not include the `select` attribute, the parser will apply whichever template seems most appropriate for the context.

The `xsl:apply-templates` can also be used to limit the XML being processed. If the `select` attribute is provided, only the elements and children that match the expression are processed. For example, given the following XML:

```
<?xml version="1.0" encoding="utf-8" ?>
```

```
<root><firstChild><secondChild>Lorem
Ipsum</secondChild><thirdChild>dolor sit
amet</thirdChild></firstChild></root>
```

you could construct this XSLT:

```
<?xml version="1.0" encoding="utf-8" ?>

<xsl:stylesheet xmlns:xsl="http://
www.w3.org/1999/XSL/Transform">

<xsl:template match="/root/firstChild">

    <xsl:apply-templates
select="secondChild" />

</xsl:template>

</xsl:stylesheet>
```

When applying the transformation, the output in this case would simply be "Lorem Ipsum," as only the `secondChild` element would be processed.

Apply Templates

① Open an XSLT document that contains the root `stylesheet` element and the `output` element.

② Type an opening `xsl:template` element.

③ Type a `match` attribute.

④ Use XPath to set the value of the `match` attribute to an element in the XML file that you plan to transform.

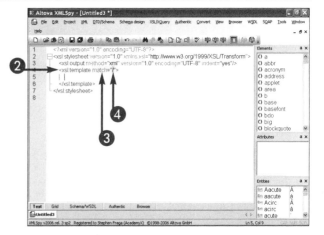

⑤ Type an `xsl:apply-templates` element.

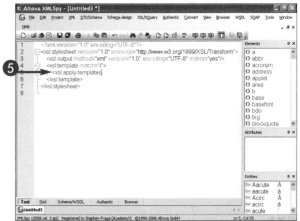

6 Type the `select` attribute.

7 Set the value of the attribute to an XPath expression.

8 Type the closing `xsl:template` tag.

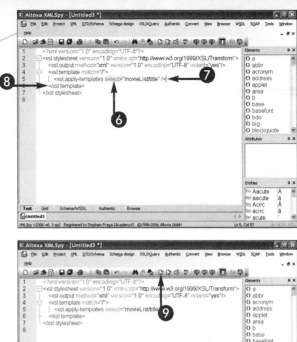

9 Click the Check Well-Formedness button to confirm that the document is well-formed.

● The Validation area opens to show if there are errors or no errors in the document.

10 Save the document with an .xsl file extension.

The file is saved.

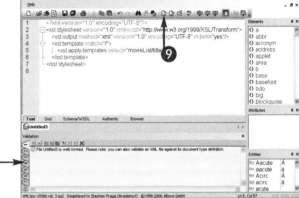

Apply It

You can also use `apply-templates` to apply the properties of a second template in your XSLT.

```
<xsl:template match="/">
                <xsl:element name="NewElem">
                    <xsl:apply-templates select="sample">
                </xsl:element>
</xsl:template>
<xsl:template match="sample">
                <xsl:copy>
                    <xsl:value-of select="." />
                </xsl:copy>
</xsl:template>
```

Loop with XSLT

Frequently, you will want to loop over elements in your XML. Almost every XML document has at least one element that repeats for each individual piece of data. If you were developing an XML phone list, you would have a root element followed, probably, by an element such as `<person>`. This element would contain the details that are contained in a phone book, such as name, address, and phone number. This element would also repeat once for each person being stored in the directory.

When transforming this kind of document, it seems obvious that you would want to have the output for each person to be the same. Instead of having to create an unknown, and unknowable, number of `xsl:templates`

for each person, you can use the `xsl:for-each` element to loop over your XML.

The `xsl:for-each` element has a required `select` attribute, in which you provide an XPath expression to the element over which you want to loop. This element can only be used within an `xsl:template` block:

```
<xsl:template match="/">

    <xsl:for-each select="person">

    <xsl:value-of select="name" />

    </xsl:for-each>

</xsl:template>
```

Loop with XSLT

① Open an XSLT document that contains the root `stylesheet` element and the `output` element.

② Type an opening `xsl:template` element.

③ Type a `match` attribute.

④ Use XPath to set the value of the `match` attribute to an element in the XML file that you plan to transform.

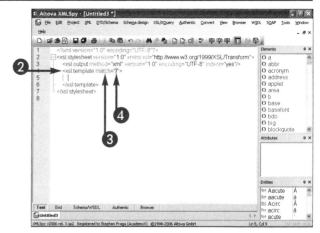

⑤ Type an `xsl:for-each` tag.

⑥ Type the `select` attribute.

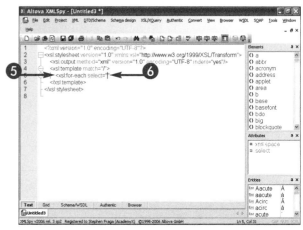

7. Set the value of the attribute to an XPath expression for the element over which you want to loop.

8. Type an `xsl:value-of` tag.

9. Type a `select` attribute.

10. Set the value of the attribute to an XPath expression.

11. Type the closing `xsl:for-each` tag.

12. Type the closing `xsl:template` tag.

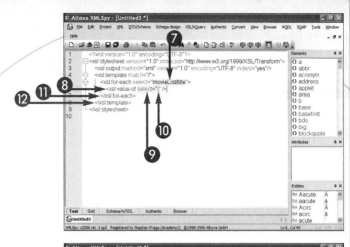

13. Click the Check Well-Formedness button to confirm that the document is well-formed.

● The Validation area opens to show if there are errors or no errors in the document.

14. Save the document with an .xsl file extension.

The file is saved.

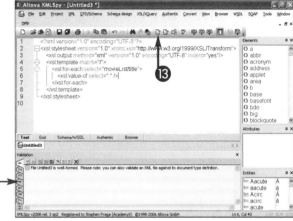

Apply It

You can nest `for-each` statements if you need to. If you have a repeating element within another repeating element, it is legal, and in that case you would need a `for-each` within a `for-each`:

```
<xsl:template match="/">
                <xsl:for-each select="person">
                    <xsl:value-of select="firstname" />
                    <xsl:text> </xsl:text>
                    <xsl:value-of select="lastname" />
                    <xsl:for-each select="phone">
                        <xsl:value-of select="phone" />
                    </xsl:for-each>
                </xsl:for-each>
</xsl:template>
```

Note that you could achieve the same effect by creating separate templates for the nested repeating element and then applying those templates instead of using `xsl:for-each`.

Sort with XSLT

Data is frequently entered in a relatively random order. In creating a customer list, you are going to add customers as you encounter them. Employee directories are usually created in the order in which employees join the organization. Even if the data is entered in a specific order, there are many occasions when a different order is needed for a particular purpose.

XSLT provides the ability to reorder data through the implementation of the `xsl:sort` element. `xsl:sort` takes a `select` attribute, which uses an XPath expression to specify the element on which sorting will occur. If omitted, the sorting will occur on the currently selected node.

By default, `xsl:sort` treats all data as text, which can return strange results if given a set of numbers with unequal digits — that is, "1, 2, 5, 10, 20, 30" will sort to "1, 10, 2, 20, 30, 5." Therefore, the element has an optional `data-type` attribute that enables you to specify a data type for the element to be sorted. To properly sort the preceding list, the `data-type` attribute would need to be set to `number`.

Multiple sort orders, such as sorting on last name and then first name, can be achieved by presenting multiple `xsl:sort` elements. The data is sorted in the order in which the tags are listed.

The `xsl:sort` element also accepts optional `order` and `case-order` attributes. The `order` attribute has possible values of `ascending`, which is the default, and `descending`. The `case-order` attribute accepts `upper-first` and `lower-first` to specify whether words with capital first letters should have sorting preference.

Sort with XSLT

① Open an XSLT document that contains the root `stylesheet` element and the `output` element.

② Type an opening `xsl:template` element.

③ Type a `match` attribute.

④ Use XPath to set the value of the `match` attribute to an element in the XML file that you plan to transform.

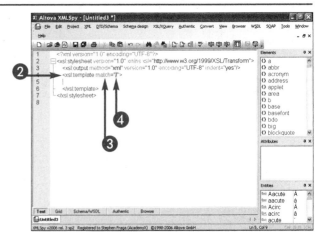

⑤ Type an `xsl:for-each` tag.

⑥ Type the `select` attribute.

⑦ Set the value of the attribute to an XPath expression for the element over which you want to loop.

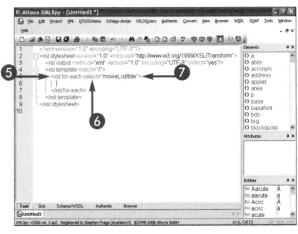

8. Type an `xsl:sort` tag.

9. Set the `select` attribute to the XPath expression of the criteria on which you want to sort.

10. Type an `xsl:value-of` tag.

11. Type a `select` attribute.

12. Set the value of the attribute to an XPath expression.

13. Type the closing `xsl:for-each` tag.

14. Type the closing `xsl:template` tag.

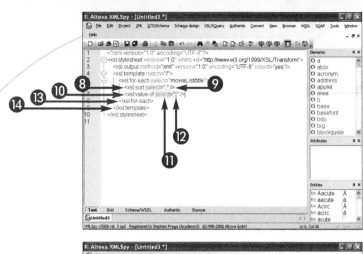

15. Click the Check Well-Formedness button to confirm that the document is well-formed.

● The Validation area opens to show if there are errors or no errors in the document.

16. Save the document with an .xsl file extension.

The file is saved.

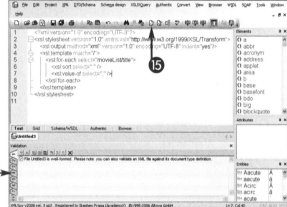

The `xsl:sort` element must be a child of either `xsl:for-each` or `xsl:apply-templates`. If the latter, you need to use an opening and closing `xsl:apply-templates` tag because that tag is normally presented as an empty tag. The `xsl:sort` tag itself will always be empty:

```
<xsl:template match="/">
            <xsl:apply-templates select=".">
                <xsl:sort />
            </xsl:apply-templates>
</xsl:template>
```

Although you will almost always want to sort on an element, the `xsl:sort`'s `select` attribute can take any valid XPath expression, including an attribute reference, so `<xsl:sort select="@rating">` would sort by the value in the `rating` attribute of the element selected by the `xsl:apply-templates` or `xsl:for-each` element.

Using Conditional Logic in XSLT

XSLT has the capability to make simple decisions in the course of applying a transformation. The language provides for two elements to perform conditional logic: xsl:if and xsl:choose.

The xsl:template, xsl:value-of, and xsl:apply-templates elements have implicit conditional logic: They will only apply if the element exists. However, it is often necessary to build more specific, explicit logic into your transformations. xsl:if has a required test attribute, which takes as its value an XPath expression that must evaluate to a true or false value. If the test is true, the elements within the xsl:if will execute; if not, they will be ignored.

```
<xsl:template match="/movieList/title">

    <xsl:if test="@rating='PG'">
```

```
    <xsl:apply-templates />

    </xsl:if>

</xsl:template>
```

The limitation of xsl:if is that it can only test on a single condition. Should you need to provide more conditions, similar to an if/else if structure in traditional programming, you use the xsl:choose element, which does not take attributes, but rather will contain a set of xsl:when elements, which like xsl:if take a test attribute, set to the value against which you want to test.

You can optionally provide an xsl:otherwise element as the last child of xsl:choose. This element will serve as a default if no xsl:when test proved true.

Using Conditional Logic in XSLT

① Open an XSLT document that contains the root stylesheet element and the output element.

② Type an opening xsl:template element.

③ Type a match attribute.

④ Use XPath to set the value of the match attribute to an element in the XML file that you plan to transform.

⑤ Type an xsl:for-each element.

⑥ Type a select attribute.

⑦ Set the value of the attribute to an XPath expression.

⑧ Type an xsl:sort element.

⑨ Set the value of the select attribute to an XPath expression.

⑩ Type an opening xsl:choose tag.

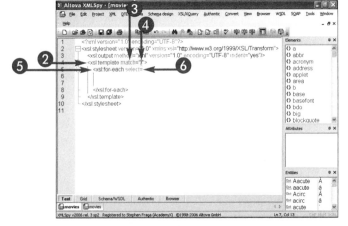

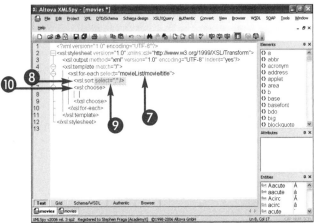

⑪ Type an `xsl:when` tag.

⑫ Type the `test` attribute.

⑬ Set the value of the attribute to an XPath expression that will evaluate to true or false.

⑭ Type an `xsl:value-of` tag.

⑮ Type a `select` attribute.

⑯ Set the value of the attribute to an XPath expression.

⑰ Type the closing `xsl:when` tag.

⑱ Repeat steps **11** through **17** for each condition.

⑲ Type a closing `xsl:choose` tag.

⑳ Type the closing `xsl:template` tag.

㉑ Click the Check Well-Formedness button to confirm that the document is well-formed.

● The Validation area opens to show if there are errors or no errors in the document.

㉒ Save the document with an .xsl file extension.

The file is saved.

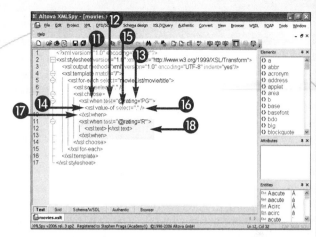

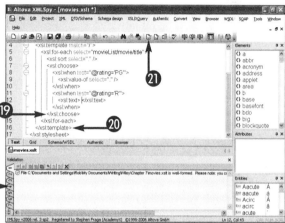

Apply It

You can achieve the same effect as `xsl:choose` by using a series of `xsl:if` statements. The amount of code required is almost identical:

```
<xsl:template match="/">
                <xsl:if test="first_condition">
                   <xsl:apply-templates select="." />
                </xsl:if>
                <xsl:if test="second_condition">
                   <xsl:apply-templates select="/childElement" />
                </xsl:if>
</xsl:template>
```

XSLT can create new elements in the result document that did not exist in the original. This is most often used in XML to XML transformations, where the new XML file needs elements not originally present.

New elements are created using the `xsl:element` element. It takes a required `name` attribute, wherein you specify the name of the element being created. If the new element requires a namespace, you use the `namespace` attribute to provide the URL to the namespace.

The contents of the new element are provided by applying a template within the `xsl:element` tag, or using `xsl:value-of` within the tag, or providing literal text:

```
<xsl:element name="fullname">

    <xsl:value-of name="firstname" />
```

```
<xsl:text> </xsl:text>

</xsl:element>
```

Attributes can be added to the element through the inclusion of an `xsl:attribute` element within the `xsl:element` tag. Like `xsl:element`, the contents of the attribute are provided within its tag:

```
<xsl:element name="title">

    <xsl:attribute name="rating">

        <xsl:value-of select="@rating" />

    </xsl:attribute>

</xsl:element>
```

Create an Element

1 Open an XSLT document that contains the root `stylesheet` element and the `output` element.

2 Type an opening `xsl:template` element.

3 Type a `match` attribute.

4 Use XPath to set the value of the `match` attribute to an element in the XML file that you plan to transform.

5 Type an `xsl:element` tag.

6 Type the `name` attribute.

7 Set the value of the attribute.

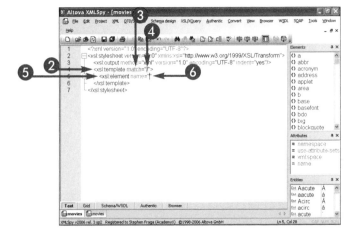

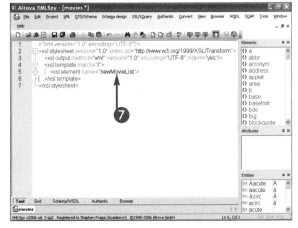

⑧ Type an `xsl:attribute` tag.

⑨ Type a `name` attribute.

⑩ Set the value of the attribute.

⑪ Type the closing slash and angle bracket of the `xsl:attribute` tag.

⑫ Type the closing `xsl:element` tag.

⑬ Type the closing `xsl:template` tag.

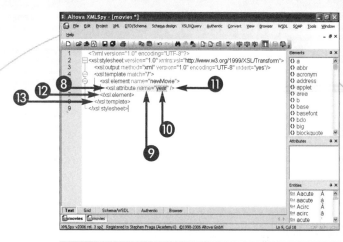

⑭ Click the Check Well-Formedness button to confirm that the document is well-formed.

The Validation area opens to show if there are errors or no errors in the document.

⑮ Save the document with an .xsl file extension.

The file is saved.

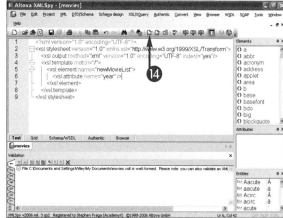

Apply It

You can create attributes that can be used on many elements, or a single reference to multiple attributes, using the `xsl:attribute-set` element, which is a top-level element and must be a direct child of the root `xsl:stylesheet` element:

```
<xsl:attribute-set name="reviewersSet">
                <xsl:attribute name="reviewers">Scott, Bill, Ted</xsl:attribute>
</xsl:attribute-set>
<xsl:template match="/">
                <xsl:element name="review" use-attribute-sets="reviewersSet">
                  <xsl:apply-templates match="." />
                </xsl:element>
</xsl:template>
```

One of the most versatile and useful capabilities of XSLT is that one XSLT document can include the contents of another. This enables you to modularize your approach to designing transformations. If, for example, you have a set of `xsl:templates` that need to be used on multiple documents, you can place them in their own file and then include them as necessary. Dividing style sheets like this also allows you to reduce development and debugging time, as portions of your style sheet will only need to be created once.

XSLT provides for two elements to include files: `xsl:import` and `xsl:include`. The `xsl:import` element takes a required `href` attribute, set to a relative or absolute path to the file being imported. All transformation instructions in the importing file will take precedence over any instructions in the file being imported in the case of a conflict. Should two or more

imported style sheets contain conflicts among themselves, the last imported will take precedence.

The `xsl:include` element also takes a required `href` attribute. As with `xsl:import`, the attribute's value must be a relative or absolute path to the file being included. Unlike `xsl:import`, instructions in the `xsl:include` file do not take precedence over those in the file doing the including.

Both the `xsl:import` and `xsl:include` elements must be direct children of the root `xsl:stylesheet` element. The `xsl:import` element must also be the first element presented after the root, before any other elements.

Imported and included files can, in turn, include other files. Be careful when doing this, however, because it can become very confusing very quickly. Also, you must take care to avoid circular references, in which file A includes file B, which in turn includes file A. Parsers will throw errors should this occur.

Include and Import Other XSLT Files

1 Open an XSLT document that contains the root `stylesheet` element and the `output` element.

2 Type an `xsl:include` element.

3 Type an `href` attribute.

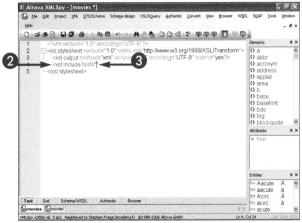

Set the value to a path to another
XSLT document.

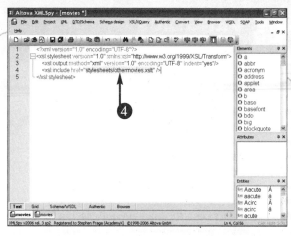

Click the Check Well-Formedness
button to confirm that the document
is well-formed.

- The Validation area opens to show if
there are errors or no errors in the
document.

Save the document with an .xsl file
extension.

The file is saved.

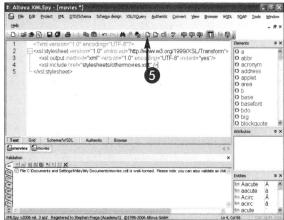

Extra

Imported and included documents may import or include other documents. So it is possible to have one style
sheet include or import a second style sheet. There is in theory no limit as to how many levels of importing or
including you can have: Style sheet A can import style sheet B, which in turn imports style sheet C. You could
even have a style sheet that imports another, which in turn includes a third, or vice versa. For example, style
sheet A could import style sheet B, which already includes style sheet C. Keep in mind that the key difference
between importing and including is that the former establishes precedence whereas the latter does not.

Be aware that recursive importing or including is not allowed, directly or indirectly. If style sheet A imports or
includes style sheet B, and B then imports or includes A, an error will occur. Care needs to be taken to avoid
this when more than one level of importing or including is happening, so an error will also occur if style sheet
A imports or includes style sheet B, which imports or includes style sheet C , which in turn imports or
includes style sheet A.

XSLT provides support for basic variables and parameters to represent data in your documents. Although the two are slightly different, their basic purpose is the same.

`xsl:variable` enables you to create a named variable that can be used elsewhere in your document. It has one required attribute, `name`. The value of the attribute can either be presented between the opening and closing `xsl:variable` tags or through the use of an XPath expression in the optional `select` attribute. The tag must be empty if using `select`.

Once set, the variable can be referenced elsewhere in the document through the `$name` syntax, where `name` is the value given in the `name` attribute. A variable's value cannot be changed later in the code:

`<xsl:variable name="rating">PG</xsl:variable>`

`<xsl:value-of select="$rating" />`

Parameters serve a similar purpose to variables, but although variables have their value set within the XSLT document itself and then cannot change, parameters can have their values set and changed externally, either from within the document or at runtime.

Parameters are set with the `xsl:param` element and a `name` attribute. Just as with variables, you can use either a value within the tags or a `select` attribute. A parameter's initial value can be overridden from within the style sheet, usually in an `xsl:apply-templates` construct with an `xsl:with-param` element, which takes a `name` attribute equal to the parameter being set, and a new value provided either within the tags or using `select`. Many XSLT parsers also allow for the setting of parameters at runtime. Consult your parser's documentation for details as to how to accomplish this.

Using Variables and Parameters

① Open an XSLT document that contains the root `stylesheet` element and the `output` element.

② Type an opening `xsl:variable` element.

③ Type a `name` attribute.

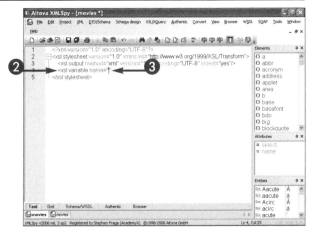

④ Set the value of the name.

⑤ Type in literal text for the value of the variable.

⑥ Type a closing `xsl:variable` tag.

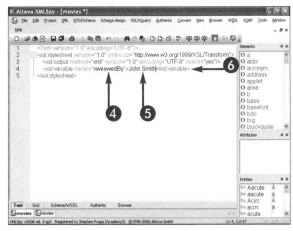

7 Type an opening `xsl:template` element.

8 Add an appropriate `match` attribute.

9 Type an `xsl:element` tag.

10 Type the `name` attribute.

11 Add an `xsl:value-of` tag.

12 Add a `select` attribute.

13 Set the value to the variable that you created.

14 Close the `xsl:element` element.

15 Type the closing `xsl:template` tag.

16 Click the Check Well-Formedness button to confirm that the document is well-formed.

● The Validation area opens to show if there are errors or no errors in the document.

17 Save the document with an .xsl file extension.

The file is saved.

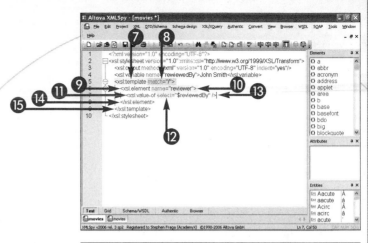

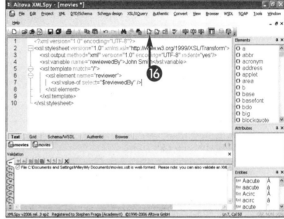

Apply It

You can use XPath expressions for purposes other than to reference paths to other nodes in XML. Instead, they can be regular mathematical expressions and leverage XPath's function libraries. This is particularly useful in the case of setting variables, as these can perform calculations:

```
<xsl:variable name="grossPay" select="6*8" />
<xsl:variable name="sumOfValues" select="sum(35,5,2)" />
```

If you need to set the value to the literal text of the expression rather than its calculated value, you can enclose the expression in both double and single quotation marks:

```
<xsl:variable name="formula" select="'8*(4+2)'" />
```

Run the Transformation with a Web Browser

After you have written the XSLT document and confirmed its well-formedness and validity, you will need to associate the XSLT file with an XML file and then parse the XML in a parser that can perform the transformation.

To associate the XLST with an XML file, you need to add an `xml-stylesheet` processing instruction to the XML. This should be at the top of the file, immediately below the XML declaration. In the processing instruction, you specify the type of style sheet you are using and the path to it:

```
<?xml-stylesheet type="text/xsl"
href="path_to_xslt_document" ?>
```

Modern Web browsers are, to a point, capable of performing the transformation. An XML-to-XML

transformation displays a single block of unformatted text, as the browser will no longer be using its built-in style sheet that allows it to display the tree structure of the XML. An XML-to-XHTML or XML-to-HTML transformation will display the properly structured and formatted Web page.

However, viewing the source of the page will show the original document's XML instead of the transformed HTML or XML in Microsoft Internet Explorer. Microsoft does have a free extension to the browser, called the Internet Explorer Tools for Validating XML and Viewing XSLT Output, which enables developers to right-click in the browser window and view the resulting document.

Run the Transformation with a Web Browser

① Open an XML document in your editor.

● In Altova XMLSpy, click File → Open.

The file opens.

② Add a processing instruction to attach an XSLT style sheet to the XML document.

③ Click File → Save.

The file is saved.

④ Open Internet Explorer.

⑤ Navigate to www.microsoft.com/downloads/details.aspx?FamilyId=D23C1D2C-1571-4D61-BDA8-ADF9F6849DF9&displaylang=en.

⑥ Follow the instructions to install the Internet Explorer Tools for Validating XML and Viewing XSLT Output.

⑦ Click File → Open.

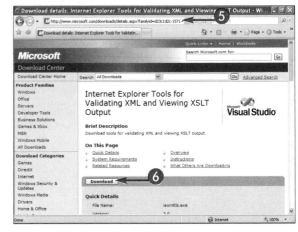

8 Open the XML document that you saved in step **3**.

The transformed file is displayed in the browser.

9 Right-click the document.

10 Click View XSLT Output.

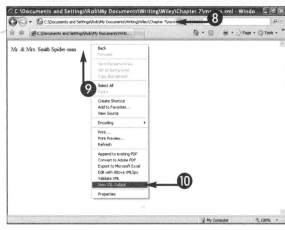

The output appears in the XSLT Transformation Output window.

Extra

XSLT that results in properly formed HTML will be displayed correctly in other modern browsers such as Mozilla Firefox. However, as of the time of this writing, Firefox lacks the add-on functionality provided by Microsoft's Internet Explorer Tools for Validating XML and Viewing XSLT Output, so although the resulting HTML will be properly displayed in the browser window, you cannot view or save the resulting HTML source. In fact, if you use Firefox's View Source functionality, you will see the original, untransformed XML file. Like Internet Explorer, Firefox will generally render transformed XML as plain text in the browser window.

Unfortunately, even Internet Explorer with the add-on installed makes saving the resulting output difficult as it opens it not in Notepad, the way normally viewing source on a Web page would, but rather in a new browser window that lacks the menu bar to enable saving. Therefore, if you need to generate XSLT output and save the result, you will need to use a dedicated XSLT processor, such as the one built into XMLSpy, which nicely is able to both display the results and save the output.

Run the Transformation Using Altova XMLSpy

ltova XMLSpy is the XML editor of choice among many professional XML developers — in part because of the powerful additional tools it contains for designing and running XSLT transformations.

At a simple level, XMLSpy enables users to run an XSLT transformation by clicking a single button on the toolbar. This causes the program's built-in parser to perform the transformation and display the resulting document. By default, the transformed document is displayed in XMLSpy's built-in browser, which runs the Internet Explorer rendering engine, but unlike running the transformation directly in Internet Explorer, XMLSpy gives developers the choice to also view and save the source code resulting from the transformation by simply switching to Text view.

More complex transformations, such as those which rely on variables and conditional logic, can often require debugging. Syntax errors will be caught by the parser and

return as well-formedness or validation errors, which are fairly easy to fix. However, when using conditional logic, XSLT documents can sometimes suffer from logical errors, in which the syntax is correct but the transformation returns unexpected results. To help with this, XMLSpy includes a full-featured debugger for XSL, including the ability to step into code and set breakpoints. Depending on the complexity of the transformation, these can be invaluable to developers.

XMLSpy enables developers to provide new values for parameters at runtime, so it is possible to set up an XSLT document that will perform differently each time that it is run, based on the parameter value set.

XMLSpy contains the capability to run both XSLT and XSL-FO transformations, although the latter requires an additional free plug-in, called *Apache FOP*, which is available for download from the Altova Web site, www.altova.com.

Run the Transformation Using Altova XMLSpy

① In XMLSpy, click File ➔ Open.

② Open an XML file.

   The file opens.

③ Click XSL/XQuery ➔ Assign XSL.

④ Click OK in the message.

⑤ Click Browse.

⑥ Select the XSLT document.

⑦ Click Open.

⑧ Click OK.

● The `xml-stylesheet` processing instruction is added to the document.

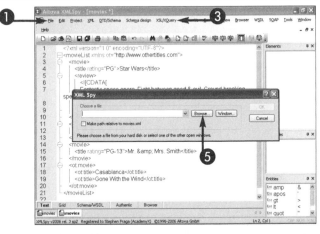

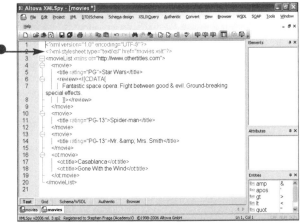

9 Click XSL/XQuery → XSL Transformation.

The transformed document opens in a new window.

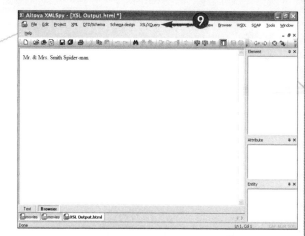

10 Click Text.

The view changes to show the transformed code.

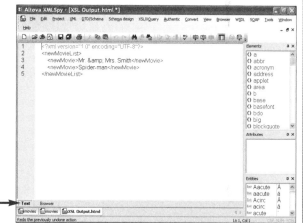

Extra

Altova has a companion product available called *StyleVision* that is designed specifically to create XSLT documents. StyleVision supports output in both XSLT 1 and 2, as well as XSL-FO and cascading style sheets. It can generate transformations to HTML, PDF, Rich Text Format, and Authentic forms. It also supports input from XML and most major databases.

StyleVision uses a graphical design interface, so developers do not need to write code in order to generate the output that they want. Its interface supports drag-and-drop functionality from the source XML file, and helper screens similar to those in XMLSpy make applying formatting easy. The program will simultaneously generate XSL style sheets for each of its output formats, so you do not need to specify one and worry that you may end up needing another. StyleVision includes an integrated preview window for HTML, PDF, and RTF output and enables you to quickly switch between the preview and source code for each.

As with XMLSpy, Altova offers a fully functioning 30-day trial version of StyleVision from its Web site at www.altova.com. In addition, Altova offers free online instructor-led training courses for its products.

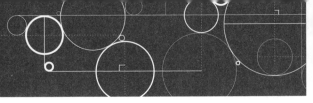

PHP, the extremely popular open source server-side Web scripting technology, has the capability to perform XSLT transformations at the server, delivering a regular HTML document to the user's browser. PHP, which is currently in version 5.2, can be downloaded free of charge from www.php.net. PHP 5 performs XSLT transformations by way of the XSL extension, which is included by default in the PHP installation.

The first step in performing the transformation in PHP involves creating an XSLT processor resource object:

```
$xmlProc = new XsltProcessor();
```

Then you need to load the XSLT document into an instance of the DomDocument object:

```
$xslt = new DomDocument();

$xslt -> load("xslt_stylesheet.xsl");
```

Next, import the style sheet into the processor resource object:

```
$xmlProc -> importStylesheet($xslt);
```

Now, you need to load the XML into another instance of DomDocument.

```
$xml = new DomDocument();

$xml -> load("xmlfile.xml");
```

Finally, you invoke the transformToXML method. It is a good idea to do this within an if statement, allowing you to gracefully handle errors that may occur in the process:

```
if ($html = $xmlProc->transformToXML($xml)) {

        echo $html;

} else {

        trigger_error(E_USER_ERROR);

}
```

Run the Transformation Using PHP

① Create a new PHP document in your PHP editor.

② Create an instance of the XsltProcessor object.

③ Create an instance of the DomDocument object for the XSLT document.

④ Load the XSLT document into the DomDocument instance.

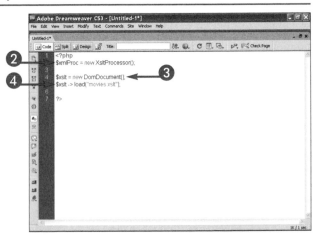

⑤ Call the importStylesheet method of the XsltProcessor object.

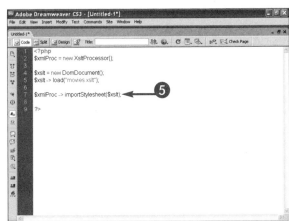

6 Create an instance of the `DomDocument` object for the XML file.

7 Load the XML file into the `DomDocument` instance.

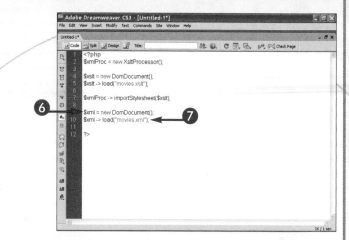

8 Create an `if` statement.

9 In the test of the `if` statement, set a variable equal to the `XsltProcessor` calling the `transformToXML` method on the XML variable.

10 Use an `echo` statement to output the variable.

11 Add an `else` block.

12 Use `trigger_error` to gracefully handle errors.

13 Click File → Save.

The file is saved.

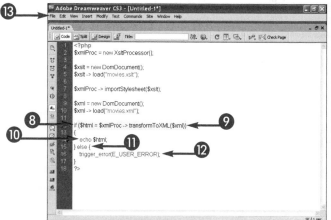

Apply It

You can pass parameter values to the XSLT at runtime in PHP. In version 5, you must create each parameter individually:

```
$xmlProc -> setParameter($namespace, "param_name", "value");
```

In version 5.1 and later, you can create an array to hold the parameters and then pass the array to the `XsltProcessor` object:

```
$params["param_name"] = "value";
$xmlProc -> setParameter($namespace, $params);
```

Run the Transformation Using Adobe ColdFusion

Adobe ColdFusion is a Web application server. The most current version, ColdFusion 8, was released in the summer of 2007.

ColdFusion has many advantages over other Web applications. First, and perhaps most important, it uses a relatively simple yet extremely powerful language, CFML, which closely resembles HTML in structure and syntax. Thanks to this, developing applications in ColdFusion takes a fraction of the time and code needed by other languages. ColdFusion also provides the ability to quickly develop Flash-based forms and dynamically generate PDF documents on-the-fly. A free version of the ColdFusion server is available at www.adobe.com/products/coldfusion; download the trial edition and install it as the free developer edition. CFML documents are, like HTML, plain text, but Adobe's Dreamweaver CS3 product has many features in it to enable developers to create ColdFusion

applications even more quickly. A 30-day trial of Dreamweaver can be downloaded from www.adobe.com/products/dreamweaver.

Performing XSLT transformations in ColdFusion is extremely simple. First, you use the `cffile` tag to load the XSLT document into a variable:

```
<cffile action="read" file="path_to_xslt_
document" variable="xsltDoc">
```

Then you call ColdFusion's `XMLParse` function to read the XML file into another variable:

```
<cfset xmlDoc = XMLParse
("path_to_xml_document")>
```

Finally, you call the `XMLTransform` function, passing the XML document and the XSLT document variables to it:

```
<cfoutput>#XMLTransform(xmlDoc,
xsltDoc)#</cfoutput>
```

Run the Transformation Using Adobe ColdFusion

① Create a new ColdFusion document.

● In Adobe Dreamweaver, click File → New.

  In the Page Type column, select ColdFusion and click Create.

● Click View → Code and delete all the existing code on the page.

② Create a `<cffile>` tag.

③ Set the `action` attribute to **read**.

④ Set the `file` attribute to a path to an XSLT file.

⑤ Set the `variable` attribute to a valid ColdFusion variable name.

⑥ Create a `<cfset>` tag.

⑦ Set a variable name equal to the `XMLParse` function.

⑧ Pass the path to an XML file as the function's argument.

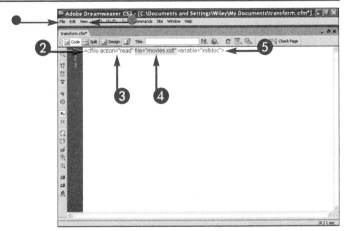

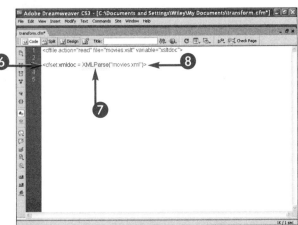

9 Create a `<cfoutput>` tag.

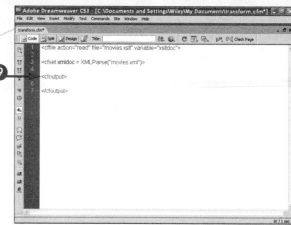

10 Output the `XMLTransform` function.

11 Pass the XML document variable and the XSLT document variable as the function's arguments.

12 Click File ➔ Save.

The file is saved.

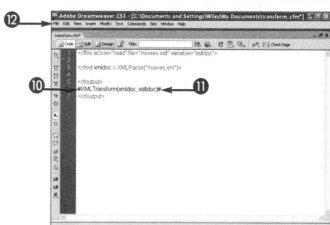

Extra

Another exciting implementation of XML and XSLT with ColdFusion is the implementation of XForms. XForms is actually a Web standard developed by the W3C to provide a newer, much more powerful implementation of Web forms by using XML to describe the form controls and XSLT to describe the layout. When you separate the form controls from their content, it is much easier to reorganize, repurpose, and redesign forms. Additionally, XForms provide many form controls that are not supported by regular HTML forms, such as combo boxes and date pickers, as well usability improvements such as input masks. Unfortunately, there are very few browsers with native support for XForms at this time.

ColdFusion, through its native `<cfform>` tag set, can automatically generate the XML for XForms and provide the XSLT transformation on the server, so developers do not need to worry about browser support for them. Although creating the form itself is very easy in ColdFusion, the language does not provide any help in generating the XSLT for the presentational side of things. However, you can use the XSLT you now know to create the necessary XSLT code to use this powerful feature in ColdFusion.

ASP.NET applications can run XSLT transformations via the `XslTransform` class. To use this class, developers must first import several additional libraries into their code:

```
<%@ Import Namespace="System.Xml" %>

<%@ Import Namespace="System.Xml.Xsl" %>

<%@ Import Namespace="System.Xml.XPath" %>
```

Then a subroutine is created to contain the code:

```
<script language="C#" runat="server">

    public void Page_Load(Object sender,
EventArgs E) {
```

Next, the `MapPath` method is called to retrieve the XML and XSL documents:

```
    string xmlPath =
Server.MapPath("path_to_xml");
```

```
    string xslPath =
Server.MapPath("path_to_xsl");
```

Following that, the `XPathDocument` class is instantiated, taking the XML document as a property:

```
    XPathDocument doc = new
XPathDocument(xmlPath);
```

The `XslTransform` class is instantiated, and the XSL file is loaded into it:

```
    XslTransform transform = new
XslTransform();
```

```
    transform.Load(xslPath);
```

Finally, the `Transform` method of the `transform` object is called, taking as its argument the `XPathDocument` object:

```
    transform.Transform(doc);

    }

</script>
```

Run the Transformation Using ASP.NET

① Create a new C# document in your ASP.NET editor.

② Import the `System.Xml`, `System.Xml.Xsl`, and `System.Xml.Xpath` libraries.

③ Create a `script` tag.

④ Set the `language` attribute to **C#**.

⑤ Set `runat` to **server**.

⑥ Create a new `public` subroutine with a data type of `void` called `Page_Load`.

⑦ Set the subroutine's arguments to **Object sender, EventArgs E**.

⑧ Create a string variable, set equal to the `Server.MapPath` function.

⑨ Set the argument equal to the path to the XML file.

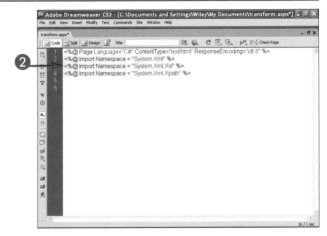

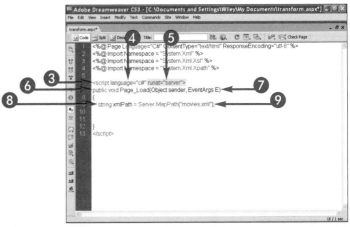

10 Create a string variable, set equal to the `Server.MapPath` function.

11 Set the argument equal to the path to the XSL file.

12 Create a new instance of the `XPathDocument` object.

13 Pass the XML file reference to `XPathDocument`.

14 Create a new instance of the `XslTransform` object.

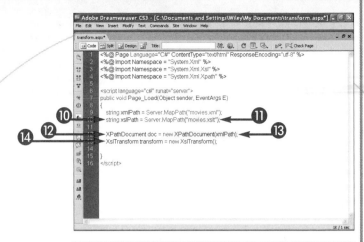

15 Call the object's `Load` method, passing to it the variable containing the path to the XSL file.

16 Call the object's `Transform` method, passing to it the instance of the `XPathDocument`.

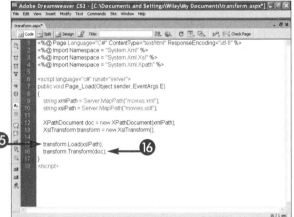

Extra

ASP.NET is Microsoft's set of Web technologies for creating dynamic Web applications. It runs on top of the .NET platform, which is an optional, albeit free component in Windows operating systems. If you are using Windows XP or Windows 2000, you can download and install the .NET platform from Microsoft's Web site. If you use Windows 2003 or Windows Vista, the platform comes preinstalled.

ASP.NET applications are written in one of two common languages: Visual Basic .NET, the latest version of Microsoft's Visual Basic programming language, and C#, pronounced "C sharp," a language the company developed for .NET based on C++. ASP.NET applications offer many advantages over other Web application languages, including precompiled code that runs much more efficiently than traditional script-based languages; Web controls based on the Windows user interface, which greatly reduces learning time for traditional Windows developers; the ability to separate presentational code from business-logic code; and more.

Create an XSLT Document Using Adobe Dreamweaver CS3

Adobe Dreamweaver offers a powerful Web design and development platform. It provides a "What You See Is What You Get" design environment that frees developers from having to write code. Its latest incarnation, now branded as part of Adobe's Creative Suite 3, lets XML developers create XSLT documents to transform XML to XSLT entirely in Design view. You can download a free 30-day trial of Dreamweaver from www.adobe.com/products/dreamweaver.

When you open a new XSLT document, Dreamweaver prompts you to find an XML source document. The program will then read this document and determine the XML tree structure. Its Bindings panel, normally used for showing database queries, will update to show the structure of the XML file, with indicators for repeating elements.

You can then design the basic HTML page as you normally would, adding text, headers, tables, images, and any other static elements. To add references to the XML, you can simply drag and drop the element that you want from the Bindings panel. In the code, Dreamweaver automatically generates the `xsl:template`, `xsl:apply-templates`, and `xsl:value-of` elements as needed.

On Dreamweaver's Insert bar, you will find an XSLT tab. On this bar are buttons to add repeat regions, which is Dreamweaver's term for an `xsl:for-each` statement, `xsl:if` statements, and `xsl:choose` instructions. In all three cases, the application will prompt you for the additional information it needs, such as which node to use for `xsl:for-each` or the condition to apply for `xsl:if` or `xsl:choose`.

Using Dreamweaver's Preview in Browser feature, you can view the results of the XSL in a Web browser via a temporary file that the application creates. You can return to Dreamweaver and make any modifications necessary before saving the file.

Create an XSLT Document Using Adobe Dreamweaver CS3

① In Dreamweaver, click File → New.

② Click XSLT (Entire Page).

③ Click Create.

A new document opens, and the Locate XML Source dialog box appears.

④ Click Browse.

⑤ Select the XML file that you want to transform.

⑥ Click Open.

⑦ Click OK.

The Bindings panel updates.

⑧ On the Insert bar, click the Common tab.

⑨ Click the Table button.

⑩ Fill out the Table dialog box and click OK.

A table is inserted.

⑪ In the Application panel, click Bindings.

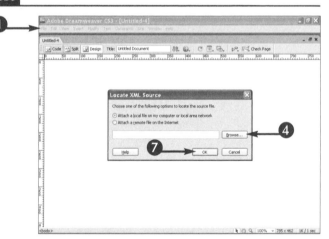

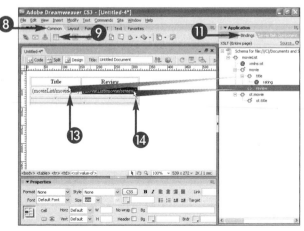

⓬ Drag the name of the element or attribute that you want to display on the page into one of the cells of the table.

The dynamic text is displayed on the page.

⓭ Repeat step **12** for any other data that you want to display.

⓮ On the Tag Chooser, click `<tr>`.

The row is selected.

⓯ On the Insert bar, click the XSLT tab.

⓰ Click the Repeat Region button.

The XPath Expression Builder (Repeat Region) dialog box appears.

⓱ Click the repeating element in the XML.

⓲ Click OK.

A repeat region is added to the document.

⓳ Press F12.

The transformed document is displayed in the default Web browser.

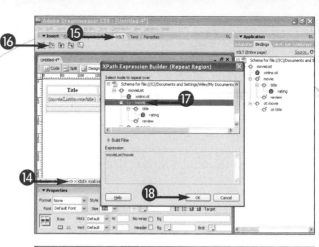

Extra

In order to support many of its traditional Web design features, Adobe Dreamweaver CS3 adds an embedded DOCTYPE to the top of the style sheet. This DOCTYPE adds general entity declarations for ten common entities used in HTML: for a nonbreaking space, © for the copyright symbol (©), ® for the registered trademark symbol (®), ™ for the trademark symbol (™), — for an em dash (—), “ for the left double quotation mark ("), ” for the right double quotation mark ("), £ for the British pound symbol (£), ¥ for the yen symbol (¥), and € for the Euro symbol (€). If you do not plan on using any of these symbols in your output, you can safely delete the DOCTYPE from the code of your document. Dreamweaver also allows you to create XSLT page fragments, when you want to include XML data on a bigger Web page. This can only be done on dynamic pages, as the transformation itself will need to be performed server-side by ColdFusion, PHP, ASP, or ASP.NET. After you create an XSLT page, you can open another page created using one of those server models and then use Dreamweaver's XSL transformation server behavior.

Understanding CSS

TML was originally conceived as a language to enable scientists to exchange information electronically with one another. As such, its original specification contained very little in terms of design elements. Rather, the early versions of the language focused entirely on structural elements, such as paragraphs, headings, lists, and tables. Fortunately, HTML and the Web did not stay solely in the realm of nuclear physicists for long. As its popularity grew in the mid-1990s, better design control, such as specifying fonts and colors, adding borders, and laying out pages, became necessary. Adapting HTML to simultaneously fill both the needs of defining structure and defining presentation turned out to be close to impossible, to the

point that many sites were horribly bloated with unnecessary code. Making matters worse, not all browsers supported all the presentational elements, forcing some designers to create multiple copies of their site for different browsers.

The World Wide Web Consortium, which oversees the development of HTML and other Web technologies, including XML, decided that the solution to the problem was to remove anything presentational from HTML, in essence taking it back to its original design goals, and instead created an entirely new language for the presentation of documents on the Web. Thus CSS (cascading style sheets) was born.

CSS Versions

The most widely supported versions of CSS are 1 and 2. CSS 1, introduced at the end of 1996, includes support for font controls, color, text spacing, text alignment, margins, borders, padding, and ID and class selectors. CSS 2, which was released in the middle of 1997, added positioning and media types. A newer version, CSS 3, is under development. It promises to add much more control over selector types and enhanced visual properties such as partial transparency, rounded corners, and shadows.

CSS Browser Support

Almost every major modern browser has near-perfect support for CSS 1. Most modern browsers support major portions of CSS 2, although many are notoriously buggy, especially in regards to many of the positioning rules. As CSS 3 has yet to be released, there is almost no support, although portions of it are already supported by some browsers, such as Apple's Safari. Due to these inconsistencies, it is vital that you test your pages in as many browsers as possible.

CSS General Syntax

CSS is not HTML, and it relies on an entirely different syntax. A style sheet is made up of a series of rules, which are in turn made up of one or more selectors, followed in curly braces by one or more declarations. The declarations are in turn made up of properties and values, separated by a colon. Each property:value pair is separated from other property:value pairs by a semicolon. The following example shows a style sheet rule in which the HTML p element is the selector, with a color:#AC3675 declaration and a font-weight:bold declaration:

```
p { color:#AC3675; font-weight:bold;}
```

Multiple Selectors

A style rule can take multiple selectors. A comma-separated list of selectors is presented, and then the style rule will apply to all elements in the list:

```
p, td, li { font-size:90%; }
```

Whitespace in CSS

CSS is completely whitespace insensitive. You can add as much or as little whitespace as you want. Some developers argue that readability is of paramount concern, especially in longer style sheets, so they advocate in favor of placing the selector on a line by itself, followed by each declaration on its own line. Others argue that each additional carriage return or tab character is adding unnecessary file size to the style sheet and should be avoided.

CSS General Syntax *(continued)*

Case Sensitivity in CSS

CSS declarations, both the properties and rules, are case insensitive. The selector, on the hand, is case sensitive. Because XHTML requires that all elements be lowercase, CSS element selectors should likewise be lowercase. Advanced selectors such as classes and IDs need to match the case in which they are typed in the XHTML document.

Units of Measurement

There is no default unit of measurement in CSS. The specification allows for a wide variety of supported units, both absolute and relative. Absolute units include inches, centimeters, millimeters, points, picas, and pixels. Relative units include percentages, ems, and exes. Units of measurement can be applied to many CSS properties, including font size, border width, element width, padding and margins, and position. Because there is no default, the unit must always be specified.

The Cascade

The *cascade* specifies how conflicts in multiple rules applied to the same element are resolved. In general, style rules that are closer to the element in question take precedence over those farther away, so a rule in an embedded style sheet will override a conflicting rule in a linked style sheet. Also, more specific rules override less specific rules, so ID selectors take precedence over general element selectors, as an ID targets one specific element whereas an element selector targets a less-specific set of elements on a page. Only declarations directly in conflict will be overridden, so a declaration

from a less-specific selector will apply if the more-specific selector is silent on that property.

For example, take the following two rules:

```
p {color:#999999; font-weight:bold; }
```

```
p#heading {color:#000099; }
```

A paragraph with an ID of `heading` would be dark blue, using the `color:#000099` from the more-specific `p#heading` rule, but would also be bold, as the more-specific rule does not state a `font-weight` property, so the less-specific rule applies.

Inheritance

Many, but not all, CSS properties inherit from parent-to-child elements. For example, if you have a paragraph that contains a span, the span will inherit most of the parent's properties, especially those regarding text and font styles. Box model properties will not inherit to nested inline elements, however, so the parent's margins and padding would not be directly applied to the nested span.

CSS Editors

CSS documents are plain text, like XHTML, so any editor will work. Every XHTML editor has some support for CSS, from a basic understanding of the file type such as you find in XMLSpy, to advanced code hinting and visual design support such as is found in Adobe Dreamweaver.

Linking and Importing

Usually, it is best to keep your style sheet information in a separate document. This maintains the concept of separating content from presentation, one of the key considerations behind the development of CSS. It also enables you to apply the same style sheet to multiple pages, so you can create one design for your entire Web site.

CSS provides for two ways to attach a CSS style sheet to an XHTML page. The more common is to use the XHTML `link` element:

```
<link rel="stylesheet" type="text/css"
href="path_to_css_document" />
```

All three attributes are required. The value of the `rel` attribute is almost always `stylesheet`, and the value of `text` is always `text/css`.

The second method is to import your style sheet through the special CSS `@import` rule, which appears within an XHTML style tag:

```
<style type="text/css">

@import ("path_to_css_document");

</style>
```

The two methods are not mutually exclusive. If you use both, any rule in the imported style sheet will take precedence over all rules in the linked style sheet, which enables designers to force certain properties to override. Also, be aware that early CSS-aware browsers do not support `@import`.

Change the Font

In the early days of the Web, choices for typographic controls were extremely limited on the Web. Designers could change the font itself and the color and size of text. A variety of elements would cause text to be rendered as bold or italic, but certain elements such as headings could not be made unbold. CSS sought to change all of that through the implementation of two broad categories of typographic controls: font properties and text properties.

You can change the font used on text through the font-family property. All browsers use device fonts — the fonts installed on a user's system — rather than embedding fonts into the file, so if you specify a font that the user does not have, the browser will revert to its default. Therefore, it is always a good idea to specify more than one font in a comma-separated list. The font-size property enables you to set the size of the text,

either by providing an exact measurement in any unit or through one of seven absolute keywords (xx-small, x-small, small, medium, large, x-large, and xx-large) or by means of one of two relative keywords (smaller and larger). The font-weight property allows you to set text as being bold or normal, and the font-style property lets you make text italic or normal. CSS provides for a line-height property to control the space between lines of text, and font-variant allows you to render text in small-caps.

Text properties include text-align for horizontal alignment of text with values of left, right, center, and justify; text-decoration, most commonly used to remove the underline from hyperlinks with the none value; text-indent, which indents the first line of a block of text; and text-transform, which accepts uppercase, lowercase, capitalize, and none as possible values.

Change the Font

1 Create a new CSS document.

● In Adobe Dreamweaver CS3, click File → New.

From the list of page types, select CSS.

Click Create.

A new file is created.

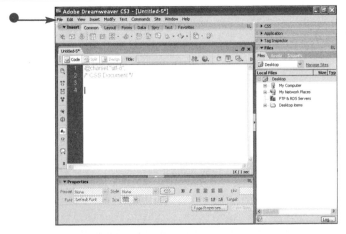

2 Type **p**.

3 Type an opening curly brace.

4 Type **font-family:**.

5 Type a comma-separated list of fonts.

6 Type a semicolon.

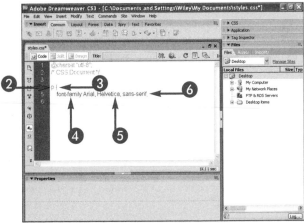

7 Type **font-size:**.

8 Type a size value.

9 Type a semicolon.

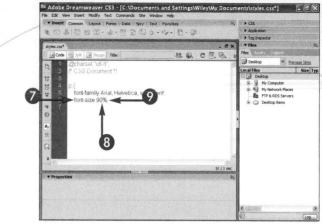

10 Type **text-align:**.

11 Type a value for the alignment.

12 Type a semicolon.

13 Type a closing curly brace.

14 Click File → Save.

The file is saved.

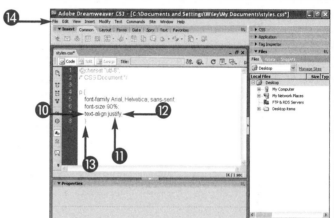

Extra

Visually impaired users can use a feature of the browser to change the size of the text on a Web page. Most browsers follow the CSS specification, which requires that browsers enable the user to scale text on a page under all circumstances. Unfortunately, however, Microsoft Internet Explorer adopted a different interpretation, whereby users can only scale text if the designer sets the font size using a relative unit of measurement — specifically, using percentages, ems, and exes. Using any other unit on your fonts will prevent users from being able to scale text in Internet Explorer.

Setting font sizes as a percentage has another advantage. When you set a font to a percentage, you are setting it to a percentage of the size of its parent element. So if you set the font-size of the body element to 90% and then the size heading level 1 to 110%, you are saying that you want the headings to be 10% bigger than the body text. This gives you enormous flexibility in your design, as you can increase or decrease the size of all text by simply changing the value of the body, causing all the other sizes to scale accordingly.

The CSS `color` property officially sets the foreground color of an object, but in practical terms, the only thing in the foreground that can change color is the text.

CSS supports three methods of determining the color of text. First, you can use one of the HTML color names. Officially, there are only 16 supported by CSS: `aqua`, `black`, `blue`, `fuchsia`, `gray`, `green`, `lime`, `maroon`, `navy`, `olive`, `purple`, `red`, `silver`, `teal`, `white`, and `yellow`. However, a total of 147 named colors are actually supported by browsers. A complete list can be found at www.w3schools.com/html/html_colornames.asp.

A much wider spectrum of colors is available if you use either the RGB or the hexadecimal method of setting colors. Either of these give you access to over 16.7 million colors. To use the RGB syntax, you state the values of the amount of red, green, and blue that you want to mix to get the color that you want. Values are expressed as a number between 0 and 255.

```
p { color:rgb(116,18,234); }
```

Much more widely used is the hexadecimal system. Hexadecimal is actually a method of counting that uses sixteen digits, rather than ten, and it enables you to count from 0 to 255 using two digits rather than three. The extra six digits are represented by the letters A through F. Hexadecimal colors are given by typing a pound sign, followed by a six-digit hexadecimal value, with the first two digits expressing the amount of red in the color, the second two the amount of green, and the third the amount of blue. The same color shown previously expressed in hexadecimal would be `#7412EA`.

Change the Color of Text

① Open a CSS document in your editor.

● In Adobe Dreamweaver, click File →
   Open.

   The file opens.

② Type an `h1` selector.

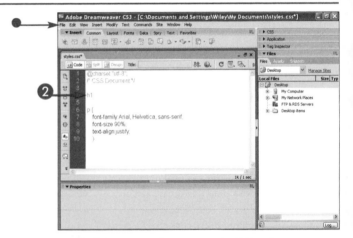

③ Type an opening curly brace.

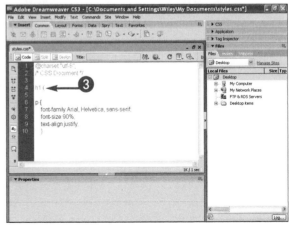

④ Type **color:**.

⑤ Type a color value.

⑥ Type a semicolon.

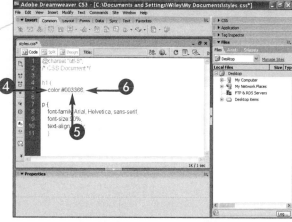

⑦ Type the closing curly brace.

⑧ Click File → Save.

The file is saved.

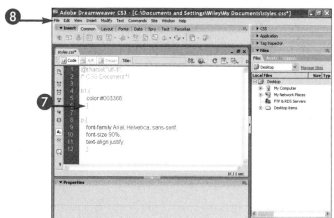

Extra

You can save typing by using one of the many shortcuts available in CSS. For colors, if you use a color where all three sets of hexadecimal digits are a pair, you can provide the color in three digits, rather than six.

```
h1 {color:#CC9933;}
```

can be expressed as

```
h1 {color:#C93;}
```

You cannot do this unless all three sets of numbers are paired, so the color #CC9934 could not be shortened.

Add a Background Color and Image

I n HTML, the only elements that can have background colors applied to them are `body`, `table`, `td`, and `th`. In CSS, any element that can be displayed onscreen can take a background color. That means the `body` element and any element that can be placed in the `body`, so it is now possible to set background colors on paragraphs, headings, lists, or anything else. Color is applied using the `background-color` property, using either a named color, RGB, or hexadecimal, although the latter is the most widely used and supported:

`body { background-color:#424242; }`

CSS also supports placing a background image on any element. Background images are by default placed in the top-left corner of the element and tile horizontally and vertically, but all three of these behaviors can be

controlled. Images are placed in the background using the `background-image` property, which takes as its value `url(path_to_image)`. You can set the placement of the image using the `background-position` property, which can take a percentage offset from the top-left corner, an exact measurement offset from that corner, or through the use of the keywords `top`, `center`, `bottom`, and `left`, `center`, `right`. Multiple measurements can be given to provide both horizontal and vertical offset. Tiling is determined by the values set on the `background-repeat` property, which can be `repeat-x`, `repeat-y`, `repeat`, or `no-repeat`:

```
table {background-image:url(watermark.gif);
background-repeat:no-repeat; background-
position:bottom left; }
```

Add a Background Color and Image

① Open a CSS document in your editor.

● In Adobe Dreamweaver, click File → Open.

The file opens.

② Type a `body` selector.

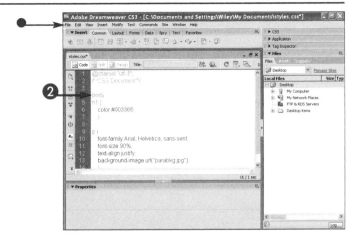

③ Type an opening curly brace.

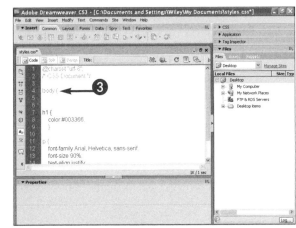

④ Type **background-color:**.

⑤ Type a color value and a semicolon.

⑥ Type the closing curly brace.

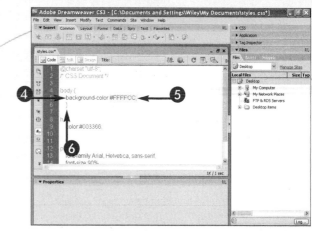

⑦ Type a p selector.

⑧ Type an opening curly brace.

⑨ Type **background-image:url(**.

⑩ Enter a path to an image.

⑪ Type the closing parenthesis and a semicolon.

⑫ Type the closing curly brace.

⑬ Click File → Save.

The file is saved.

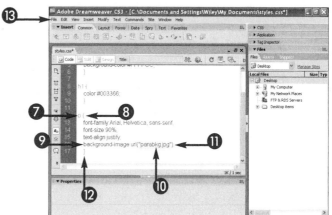

Extra

There is a lot of confusion regarding when you should use CSS to place images on your page and when you should use the XHTML img element. CSS background images are not intended to replace the img element. As their name implies, they are intended to allow you to place an image in the background of an element. Any image that is important to the content of a page should be placed in the document through the XHTML img tag.

There is a background shortcut property in CSS that enables you to specify a background color, the path to a background image, and its position and repeatability in a single line:

```
body { background: #FFF url(site-background.gif) top left no-repeat; }
```

You can also use this shorthand to set any one of the properties, so instead of using background-color:#FFF;, you can use simply background:#FFF;.

A final property of the background is background-attachment, with values of fixed or scroll. The scroll value is the default and causes the image to scroll up and down with the screen. A value of fixed will cause the image to remain in place as the text of the page scrolls over it.

Add Borders

Traditional HTML allows for borders only on tables and images. CSS allows any element to accept a border.

There are actually 15 separate properties that set borders, but they can be broken into several distinct groups. Each border is made up of three parts: its width, color, and style. Each element can take a border on one or more of each of its four sides. The combination of these properties gives us the 12 longhand border properties: `border-top-width`, `border-top-style`, `border-top-color`, `border-right-width`, `border-right-style`, `border-right-color`, `border-bottom-width`, `border-bottom-style`, `border-bottom-color`, `border-left-width`, `border-left-style`, and `border-left-color`. However, each of the seven broader categories has an associated shorthand property, so it is possible to set the width, style, and color of each side using simply `border-top`, `border-right`,

`border-bottom`, or `border-left`. You can also set the same width on each side of a border using the `border-width` shorthand or set all four styles at once with `border-style` or all four colors with `border-color`. If using one of these shorthand properties, you can provide a single value to apply to all four sides; or two values, the first of which applies to the top and bottom and the second of which applies to the left and right; or four values, one for each side, which must be listed in the order top, right, bottom, left.

The border width can be expressed in any valid unit of measurement, although pixels is by far the most common. The border color can be expressed using names, RGB, or hexadecimal. Valid border styles are `dashed`, `dotted`, `double`, `groove`, `hidden`, `inset`, `none`, `outset`, `ridge`, and `solid`. Not all browsers support all styles, but most will degrade gracefully to `solid` if they do not support the style given.

Add Borders

① Open a CSS document in your editor.

● In Adobe Dreamweaver, click File → Open.

　The file opens.

② Type an `h1` selector.

③ Type an opening curly brace.

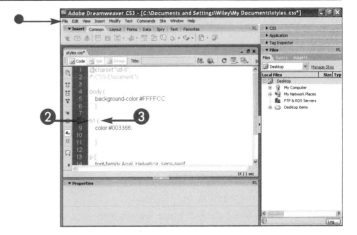

④ Type **border:**.

⑤ Type width, style, and color values in a space-separated list and then a semicolon.

⑥ Type the closing curly brace.

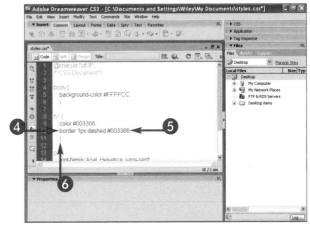

⑦ Type an `h2` selector.

⑧ Type an opening curly brace.

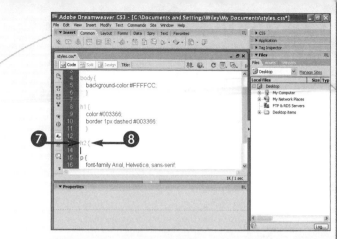

⑨ Type **border-bottom:**.

⑩ Type a color, width, and style value in a space-separated list and then a semicolon.

⑪ Type the closing curly brace.

⑫ Click File ➔ Save.

The file is saved.

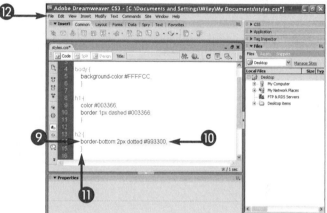

Extra

You can use the border properties in CSS to better control table borders. Instead of the XHTML `border` attribute, which adds the border to the entire grid, CSS adds borders separately to each element of a table, so setting the border on the table itself only draws it around the outside of the table, not the individual cells. They would need separate border declarations, as would table headers. It is valid to set borders on the `tr` element to draw a border around a single row of a table, or if you use the XHTML `col` or `colgroup` elements, you can draw borders around columns.

If you apply borders to the `td` or `th` elements, each cell will be drawn individually, with a small gap between the borders of adjacent cells. This space can be eliminated entirely using the `border-collapse` property with a value set to `collapse`. Conversely, the size of the gap in the border can be precisely controlled through the `border-spacing` property. These two properties apply only to tables.

Add Padding and Margins

All block elements exist in their own space on the page. This space is maintained by two primary properties in CSS: `padding` and `margin`. The padding defines the space within the block, between the content and the border, whereas the margin defines the space between blocks.

Padding is set in CSS using the `padding-top`, `padding-left`, `padding-bottom`, and `padding-right` properties. There is also a shorthand `padding` property that enables you to set padding around the entire box in one line. If you supply one value, it is applied to all four sides; two values are applied to the top/bottom and left/right; and four values are applied clockwise around the box: top, right, bottom, left. Padding can be expressed in any unit of measurement, although pixel and percent are the most common.

Margins use the same syntax as padding, so there are four longhand properties, `margin-top`, `margin-right`, `margin-bottom`, and `margin-left`, and a shorthand `margin`, which accepts the same values as padding.

One of the most confusing aspects in dealing with margins in CSS is that adjacent margins collapse into one another. Therefore, when you see two adjacent elements, the space between them is simultaneously the bottom margin of the upper element and the top margin of the lower element. Reducing or removing only the bottom margin of the upper element, for example, will not cause the elements to move closer, as you would also need to reduce the top margin of the lower element. A fairly common technique is to remove one of the two margins altogether and then use the other exclusively to control the spacing between the elements.

Add Padding and Margins

① Open a CSS document in your editor.

● In Adobe Dreamweaver, click File →
Open.

The file opens.

② Type an `h1` selector.

③ Type an opening curly brace.

④ Type **margin:**.

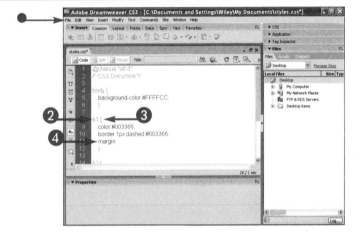

⑤ Type a value followed by a semicolon.

Note: Do not forget to specify the unit of measurement.

⑥ Type the closing curly brace.

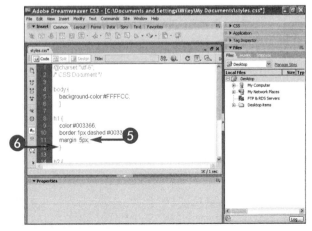

136

⑦ Type an `h2` selector.

⑧ Type an opening curly brace.

⑨ Type **padding:**.

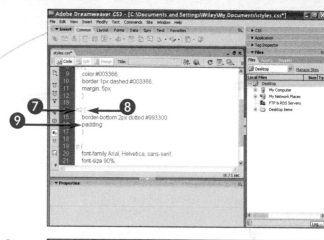

⑩ Type a value, followed by a semicolon.

Note: *Again, do not forget to specify the unit of measurement.*

⑪ Type the closing curly brace.

⑫ Click File → Save.

The file is saved.

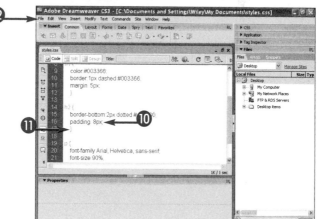

Apply It

You can use negative values for margins and padding, which is another common technique for moving elements closer together:

```
h1 { margin-bottom:-20px; }
p { margin-top:-10px; }
```

Visually, using negative margin values and reducing both values gives the same result, so it is a matter of personal preference.

Position Elements

CSS 2 introduced the ability to lay out elements on the page. Previously, the only way to achieve multicolumn layouts in Web pages was through the use of tables, which results in enormously bloated code and requires considerable time and effort to design and maintain. Unfortunately, despite the obvious evidence as to the advantages of using CSS for layout, many Web designers continue to insist on using tables.

CSS layouts are primarily achieved through the use of the position property and several related properties. The possible values of the position property are static: default, relative, absolute, and fixed. Absolute positioning, the first of these properties that most designers learn, removes the element from the flow of the page and places it in a set spot on the page, which is specified using any combination of the top, left, bottom,

or right properties. Usually, the values of these properties are given in pixels. Relative positioning is rarely used to lay out the given element, although it can accept top, bottom, left, and right properties as well. Instead, relative positioning is usually set on an element so that its child elements can be positioned absolutely within it, instead of within the browser window. Fixed positioning, which is not supported by Internet Explorer prior to version 7, causes elements to not scroll with the rest of the page.

In order to effectively position elements, you need to specify a width for them. Block elements by default have a width of 100%, which does not leave room for other elements to sit next to them. There is a height property in CSS as well, although care should be taken, as browsers are inconsistent as to how they treat elements with more content than will fit in the given height.

Position Elements

① Open a CSS document in your editor.

● In Adobe Dreamweaver, click File → Open.

The file opens.

② Type a p selector.

③ Type an opening curly brace.

④ Type **width:**.

⑤ Type a value followed by a semicolon.

Note: Do not forget to specify the unit of measurement.

⑥ Type **position:absolute;**.

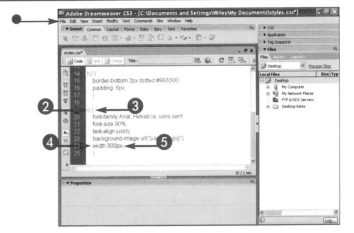

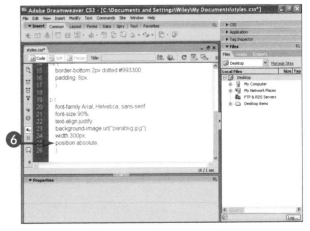

7 Type **top:**.

8 Type a value followed by a semicolon.

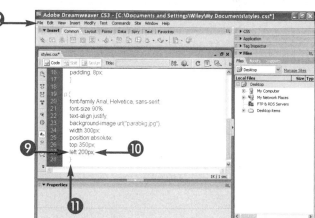

9 Type **left:**.

10 Type a value followed by a semicolon.

11 Type the closing curly brace.

12 Click File → Save.

The file is saved.

Extra

Positioning can only be applied to block elements, but you can use the `display:block` declaration to force an inline element to be displayed as a block if you need to position it.

Browsers are littered with bugs when applying positioning. Netscape 4.7 does not support it correctly at all and completely mangles positioned layouts. Internet Explorer 5 and 6 have a famous box-model bug that causes them to incorrectly calculate the width of an element, which will wreak havoc with precisely positioned layouts. This can be worked around by using the XHTML Strict DOCTYPE for Internet Explorer 6 or by using one of a number of box-model hacks. Anytime you implement a positioned layout, be sure to carefully test it in multiple browsers to make sure that your layout will not break. It is generally helpful to code for and test initially in a more standards-compliant browser such as Mozilla Firefox and then hack or modify the layout for less compliant browsers such as Internet Explorer.

Float Elements

There are a variety of approaches to creating layouts with CSS. One that is gaining more acceptance as browser support for it increases is using the CSS `float` property. Floating an element allows other elements to move up to either the right or left of the element being floated.

Floated elements must have a `width` property specified, as the default width of 100% does not allow any room for the float. If the width of the two elements in question exceeds the width of the browser window, the second element will not float, so care must be taken to ensure that the elements will fit properly even in smaller windows.

The actual values of the float often seem backwards to many developers. To have the second element on the page float to the right of the first, it is the first element

that must be floated, and you need to use `float:left` — not `float:right` as seems logical. The reasoning here is that it is actually the first element that is floating, although the opposite appears to be true.

If you have three or more elements and you want to have the third float to the right of the first two, and have those two appear as though they were not floating, keeping the second directly below the first, then you must specify a `float:left` on the first element and on the second, which allows the third element to float into the empty space. In order to keep the second element from floating next to the first, you then set the `clear` property on it, with a value of `left`: You are telling this element to float left, but not let other elements float to its left.

Float Elements

① Open a CSS document in your editor.

● In Adobe Dreamweaver, click File → Open.

  The file opens.

② Type a `p` selector.

③ Type an opening curly brace.

④ Type **width:**.

⑤ Type a value followed by a semicolon.

Note: Do not forget to specify the unit of measurement.

⑥ Type **float:left;**.

⑦ Type the closing curly brace.

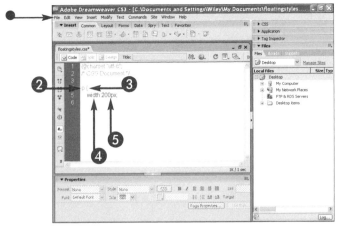

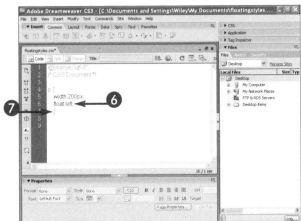

⑧ Type a `div` selector.

⑨ Type an opening curly brace.

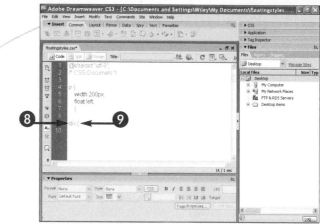

⑩ Type **width:**.

⑪ Type a value followed by a semicolon.

Note: *Make sure that the sum of the values in steps 5 and 10 do not exceed the width of the browser window.*

⑫ Type the closing curly brace.

⑬ Click File → Save.

The file is saved.

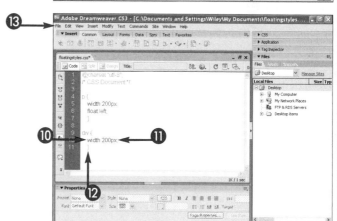

Extra

There are several well-known bugs regarding floats, especially when using Internet Explorer 6. One of the trickiest if you are unaware of its existence is the so-called Internet Explorer Double-Margin Float bug. In this case, if you apply a margin to an element on the same side as the float, the browser will double the value of the margin. In other words, if you have `margin-left:5px; float:left;` for an element, Internet Explorer 6 will render the page with 10 pixels of left margin. Fortunately, there is a fairly simple fix for this bug: Simply add a `display:inline` declaration to the same element, and the bug disappears. A quirk of the CSS specification states that floated elements are treated as block elements, regardless of what the style sheet says, so this fix will not negatively affect other browsers.

A similar bug in the same browser causes inline elements adjacent to a floated element to appear to be indented from their usual location. The same `display:inline` declaration fixes this bug as well.

Combine Floats, Positioning, and Margins for Layout

Most layouts require a combination of techniques. Using absolute positioning results in a page that is completely fixed in place and will break as soon as any additional content is added. Floats have a series of well-documented bugs and are difficult to work with throughout an entire document.

Most designers therefore rely on a combination of positioning, floats, and margins to achieve the design that they want. Consider a classic three-column design: There is a header that stretches across the top of the page. Below that, a left column contains navigation, a middle column has the content, and a right column contains additional links or information. Many designs would call for the left and right columns to be fixed in place, with the middle column expanding or collapsing to fill the remaining space, regardless of how wide the monitor.

This design can be achieved by positioning the side columns. You start by using `position:absolute` on the left column. Then, use `position:absolute` on the right column but anchor it to the right edge of the screen by providing `top` and `right` properties. Because these columns are absolutely positioned, the content column will move up to fill the space but will most likely overlap the right column while being overlapped by the left. This can be solved by simply setting the left margin of the middle column to slightly more than the width of the left column, and its right margin to slightly more than the width of the right column, thus visually keeping it out of the way. Because the right column is anchored to the right edge of the screen and the right margin of the middle column is likewise relative to that edge, as the browser expands or collapses, these two boxes will remain separated, with any additional or lost space being absorbed by the middle column.

Combine Floats, Positioning, and Margins for Layout

① Open a CSS document in your editor.

② Type a selector for the ID of the left column.

③ Type an opening curly brace.

④ Type **position:absolute;**.

⑤ Type **top:** and a value to position the element below the header and a semicolon.

⑥ Type **left:10px;**.

⑦ Type **width:**, a value, and a semicolon.

⑧ Type a closing curly brace.

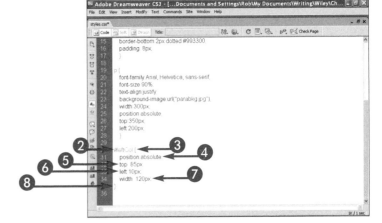

⑨ Type a selector for the ID of the right column.

⑩ Type an opening curly brace.

⑪ Type **position:absolute;**.

⑫ Type **top:**.

⑬ Type the same value you used in step **5** and a semicolon.

⑭ Type **right:10px;**.

⑮ Type **width:**.

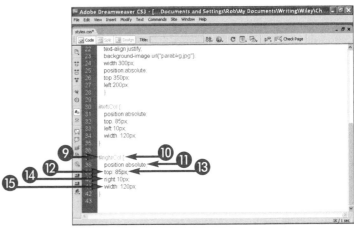

16 Type a value for the width and a semicolon.

17 Type a closing curly brace.

18 Type an ID selector for the middle column.

19 Type an opening curly brace.

20 Type **margin-left:**.

21 Type a value equal to the width of the left column plus 20 pixels and then a semicolon.

22 Type **margin-right:**.

23 Type a value equal to the width of the right column plus 20 pixels and then a semicolon.

24 Type a closing curly brace.

25 Click File → Save.

The file is saved.

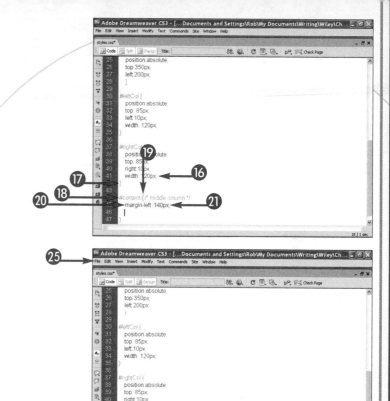

Extra

Designers need to choose between creating fixed or fluid layouts. Fixed layouts rely on specifying exact widths for each element on the page, so that the page is always precisely the same width, regardless of the width of the browser window. Fluid layouts use relative units, generally percentages, for some or all of the widths, thereby allowing the layout to expand or collapse so that it always fills the browser window.

There are advantages and disadvantages to both of these approaches. Fixed layouts are generally easier to design, but may result in the user having to scroll right and left if the browser window is too small. Fluid layouts should avoid this scrolling but are more difficult to create and may not look good on very wide screens — an increasingly common phenomenon.

The most important thing to keep in mind is that you, as the designer, have no way to detect or control your users' browser width, so you need to develop a design that will look good in as large a variety of widths as you can.

Although there are many times when styling XHTML elements directly is useful, there are many more times when you need to exercise more control over the page. One common scenario is the need to have multiple different elements styled identically, such as a series of items on a list. Even more common is the need to have an element adopt a different style in one part of the document from another. Using the same example, you may have a series of list items that you want to style a particular way, but there may be other items that you want styled differently, if at all.

The CSS class selector was created to solve these issues. When using a class selector, you create a style rule that is tied to a logical name you create, rather than be associated with a particular element. Then, you can apply the style to any element on your page through the use of

the `class` attribute, which is legal on any element that renders items to the screen.

When creating the class, you need to precede the name with a period to differentiate it from element selectors. Following the period, you must have a letter. The remainder of the name can only be made up of letters, numbers, and the hyphen character:

```
.companyName { font-weight:bold;
color:#FF9999; }
```

To apply the class to an element on the page, simply use the class name as the value of the `class` attribute, without the period:

```
<h1 class="companyName">ACME Co., Inc.</h1>
```

You can use a class selector as many times on a page as you want to.

Apply Styles with a Class Selector

① Open a CSS document in your editor.

● In Adobe Dreamweaver, click File → Open.

  The file opens.

② Type a name for a class, beginning with a period.

③ Type an opening curly brace.

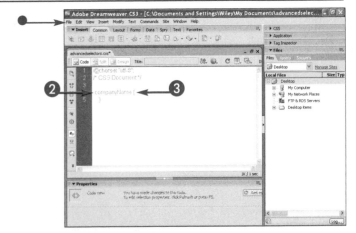

④ Type one or more CSS declarations to apply with the class.

⑤ Type the closing curly brace.

⑥ Click File → Save.

  The file is saved.

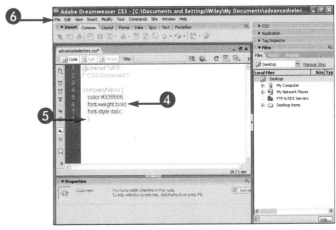

7. Open an XHTML document in your editor.

8. In the head of the document, type a `link` tag.

9. Type **rel="stylesheet"**.

10. Type **type="text/css"**.

11. Type **href="**.

12. Type the path to the style sheet that you saved in step **6**.

13. Type the closing quotation mark.

14. Close the tag by typing a slash and an angle bracket.

15. In the document, add a `class` attribute to an existing element.

16. Set the value of the `class` attribute to the name of the class you created in step **2**.

17. Click File → Save.

The file is saved.

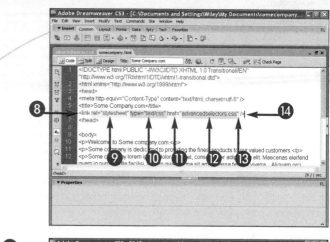

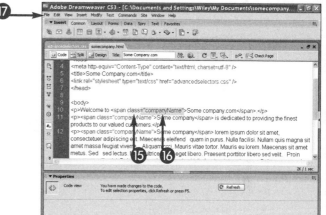

Apply It

You can apply a class to a string of text, such as a company name, even if there is no existing XHTML element surrounding it. To do this, simply add the span element. span is an inline element that was created specifically to hold style sheet instructions when no other element existed or made sense:

```
<p>Welcome to the Web site of <span class="companyName">ACME Co., Inc,</span>. We are pleased
to be able to serve you.</p>
```

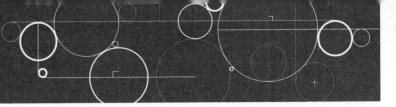

Apply Styles with an ID Selector

I f you have an element on a page that needs a specific style applied to it, and only it, you can create an ID selector. ID selectors function very similarly to classes, and in fact you can use a class instead of an ID in many cases. The key difference between a class selector and an ID selector is that a class can be used repeatedly on a page, whereas an ID must be unique to the page. Browsers may ignore any but the first application of an ID on a single page.

Because they require uniqueness, ID selectors are considered to be more specific than class selectors. In fact, they are one of the most specific selectors in CSS, so their rules will apply over almost any other rule in the style sheet.

To use an ID, you create a rule on your style sheet. The name of the ID must begin with a pound sign, followed by a letter, followed by any combination of letters, numbers, and hyphens. You can apply an ID to an element on the page by using the id attribute in XHTML, which is allowed on all elements that render items to the screen.

It is both possible and sometimes necessary to apply both an ID and a class to the same element, by using both attributes. Remember, however, that the ID rule will override conflicting class rules.

ID selectors are most often used on block-level elements such as div and the heading tags, but they can be used on any element, including hyperlinks and images. Anytime you need to uniquely identify an element on the page, you can use an ID.

Apply Styles with an ID Selector

① Open a CSS document in your editor.

● In Adobe Dreamweaver, click File ➔ Open.

   The file opens.

② Type a name for an ID, beginning with a pound sign.

③ Type an opening curly brace.

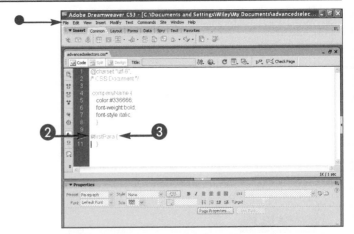

④ Type one or more CSS declarations to apply with the class.

⑤ Type the closing curly brace.

⑥ Click File ➔ Save.

   The file is saved.

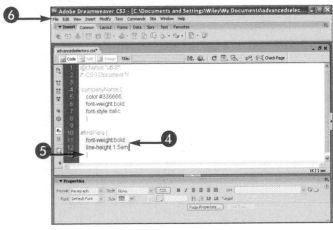

⑦ Open an XHTML document in your editor.

⑧ In the head of the document, type a `link` tag.

⑨ Type **rel="stylesheet"**.

⑩ Type **type="text/css"**.

⑪ Type **href="**.

⑫ Type the path to the style sheet that you saved in step **6**.

⑬ Type the closing quotation mark.

⑭ Close the tag by typing a slash and an angle bracket.

⑮ In the document, add an ID attribute to an existing element.

⑯ Set the value of the ID attribute to the name of the ID that you created in step **2**.

⑰ Click File → Save.

The file is saved.

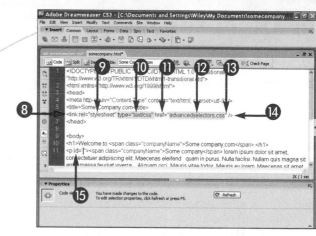

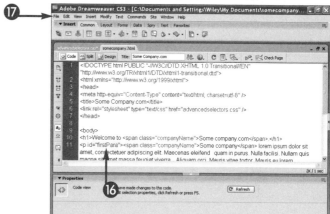

Extra

The ID attribute in XHTML has many uses beyond applying styles. JavaScript relies very heavily on the ID to identify the specific element that it is trying to manipulate. In fact, it is common to see JavaScript developers rely heavily on the `getElementByID()` function in the language for this exact purpose.

An element with an ID can also be the target of a hyperlink. In fact, hyperlinks reference IDs in the same way that CSS does, by appending the name of the ID with a pound sign. So `<a href="#content">` would take a user to an element on the same page that had an ID of `content`, and `<a href="contactus.html#directory">` would take the user to the contactus.html page and then scroll the browser to the element with the ID of `directory`.

IDs can be used as a form of self-documentation within an XHTML page. By using a descriptive ID on headings, paragraphs, and especially `div`s, you and other developers can scan through the document and get an idea of what each element's purpose is based on its ID, which may save you from needing to add XHTML comments to the document.

Using Contextual Selectors

CSS contains several methods to reference an element by its position in the document. The most common and most widely supported is a contextual selector, whereby you provide a list of elements and the browser applies the style rule to the element based on its position in that list.

For example, say you have a paragraph on a page that is inside a `div` with an ID of `mainContent`, and you want to apply a style to only that paragraph. You could apply either a class or ID selector to the paragraph and reference it directly, but it would be easier to not have to manipulate your XHTML, so instead you can use the following syntax:

```
#mainContent p { color:#cc9966; }
```

This says that a paragraph inside the element with the `mainContent` ID should have this rule applied to it. You can use any combination of elements in a contextual selector, including IDs, classes, and elements:

```
#mainContent p span.links a { background-
color:#eee; }
```

This rule says that a light-gray background should be applied to an anchor located within a span that has class links, which in turn is in a paragraph, which is in turn in an element with an ID of `mainContent`. In this case, an anchor somewhere else on the page would not get the background color, even if it was located within the classed span and a paragraph, because the anchor would not be inside that element with the ID.

Using Contextual Selectors

① Open a CSS document in your editor.

● In Adobe Dreamweaver, click File → Open.

The file opens.

② Type a contextual selector as a space-separated list of elements, IDs, or classes.

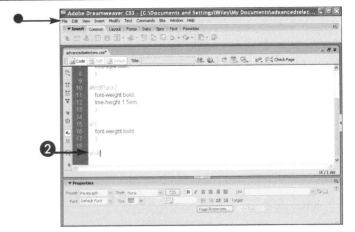

③ Type an opening curly brace.

UNIVERSITY OF WOLVERHAMPTON
Harrison Learning Centre

ITEMS ISSUED:

Customer ID: 7605489741

Title: XML : your visual blueprint for building
expert Web sites with XML, CSS, XHT
ID: 7624433241
Due: 22/04/2010 23:59

Total items: 1
15/04/2010 17:32
Issued: 2
Overdue: 0

Thank you for using Self Service.
Please keep your receipt.

Overdue books are fined at 40p per day for
week loans, 10p per day for long loans.

④ Type one or more CSS declarations to apply with the class.

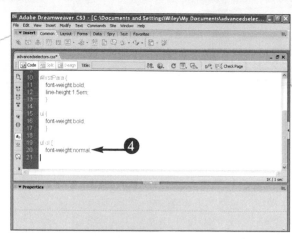

⑤ Type the closing curly brace.

⑥ Click File → Save.

The file is saved.

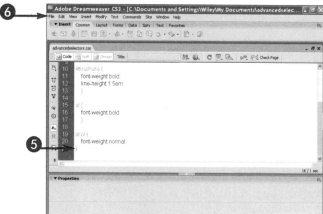

Extra

Two other special selector types in CSS are attribute and direct-descendant selectors. An attribute selector enables you to target an element if it has a specific attribute or if that attribute is set to a specific value. If you wanted to target only single-line text fields, for example, you can have a CSS selector:

```
input[type="text"] { background-color:#ccc; }
```

CSS also supports the direct-descendant selector, whereby you can target an element only if it is the direct descendant of another element:

```
#mainContent > p { font-size:85%; }
```

In this case, a paragraph is only going to have `font-size` applied if it is the direct descendant or nested directly inside of the `mainContent` element and not contained within some other element.

Neither of these selectors has been used widely yet due to lack of support from Microsoft Internet Explorer. However, both are now supported in Internet Explorer 7.

Style Headings

Almost all Web pages should have headings. They help organize the content on the page into sections both visually and semantically. Modern search engines rely on them, giving more weight to text found in headings than in regular paragraphs and other elements, so pages that properly use headings, beginning with h1, will get better search engine rankings than those that do not.

For years, Web designers shied away from using headings properly, in large part because the default display of some of the headings was far too big. Most browsers display h1 text by default at around 36 pixels, which most designers agree is far larger than it should be. XHTML also does not provide a way by which you can have headings that are not bold text. Fortunately, both of these problems can be solved with CSS, enabling you to use the proper semantic heading markup while still achieving the visual appearance that you want for your site.

Common styles applied to headings include choosing to make the text not bold, particularly in lower-level headings; changing the font family to visually differentiate the headings from the text; changing the color and size to better fit the overall design; applying borders to make the headings stand out better; and adjusting the margins and padding.

Many designers also use an image-replacement trick in CSS to display an image such as a logo on the page visually but have a heading in the code to improve accessibility and search-engine placement. Although the XHTML contains the heading text, the CSS is used to display a background image in place of the heading, and by using a text indent of some large negative number, you can place the actual text well off the screen in visual browsers.

Style Headings

1. Open a CSS document in your editor.

2. Type an h1 selector.

3. Type an opening curly brace.

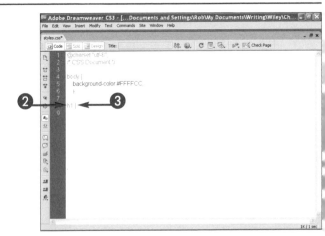

4. Type one or more style rules to apply to the h1.

5. Type a closing curly brace.

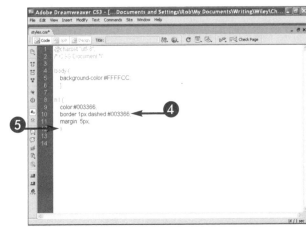

6 Type an h2 selector.

7 Type an opening curly brace.

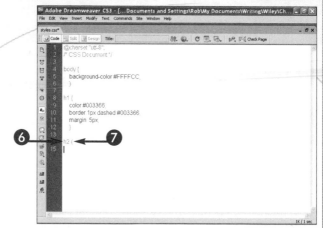

8 Type one or more style rules for the h2.

9 Type a closing curly brace.

10 Click File → Save.

The file is saved.

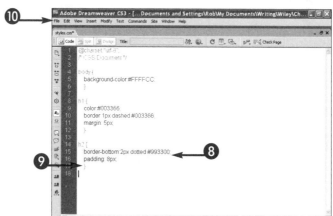

Extra

By using IDs, classes, or contextual selectors, you can have headings in one section of your document appear different from headings in another section. Be sure to test your page in a browser with styles disabled to be certain that the use of headings still makes sense logically, even if their appearance on the document may offset that.

Do not use CSS to try to cheat the search engines. Many unscrupulous designers will attempt to place much, if not all, of the text on their pages within heading tags and then use CSS to force the page to look somewhat normal, thereby hoping that because search engines like Google give higher priority to text within headings, their page will get a better search result. The problem with this approach is that doing this destroys the semantic meaning of your page, thereby ruining any thoughts you may have had to make the document accessible or easy to maintain later. In addition, search engines are consistently upgrading their systems to attempt to root out sites that try to cheat the system through techniques like this.

Style
Lists

Most Web pages rely heavily on lists. It is now easier than ever to use lists properly because CSS can quite easily make your list appear in almost any format.

You can change the bullet or number from the list by applying the `list-style-type` property to the `ul` or `ol` element. A common value to set here is `none`, which removes the bullet or number altogether, hiding the fact that you are using a list at all, and other values are `disc`, `circle`, `square`, `decimal`, `decimal-leading-zero`, `lower-roman`, `upper-roman`, `lower-greek`, `lower-alpha`, `lower-latin`, `upper-alpha`, `upper-latin`, `hebrew`, `armenian`, `georgian`, `cjk-ideographic`, `hiragana`, `katakana`, `hirogana-iroha`, and `katakana-iroha`. An idiosyncrasy of `list-style-type` is that you can apply numeric values to unordered lists and graphic values, such as `disc` or `square`, to ordered lists.

Alternatively, you can use `list-style-image` to change the bullet to display an image of your choosing. Care needs to be taken that the image you are applying is not too big for the list items, as there is no way to specify the size of the image in your CSS.

If your list items are long enough to wrap on multiple lines, you can use the `list-style-position` property, set to `inside`, to remove the hanging indent appearance of the list, or `outside`, which is the default.

All the list styles mentioned here inherit to nested lists, so if for instance you apply `list-style-image` to an unordered list, that image will also appear on items in a nested ordered list, which may require you to specify a `list-style-image` of `none` to override it.

List items, styled via their `li` element, have many styling possibilities. Any text or font property can be applied to them. As block elements, you can also work with borders, margin, and padding.

Style Lists

1 Open a CSS document in your editor.

2 Type a `ul` selector.

3 Type a curly brace.

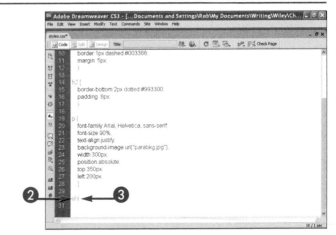

4 Type a `list-style-type` property.

5 Type a value and a semicolon.

6 Type a `list-style-position` property.

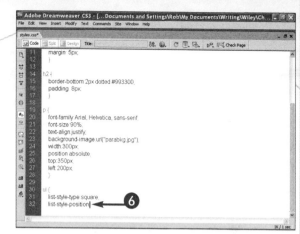

7 Type a value and a semicolon.

8 Type a closing curly brace.

9 Click File → Save.

The file is saved.

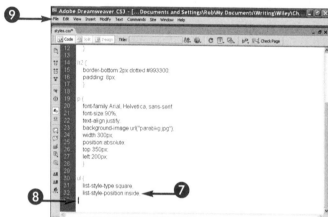

Extra

Browsers unfortunately disagree on what property exactly is being used to indent the items in a list. Internet Explorer and Opera use the left margin to indent the list, whereas Mozilla-based browsers such as Firefox and Netscape use left padding. Therefore, you will need to set both `margin-left` and `padding-left` on the `li` element to the value that you want to use to increase, or more often, decrease the indentation of the list items.

One extremely useful property for dealing with lists is `display`. List items are defined as being block elements, but applying a `display:inline` style rule to them causes the list to be displayed horizontally rather than vertically. This is particularly useful when designing navigation systems that rely on lists. A technique called "sliding doors," developed by Douglas Bowman, uses this `display:inline` rule, along with layered background images on list items and their contents to create tabbed navigation bars. You can read about the sliding-doors technique at http://alistapart.com/articles/slidingdoors/.

Style
Links

L inks are perhaps the most common element on Web pages. Links provide an extra challenge stylistically because they have several different states in which they exist. At a minimum, a designer needs to consider what the links will look like when the page is initially encountered — the state of the link that is by default blue and underlined. They may also want to style the links when they have been visited, when they are actively being clicked, and when the user moves the mouse pointer over them.

All of these states of links are exposed to CSS through a pseudo-class. *Pseudo-classes* tell the browser to act as if a class existed on the element, but only in certain situations. For styling links, there are four pseudo-classes commonly available: `:link`, `:visited`, `:hover`, and `:active`.

The `:link` pseudo-class applies its style rules to the hyperlink when it is in its normal state. The `:visited` pseudo-class applies when the target of the link exists in the browser's history. `:hover` is the pseudo-class that applies its styles when the mouse is moved over the link, giving designers the ability to create rollover effects without the need for additional scripting.

Officially, the `:active` pseudo-class is supposed to apply when the user presses and holds their mouse button down on the link — when they are activating it — and this is how Mozilla-based browsers implement it. However, Internet Explorer chooses to display the active state whenever the link has the focus, meaning that it will display a link as active when the user tabs to it, or in situations when a user clicks the link and then uses the browser's Back button to return to the page. Whichever link was clicked will in this case still be displayed as active in Internet Explorer.

Style Links

① Open a CSS document in your editor.

② Type an `a:link` selector.

③ Type an opening curly brace.

④ Type one or more style rules to apply to the link.

⑤ Type a closing curly brace.

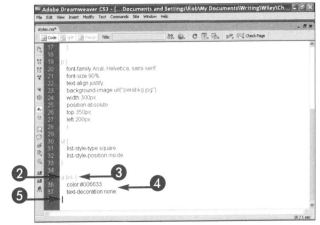

⑥ Type an `a:visited` selector.

⑦ Type an opening curly brace.

⑧ Type one or more style rules.

⑨ Type a closing curly brace.

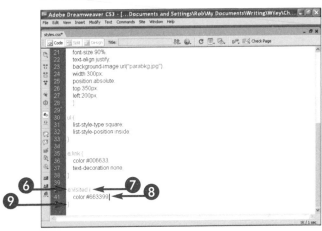

⑩ Type an `a:hover` selector.

⑪ Type an opening curly brace.

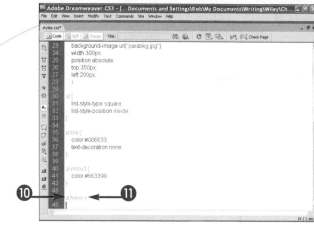

⑫ Type one or more style rules.

⑬ Type a closing curly brace.

⑭ Click File → Save.

The file is saved.

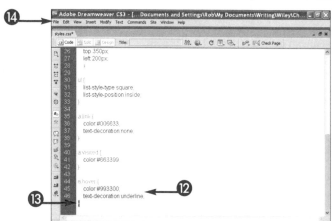

Extra

If you use more than one of these pseudo-classes, your style sheet must list the `:link` pseudo-class first, followed by `:visited`, then `:hover`, and finally `:active`.. The `:hover` pseudo-class by necessity applies at the same time as either `:link` or `:visited`, as a link that is visited does not stop being visited when it is being hovered over. In this case, the browser needs to try to display both the rules for `:visited` and for `:hover`. In the case of conflicting rules, the `:hover` rules will only apply if they were specified in the style sheet after the `:link` or `:visited` rule. Because it is likely that an active link will need to simultaneously display the properties of `:link` or `:visited` and `:hover` and `:active`, it must be given last.

Be careful when applying styles to `:hover` that may cause the size of the text to change, as this may cause the text to wrap onto two lines where before it was only one and result in a strange shifting or blinking effect as the browser redraws the page to accommodate the new longer text and again redraws it when the text reverts to one line. Changing the font family, font size, font weight, or font style can all cause this.

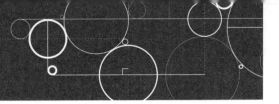

Using Other Pseudo-Classes and Pseudo-Elements

Although the pseudo-classes for hyperlinks are the most commonly used, there are a few others of which you should be aware. The `:first-child` pseudo-class enables you to style an element's first child element, whatever that may be, and the `:focus` element is useful for visually identifying currently selected form elements.

Pseudo-classes apply their style to the entire element in question. Another category of selector available in CSS is the *pseudo-element,* which applies its style to only a portion of the selected element. The two most widely supported pseudo-elements are `:first-letter` and `:first-line`. The former applies styling to only the first character within an element and can be used to create drop-cap effects. The latter applies to the entire first line of the element, which may be helpful in some formats to make the first line bold or otherwise stand out. The exact text being styled by

`:first-line` may change as the browser is resized, if such resizing causes the text to wrap differently.

Two additional pseudo-elements are `:before` and `:after`, which apply only with the CSS `content` property. The `content` property in CSS adds actual content to the page via CSS and is useful for placing icons or special symbols before text. Be aware that the generated content cannot be read by accessibility devices or search engines.

Browser support is a big issue with each of these selectors. The `:first-child` pseudo-class is not supported by Internet Explorer prior to version 7, and all versions of Internet Explorer apply `:focus` not just to form field elements but also to the currently selected hyperlink if the user is tabbing through the page. The `:first-line` and `:first-letter` pseudo-elements are widely supported by modern browsers, but no version of Internet Explorer supports generated content at all, thereby rendering support of the `:before` and `:after` pseudo-elements meaningless.

Using Other Pseudo-Classes and Pseudo-Elements

① Open a CSS document in your editor.

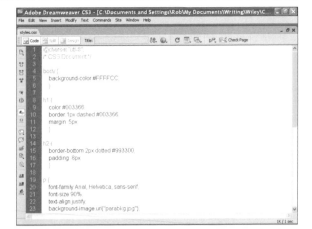

② Add a paragraph selector with a `first-line` pseudo-element.

③ Type an opening curly brace.

④ Type **font-weight:bold;**.

⑤ Type a closing curly brace.

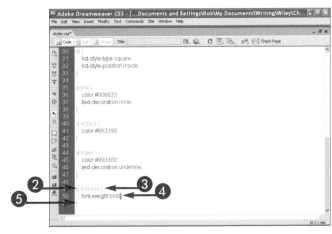

6. Type: **input[type="text"]:focus**.

7. Type an opening curly brace.

8. Type **background-color:**.

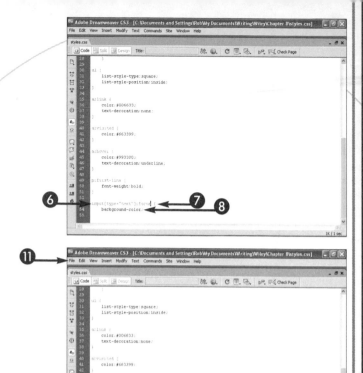

9. Type a color value for the background-color property and a semicolon.

10. Type a closing curly brace.

11. Click File → Save.

   The file is saved.

Extra

The :first-letter and :first-line pseudo-elements only allow certain CSS properties to be used. The allowed properties for :first-letter are as follows: font-variant, font-style, font-weight, font-size, font-family, font, color, background-color, background-image, background-repeat, background, float, clear, vertical-align, line-height, text-decoration, text-transform, text-shadow, word-spacing, letter-spacing, margin-top, margin-bottom, margin-left, margin-right, margin, padding-top, padding-left, padding-right, padding-bottom, and padding. The :first-line pseudo-element allows the following: font-variant, font-style, font-weight, font-size, font-family, font, color, background-color, background-image, background-repeat, background-attachment, background, clear, vertical-align, line-height, text-decoration, text-transform, text-shadow, word-spacing, and letter-spacing.

One final albeit rarely used pseudo-class is :lang(n), where n is a specified language code. This works in conjunction with the lang attribute supported by all rendering XHTML elements. The attribute enables designers to specify that the contents of a particular element are in a specified foreign language; the pseudo-class applies styles to elements with that language attribute set.

Design Content Sections

When developing a CSS-based layout, you will generally want to organize your page into logical sections. Many sites have a banner or heading area at the top, primary navigation below that, a left column with secondary navigation, a main content area, and a footer of some sort.

The XHTML div element is designed to let you style content sections. The div element is a block-level element that can contain any other block element. Each div is usually then given an ID. Styles can be applied directly to the ID to set backgrounds or borders on the section as a whole, or you can use contextual selectors to apply specific styles to elements within that section.

Although div is an extremely powerful element for styling pages, be careful not to overuse it. A common mistake is to begin thinking that the div is a universal replacement for any other tags, so designers begin using it in place of paragraphs or headings or, perhaps most commonly, lists. This is commonly referred to as "divitis," and the cure is simple: Use the right element for the right purpose. The right use of a div is in a place where no other XHTML element makes sense. Its name is short for "division," so it was specifically designed to create content sections, or divisions, on the page. No other block element is designed to wrap around a group of other elements for the purpose of applying styles. That is the job of the div — nothing else.

Design Content Sections

① Open an XHTML document in your editor.

② After the opening body tag, add an opening div tag.

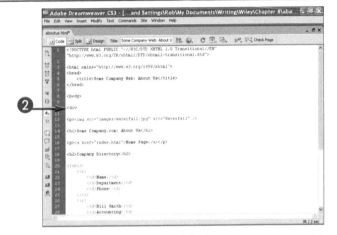

③ Add an ID attribute.

④ Set the value of the attribute to a meaningful description of the section.

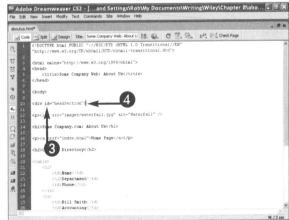

5 After the section, add a closing
`div` tag.

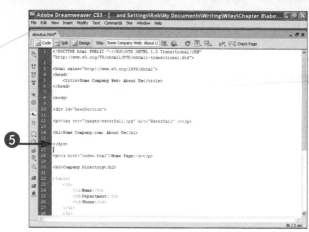

6 Repeat steps **2** to **5** as needed to
divide your document into sections.

7 Click File → Save.

The file is saved.

Extra

Having a lot of `div`s or nesting `div`s within other `div`s is not "divitis." There are many times when it is
entirely appropriate and in fact necessary to have layered `div` elements. For example, you may decide that
you need a section within a section, such as having a set of navigation links within a content section. The
problem with `div`s is not simply overusing them, but rather using them when some other element would
make more sense. Do not, for instance, mark up each item of your navigation with a `div` simply because you
want them on separate lines. An unordered list with `list-style-type` set to `none` would accomplish the
same task with roughly the same amount of code but makes more sense logically.

Creating content sections can make your code much more readable. By using meaningful ID attributes, you
are in effect creating a sort of self-documentation for the document, as you or other designers can get an idea
of what content is where on the page from simply noting the parent `div`'s ID.

Create a Style Guide

CSS enables you to create styles that can be applied to your entire site. However, some amount of initial planning is still important to ensure that the styles throughout the site work well together and present the right visual message for the site.

A formalized style guide will assist both you and other developers and designers to ensure that you remain consistent throughout the development of the site. Exactly how formal this document needs to be, or in what format it should be created and presented, will vary from one organization to the next. Many smaller companies find a less formal document, possibly created in something such as Microsoft Office Word, works well, whereas many larger organizations create Web pages to serve as the style guide, allowing offsite designers easy access to the guide. A Web search will often turn up

some of these online guides, which can serve as a useful template to follow in designing your own.

At a minimum, the style guide should set out basic properties such as which fonts are acceptable; what size fonts should be in various uses, such as in headings, paragraphs, and table cells; and what colors will be used for various elements. More detailed style guides often lay out naming conventions for ID and class selectors; specific allowed settings for borders, margins, and padding on elements; guidelines for line height and the use of bold and italic; and other details that designers will find of use.

The key to remember is that the style guide is being designed primarily as an internal document for you and others to maximize the ability to have pages designed by different people look the same.

Create a Style Guide

1 Open a new document in Microsoft Office Word.

In Word 2003 or earlier, click File ➔ New.

● In Word 2007, click the Office button ➔ New.

2 Type an introductory paragraph explaining the goals of the style guide.

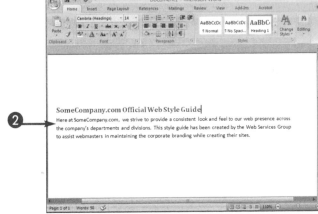

③ Type a list of the fonts, colors, and other properties to be enforced by the guide.

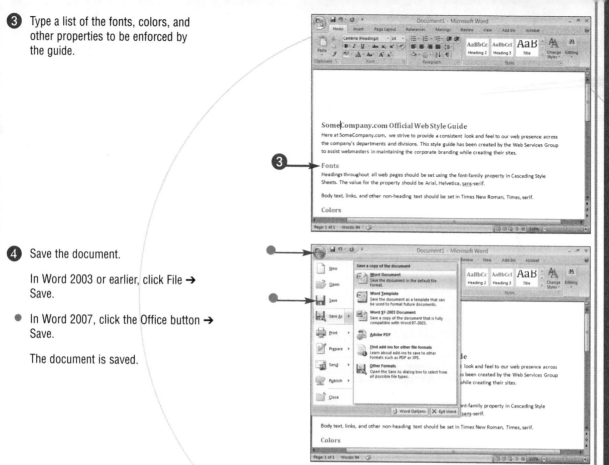

④ Save the document.

In Word 2003 or earlier, click File → Save.

● In Word 2007, click the Office button → Save.

The document is saved.

Extra

Good spelling and grammar are as important to the success of a Web site as visual design. Unfortunately, even casual examination of many Web sites will reveal that these two aspects are more often than not ignored.

Most dedicated XHTML editors, such as Adobe Dreamweaver, provide some sort of spell check utility, and some even allow for checking of spelling across multiple documents. However, no computer program is going to be perfect, so it will always be necessary to have someone proofread your documents. Computerized grammar checkers are even more unreliable than spell checkers, so it is absolutely necessary to have someone proof for that as well.

Your style guide should ideally address such writing issues as the use of parentheses on the site, how much "author voice" will be acceptable, the overall tone of the writing, the recommended or possibly required length of the content, and so on. Most Web sites want to present the appearance of being created by a single individual, even if they are not, so addressing these issues upfront will save considerable editing time later.

Create a Printable Version of Your Web Pages

The Web is an entirely different medium from print. Although many of the considerations that you need to take into account in print design do apply to the Web, there are many other issues that are specific to one medium but not the other. For example, a printed document is always going to be printed at the exact same size and can therefore be designed with set dimensions in mind, whereas Web designers have absolutely no way to know or control the size of their user's browser window.

Although many Web designers create pages that will only be viewed online and are thus free to design just for the one medium, most designers have to take into account the possibility that their users may want to print their pages. This creates a challenge, especially because Web browsers do a notoriously poor job of printing pages, often cutting off some of the page seemingly at random.

In the past, designers were often forced to create and maintain a complete second copy of their pages that were redesigned specifically for printing. Fortunately, that is no longer necessary, as CSS provides the ability to allow designers to repurpose documents for print.

Creating a print style sheet is as simple as creating a new CSS document and specifying what properties you would like to see applied to the printed document. Keep in mind that the browser is going to apply both the main style sheet and the print style sheet, so much of the print document will contain specific overrides for style rules in the main style sheet.

The browser will apply the print style sheet only when the browser's Print functionality is selected. It is capable of knowing which style sheet to use through the addition of a `media` attribute in the `link` tag, set to a value of `print`.

Create a Printable Version of Your Web Pages

① Create a new CSS document in your editor.

② Type a `body` selector.

③ Type an opening curly brace.

④ Type **font-family:Arial, Helvetica, sans-serif;**.

⑤ Type **font-size:12pt;** .

⑥ Type a closing curly brace.

⑦ Click File → Save.

The file is saved.

⑧ Open an XHTML document in your editor.

⑨ In the head of the document, below the current `link` tag, add another `link` tag.

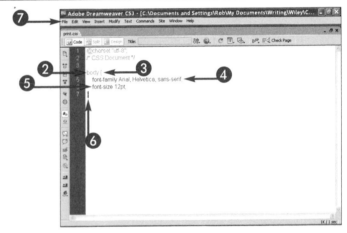

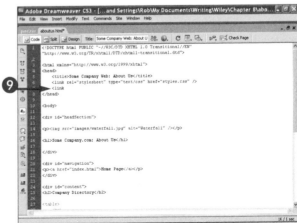

10 Set the `rel` attribute to **"stylesheet"**, the `type` attribute to **"text/css"**, and the `href` attribute to the path of the document that you saved in step **7**.

11 Add a `media` attribute, set to the value of **"print"**.

12 Click File → Save.

The file is saved.

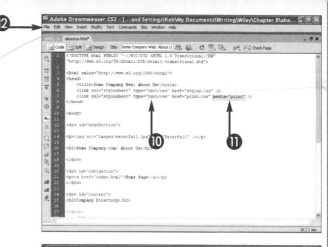

13 Open the document in a Web browser.

14 Click File → Print Preview.

Print Preview shows how the document will appear when it is printed.

Extra

There may be elements on your page that work nicely onscreen but are going to be meaningless on paper, such as navigation. These elements can be hidden when printing by CSS by using `display:none` or `visibility:hidden`. The former removes the element from the page entirely, allowing other elements to move into its space, whereas the latter merely hides the element, forcing its space to remain empty.

A few other considerations to keep in mind when designing your print style sheet are font sizes and element sizes. Points are perhaps the most logical unit of measurement to use for text when printing, as they are the normal unit used in print. Browsers behave erratically when elements are set to a width of 100% when printing — many will interpret this as 100% of the width of the browser window, not the paper. Therefore, you should set the widths of elements to exact units, using inches or some other unit with which you are familiar.

Create a Version of Your Page for Handheld Devices

These days, more and more people are browsing the Web on alternative devices other than a traditional computer. Although Web developers have always had the challenge of needing to design pages that fit on various size screens, today they must figure out how to not only accommodate everything from small 15-inch to widescreen 21-inch monitors, but also deal with the 2- and 3-inch screens on personal digital assistants (PDAs) and cell phones.

The main content of the page should be fairly easy to scale if your layout relies only on CSS. Table-based layouts are essentially unusable on these small screens. Most PDAs and phones scale images to fit in their window, so they should not pose major problems. Data tables are an issue,

as the very structure of the table may pose problems, although using CSS to set the widths of elements of the table at least gives you control as to how it scales.

An alternative style sheet for these devices can be constructed and then linked to the XHTML using a `link` tag with a `media` attribute set to **"handheld"**. Unfortunately, not all PDAs and phones recognize the `"handheld"` media type. Some may ignore CSS altogether, which should not pose too big of a problem if your XHTML is semantically valid, as the point of standards-based XHTML is that the document will make sense even without styles. Other devices may choose to attempt to display the page using the normal style rules, and there is really very little you can do about that.

Create a Version of Your Page for Handheld Devices

① Create a new CSS document in your editor.

② Type a `body` selector.

③ Type an opening curly brace.

④ Type **font-family:Arial, Helvetica, sans-serif;**.

⑤ Type **margin:0;**.

⑥ Type a closing curly brace.

⑦ Click File → Save.

The file is saved.

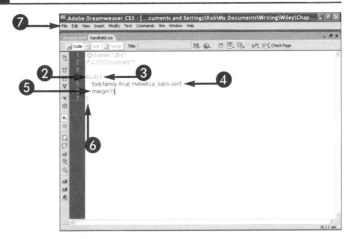

⑧ Open an XHTML document in your editor.

⑨ In the head of the document, below the current `link` tag, add another `link` tag.

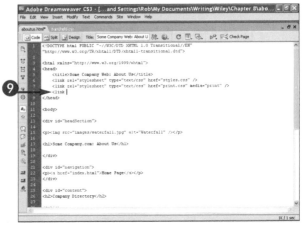

⑩ Set the `rel` attribute to **"stylesheet"**, the `type` attribute to **"text/css"**, and the `href` attribute to the path of the document that you saved in step **7**.

⑪ Add a `media` attribute, set to the value of **"handheld"**.

⑫ Click File → Save.

The file is saved.

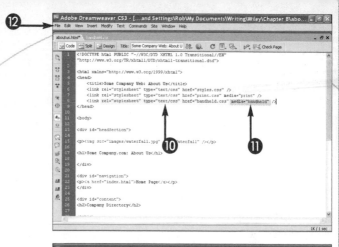

⑬ Browse to the page on a handheld device.

Extra

Testing pages for handheld devices is perhaps the biggest challenge in design, as each device is slightly different and it would be clearly cost-prohibitive to own each possible device. One solution is to use the Opera browser, which is in fact the browser used by many handheld devices. Opera provides a way to display the size of the browser window in the title bar, so you can size it down to the 320x240 used by most phones. Also, it has a small-screen-rendering mode that will use your handheld CSS page to render the page as it would on a phone or PDA.

Another solution has been recently provided by Adobe. The Creative Suite 3 bundles, released in early 2007, include an application called *Device Central CS3*, which functions as a plug-in to other applications in the suite, including Dreamweaver, Flash, and Photoshop. Device Central includes emulators for most of the major cell phone and PDA devices on the market that look and act exactly like their real counterparts. In addition, Dreamweaver CS3 includes the ability to build handheld and print style sheets visually in its Design view.

Clean Up HTML with Tidy

HTML Tidy is a simple tool for checking and cleaning up HTML documents. It was originally developed by Dave Raggett of the World Wide Web Consortium, but today, it is maintained by a group of volunteer developers.

Tidy does many things to improve the validity of HTML code. It will find and correct tags that are either lacking a closing element or have the wrong closing element; find and correct improperly nested tags; properly nest inline elements inside block elements; fix instances where block elements are nested within other block elements; add the slash to closing tags if needed; add missing quotes around attribute values; and report on unknown or browser-specific elements and attributes that are not a part of the official specification. Tidy will reformat your source code, but you can choose whether it should indent all the code, which results in a slightly bigger but more

readable file, or not. Tidy will generate an accessibility report pointing out those areas that may need to be improved to make the document accessible. It will also remove any presentational markup, such as the use of font, center, and other purely presentational elements, and replace them with equivalent CSS rules. The program has limited support for pages that contain server-side scripting, and it can parse and clean up XML files as well.

The biggest downside for most users is that although it runs on the Windows operating system, Tidy does not have a graphical user interface. Instead, you need to use the command line to execute Tidy. At its most basic, the program can be run by typing the command **tidy -f errors.txt -m index.html**, which runs the program on the index.html file, editing it in place and generating an errors.txt file with a list of what corrections were made.

Clean Up HTML with Tidy

1 Download the Tidy executable from www.paehl.com/open_source/?HTML_ Tidy_for_Windows.

2 Extract the file into the directory that contains your XHTML files.

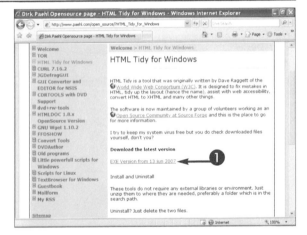

3 Open a Command window.

In Windows XP, click Start ➔ Run and type **cmd**.

The Command window opens.

4 Type **cd**, followed by a path to the folder into which you extracted Tidy.

5 Type **tidy −f errors.txt −m index.html**.

6 Press Enter.

7 Open the index.html file in your editor and observe any changes.

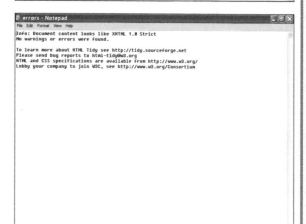

8 Open errors.txt in your editor.

If any corrections were made, they appear in the document.

Apply It

You can create a configuration file to store common settings that you want to have Tidy use. Simply save the file in the folder in which you run Tidy and then let Tidy know that you want to use it by issuing the `-config` command with the name of the file. A sample configuration file may look like this:

```
indent: auto
indent-spaces: 4
wrap: 80
markup: yes
output-xml: yes
input-xml: yes
show-warnings: yes
numeric-entities: no
uppercase-tags: no
uppercase-attributes: no
char-encoding: latin1
```

Convert HTML to XHTML Using Adobe Dreamweaver

Adobe Dreamweaver CS3, the latest version of the versatile Web development tool, creates XHTML pages by default. That is to say that when you use Dreamweaver and simply create a new document, it will use XHTML Transitional. The application automatically adds the appropriate document type declaration and the `xmlns` attribute to the `html` tag and writes all the code following the XHTML specifications.

Dreamweaver has been able to create XHTML for the last several versions and has taken the approach of creating XHTML by default for the last three versions. If you have a legacy document that was either created in an older version of Dreamweaver or created outside Dreamweaver in some other editor and is using HTML instead of XHTML, Dreamweaver provides a very easy conversion tool. The XHTML converter adds or modifies the

document type declaration, adds the `xmlns` attribute if needed, rewrites any HTML tags to lowercase, closes any tags that are not closed, fixes invalidly nested tags, adds character entities if needed, and puts quotation marks around attribute values. It will not, however, remove tags that are not valid XHTML, even if you choose to have Dreamweaver convert to XHTML Strict.

To perform this transformation, simply open the legacy HTML document in Dreamweaver and then select the appropriate version of XHTML from the Convert submenu on the File menu. You can convert a document to XHTML 1 Transitional, XHTML 1 Strict, or XHTML 1.1.

You should note that you cannot convert a document that is based on a Dreamweaver template. Instead, you need to convert the template document itself, which will then update pages created from it.

Convert HTML to XHTML Using Adobe Dreamweaver

① Open a legacy HTML document in Adobe Dreamweaver.

● Click File → Open.

Navigate to the file.

Click Open.

The document opens.

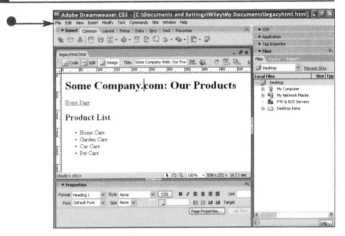

② Click View → Code.

The Code view is displayed.

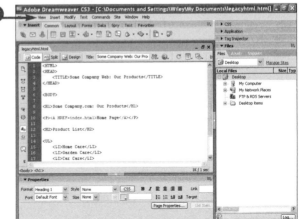

③ Click File.

④ Click Convert.

⑤ Click XHTML 1.0 Transitional.

The document is converted.

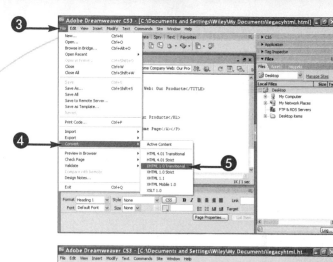

⑥ Note the changes in the code on the page.

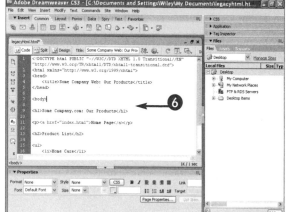

Extra

You can convert frames-based pages by selecting each frames page individually and converting it to the version of XHTML that you want. Then you can select the frameset document itself and convert it to XHTML 1 Frameset.

You can change the default document type used by Dreamweaver when it creates new pages by choosing Preferences from the Edit menu. In the New Document category, choose the version of XHTML that you want from the Default Document Type (DDT) drop-down list. The Preferences dialog box also enables you to control how Dreamweaver encodes special characters in the Code Rewriting category and modify settings such as how far code should be indented and when code lines should wrap in the Code Format section.

Dreamweaver can also validate your code to make sure that you are using valid XHTML, based on your document type declaration. Using the Validate Markup button on the document toolbar, you can have Dreamweaver check that your code is valid. When you run this validation, the Validation panel will appear with a report of any errors, including the line number and a description of the problem. You can double-click the error to jump to that line of code.

Remove Presentational Markup Using Dreamweaver's Find and Replace

Adobe Dreamweaver CS3 contains an extremely powerful find-and-replace tool. Although this tool serves the same purpose as most find-and-replace tools in that it enables you to search for strings of text and replace them, it also has many more capabilities.

Dreamweaver Find and Replace, accessible from the Edit menu or by using the Ctrl+F keyboard shortcut, allows you to search either the currently selected text, the currently active document, all open documents, documents within a specified folder, selected documents within a site, or all documents within a site. It further allows searching through the source code of a document, the visible text, text inside or outside of tags or attributes, and specific tags. You have the option to match case in your search, match whole words only, ignore whitespace, or use regular expressions. Complex searches can be saved and reused later.

The ability to search for specific tags creates the possibility to use Find and Replace to remove presentational markup from legacy HTML documents in preparation for converting them to using CSS for presentation instead. In the Find and Replace dialog box, you can select the tag that is used for presentational purposes only, such as font. You can search for all instances of the tag, regardless of their attributes, and then choose to strip the tag. To remove presentational attributes such as align, select the tag that contains the attribute and set it to be removed. You can also remove all instances of the tag or attribute from the document. If performing this on an entire folder or site, Dreamweaver will warn you that the changes will not be undoable on documents that are not currently open.

Remove Presentational Markup Using Dreamweaver's Find and Replace

① Open an HTML document with presentational markup in Dreamweaver.

● Click File → Open.

Navigate to the file.

Click Open.

The document opens.

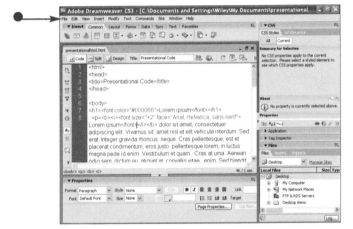

② Click Edit → Find and Replace.

The Find and Replace dialog box appears.

③ Click the Search down arrow and select Specific Tag.

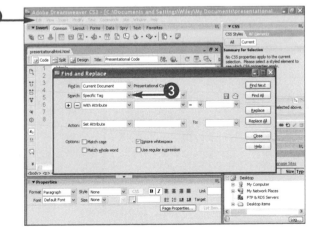

4 Select the tag that you want to remove.

5 Click the –.

6 Click the Action down arrow and select Strip Tag.

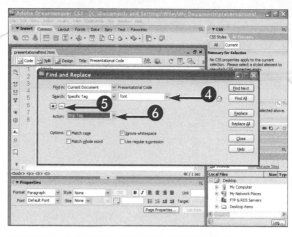

7 Click Replace All.

The Results panel opens, showing that the tag has been stripped.

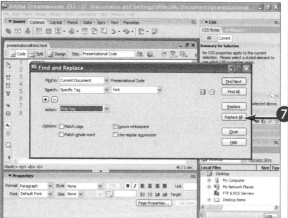

Extra

One of the more powerful features of Dreamweaver's Find and Replace is the ability to use regular expressions. Regular expressions are used by most programming languages and many tools such as Dreamweaver to allow you to search for matching strings. For example, if you had a page that listed employee email addresses, and you wanted to replace the simple text of the email address with an actual link to it, you could not use a traditional find and replace. Each email address follows a basic structure: one or more characters, the @ symbol, one or more characters, a dot, and two or more characters. Regular expressions enable you to construct a string that matches exactly that pattern.

Regular expressions are semistandardized, meaning that although there is a core set of expressions that every language or program uses, there are many variations as well. In Dreamweaver, you can search the Help file for details on using them in Find and Replace. Many resources also exist online at sites such as the Regular Expression Library at www.regexlib.com. Initially, learning regular expressions can seem daunting, but after you become familiar with them, they are fairly easy to use yet extremely powerful.

Strip Tables in Dreamweaver

converting legacy HTML documents to standards-compliant XHTML documents involves not only converting HTML tags and removing purely presentational markup such as the `font` tag, but also removing any tables that are being used for layout and replacing them with cascading style sheets and positioned elements.

Adobe Dreamweaver CS3's powerful Find and Replace feature makes stripping presentational tables out of a document quite easy. Tables are made up of three basic elements: `table`, `tr`, and `td`. Data tables make use of other elements such as `caption`, `th`, `col`, and `colgroup`, but these are rarely used for layout tables.

Before beginning the process of stripping tables, you should examine the layout of your document and decide how you plan to implement the layout in CSS. Most

likely, you will replace many of the table cells with `div` tags that contain IDs. By examining the layout in its existing form, you can get a better idea of how to rebuild the site.

Using Find and Replace, you can, one at a time, strip all instances of `table`, `tr`, and `td`. Then you can use the Wrap with Div feature in the program to add opening and closing `div` elements around selected blocks of code, complete with the IDs that you want to assign. Finally, you can go into your style sheet and add the necessary CSS to re-create the layout.

CSS layouts are not identical to table-based layouts. Although it is possible to nearly re-create the previous layout, most designers choose to take the opportunity of converting to CSS to leverage other properties of the language to improve on the overall design of the page.

Strip Tables in Dreamweaver

① Open an HTML document with presentational markup in Dreamweaver.

● Click File → Open.

Navigate to the file.

Click Open.

The document opens.

② Click Edit → Find and Replace.

③ Click the Search down arrow and select Specific Tag.

④ Click the Tag down arrow and select `table`.

⑤ Click the – to search for tags without regard to attributes.

⑥ Click the Action down arrow and select Strip Tag.

⑦ Click Replace All.

Dreamweaver strips the table tags.

⑧ Repeat steps **2** to **7**, stripping the `tr` and `td` tags.

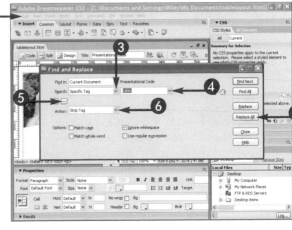

⑨ Select a block of text that you want to designate as a `div`.

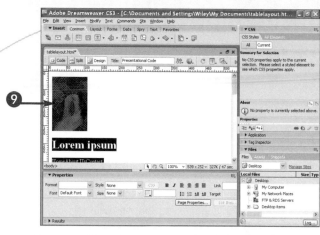

⑩ Click Insert → Layout Objects → Div Tag.

The Insert Div Tag dialog box appears.

⑪ Click the Insert down arrow and select Wrap Around Selection.

⑫ Type an appropriate ID.

⑬ Click OK.

Opening and closing `div` elements and the ID are added to the code.

⑭ Repeat steps **10** to **13** to add other `div`s to the page.

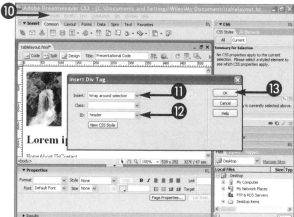

Extra

Not all tables are bad. Tables are a perfectly valid part of XHTML, provided that they are used to mark up data and not as a layout tool. Stripping tables using Dreamweaver can unfortunately be a too-powerful tool on pages that use tables both for layout and for data, as it will not be aware which tables on the page should be stripped and which should be left. This problem can be solved in one of several ways. First, you can click Find to move to each instance of the `table` tag and then click Replace to strip it and move to the next, or click Find again to skip the tags used for data. Second, you could add an ID or `class` attribute to the data table and each of its child tags and then search for instances of the tags without that attribute, which Find and Replace allows you to do. Third, you could cut the data table from the document, then use Find and Replace to strip the rest of the tables, and then paste the data table back in. Whichever method you use is a matter of personal preference.

Add Alternative Text to All Images

As the Web is primarily a visual medium, images are of course important in Web design. However, they present challenges to search engines cataloging pages because the software used by them cannot "see" the images and interpret what they represent, and they present challenges to visually impaired users who likewise cannot directly view pictures.

The XHTML `img` element has an `alt` attribute to help solve these issues. Originally, `alt` text was optional for images, but with XHTML 1 and 1.1, it is a required attribute for all images. Alternative text provides a description of the image for search engines, screen readers for the blind, and other technologies to understand the image and appropriately catalog or describe it.

Merely adding text to the `alt` attribute is not sufficient. The point here is to describe the image, so the alternative text must be a meaningful description of the image. Many online newspaper sites make the mistake of using the headline as alternative text on the main image of the page; although this may help them get better search results, it does nothing to describe the image to their blind users. Instead, care needs to be taken to make sure that images are properly described.

Occasionally, images may appear on the page that do not add to the overall content, such as decorative bullets used to set off headings or curved borders on boxes. Although it would be better to add these purely presentational images through CSS, you should make sure that you set empty `alt` text on them, using `alt=""`, if you must add them through XHTML.

Microsoft Internet Explorer on Windows will display `alt` text as a ToolTip when a user moves the mouse pointer over an image. Internet Explorer is the only browser that does this, so there is nothing wrong with your code when you view your page in Firefox or any other browser and do not see the ToolTip.

Add Alternative Text to All Images

① Open an XHTML document with images in it in your editor.

② Add an `alt` attribute to each image.

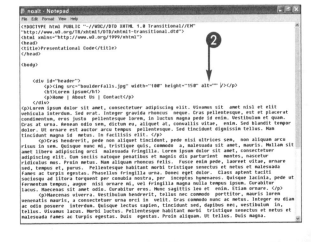

③ Add a meaningful description as the value of the `alt` attribute.

④ Save the page.

⑤ Open the page in Internet Explorer.

⑥ Move the cursor over the image.

The `alt` text appears as a ToolTip.

Extra

Alternative text is also required for the `area` element, if you are using an image map. Be sure to provide a meaningful description of the portion of the image defined in the `area` element. Alternative text is optional for the `input` tag and is rarely used because the proper use of the `label` element will generally provide a better description of the tag. It is also optional for the `applet` element, but as the use of `applet` to embed Java applets has fallen by the wayside in favor of `object`, it is also rarely an issue.

If you have a complicated image that cannot be accurately described in a few words through alternative text, you can use the `longdesc` attribute, in which you provide the URL to a separate document that describes the image in detail. Few if any visually impaired users are likely to take the time to examine this document for most images, so it is not required and is only recommended for images such as charts and graphs.

Lay Out Your Folder Structure

Many Web designers conceive a simple notion for a Web site — four or five pages about themselves. Because the site will be so small, they give little or no thought to organizing the files. Eventually, the site starts to grow, as the developer comes up with new ideas or expands their knowledge of the Web. Before long, what started as a simple set of pages has expanded into a complex Web site, but the organization is still not there, especially if the site grew incrementally.

In these situations, the Web designer can quickly become overwhelmed by the mass of pages and begin to waste valuable development time searching for files. Organizing a large site after the fact can be difficult because file paths will change and possibly break links and bookmarks within the site.

These potential problems can be avoided by carefully planning the site from the very beginning. Regardless of how small the site begins, having a logical folder structure to follow will assist in keeping track of pages and make the site more scalable in the long run.

At the very least, a Web site should contain a root directory with the index, or home page, and at least one folder for the images. Each logical section of the site may benefit from being in its own folder. Make sure that your folders have logical names, which will not only help you keep track of them but will also give your users a sense of where they are in the site and help with search-engine rankings.

The exact folder structure that you decide to use is ultimately a personal decision. The only thing that you absolutely must do is develop a system that makes sense to you.

Lay Out Your Folder Structure

① Open Windows Explorer.

   In Windows XP, click Start → My Computer → Local Disk (C:).

② Navigate to the folder in which you will store your Web files.

③ Create a new folder named "images."

   In Windows XP, right-click in Windows Explorer and choose New → Folder.

   Type **images** and press Enter.

   A new folder is created.

④ Create a new folder called "info."

   In Windows XP, right-click in Windows Explorer and choose New → Folder.

   Type **info** and press Enter.

   A new folder is created.

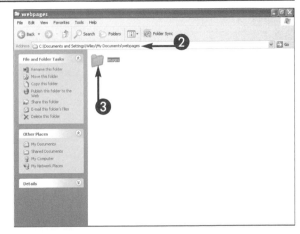

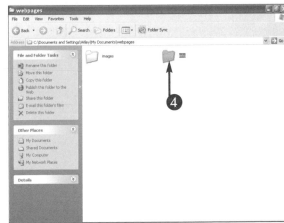

⑤ Create a new XHTML file in your editor.

● In Adobe Dreamweaver CS3, click File → New.

Click Create.

A new file opens.

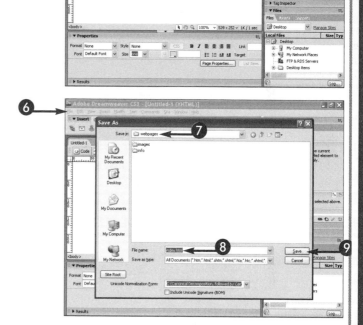

⑥ Click File → Save As.

The Save As dialog box appears.

⑦ Go to the folder that you navigated to in step **2**.

⑧ Type **index.html** for the filename.

⑨ Click Save.

The file is saved.

Extra

You will need to make sure that the folder structure that you create on your local hard drive exactly matches the folder structure on the server. When you get ready to upload your files to the Web server, you will need to create folders with identical names as those you used locally. Otherwise, your links will not work when you upload.

As you develop your site, you will have certain assets that you use locally but do not want to upload to your server. These may include the original image files from your graphics program or original source documents for the content of your site. It is recommended that these files be stored completely outside of the Web site's directory to prevent them from being uploaded accidentally, but in case they cannot be, you should at least store them all in a single, clearly labeled folder.

Plan Your Site's Navigation

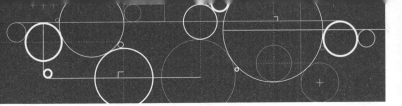

S ites that have well-thought-out navigation are easy to spot on the Web. Sites with poorly designed navigation are more difficult to find. The reason is simple: Good navigation is one of the keys to an excellent, successful site, whereas poor navigation can often lead to the failure of your site. So sites with good navigation tend to stick around, and those with bad navigation do not.

Good, effective navigation does not happen by accident. Only through careful planning and testing can you create an effective navigation structure for your site.

The first, most important thing to keep in mind in planning navigation is to put yourself in your user's place. The Web is a user-centric environment. Because it is so easy to simply go somewhere else and find the information you want, very few users will tolerate bad

design, either on the page as a whole or particularly in a site's navigation. You should not make your users think about what they are doing; instead, your site's navigation should be laid out so that it is practically intuitive for them to get where they need to go. Do not hide your navigation; make it obvious and make it stand out on the page. Do not buck conventions simply for the sake of bucking them; most sites place navigation on the top and left of the page, not because the designers are too lazy or lack the creativity to come up with something different, but because that is where users expect to find it.

After you have your site designed, test it with as wide a variety of users as you can. If they have problems navigating the site or finding the information on it, the fault is yours, not theirs, and the site's navigation needs to be redesigned to fit.

Plan Your Site's Navigation

EXAMINE SITES WITH GOOD NAVIGATION

① Open a Web browser.

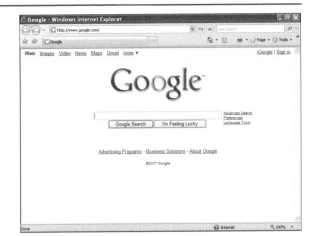

② Navigate to www.amazon.com.

③ Observe how the site organizes its navigation structure.

④ Navigate to www.ebay.com.

⑤ Observe how the site's navigation is organized.

PLAN YOUR SITE'S NAVIGATION

⑥ Create a sketch or diagram of the top-level navigation of your site.

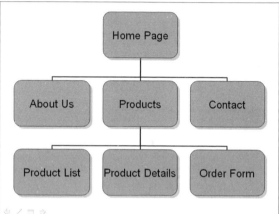

Extra

Your site will most likely rely on two levels of navigation. The top level will contain links to the key sections of your site and will most likely appear on all pages in the site. Second-level navigation will be specific to a section of the site and will change based on the section in which is appears.

Common practice is to place the top-level navigation either along the top of the page or in the left-hand column, with second-level navigation either nested within the top level or below it. Although there is no requirement that these conventions be followed, be careful in varying from them too much. Although it is possible to design a page with effective navigation placed elsewhere, you need to be sure that your users can find the links that they need without having to hunt for them.

You should also try to maintain consistency in the layout and wording of second-level navigation from one section to the next to avoid user confusion.

Create an
Index Page

The first page in a site is the home page, also called the *index page.* The home page needs to make a good first impression on your users because if they are dissatisfied with the home page, they are unlikely to continue on from there.

Creating a successful home page is an art unto itself. There needs to be a balance between presenting enough information to your users that they will feel that your site is something that they can use, but at the same time, you do not want to overwhelm them. You need to provide good navigation to the other main sections of the site.

Often, the home page will require an entirely different layout from the rest of the site. Although this is acceptable and actually a fairly common practice, you need to make sure that the design of the home page is

close enough to the design of the rest of the site that there is continuity: Your users need to feel like they are on the same site when they navigate to other pages, even if the layout is different. Using consistent colors, fonts, and images can be helpful in maintaining this continuity.

Spending some time browsing the Web and taking a critical, design-oriented look at popular Web sites or sites that you personally like can be very helpful in designing your home page. At the same time, it can be just as helpful to look at sites that you do not like to analyze what they are doing wrong.

Keep in mind as well that search engines, like your users, will start at your home page, so you need to be sure to provide enough keyword-oriented content on your pages so that they will catalog it properly.

Create an Index Page

① Create a new XHTML file in your editor.

● In Adobe Dreamweaver CS3, click File ➜ New.

Click Create.

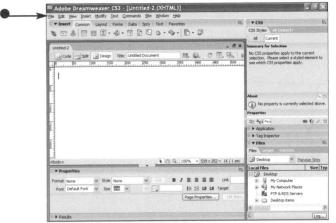

② Enter a main heading for your site.

③ Use the XHTML heading 1 element to mark up the heading.

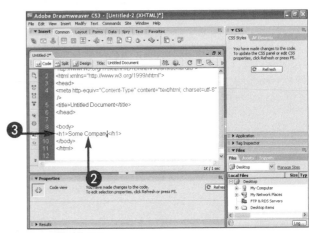

④ Type a brief paragraph describing your site.

⑤ Add your navigation.

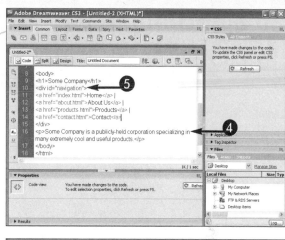

⑥ Use CSS to lay out and design your site.

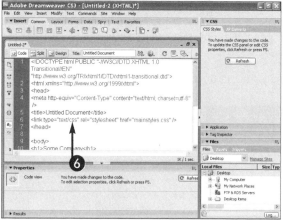

Extra

Avoid creating a home page that is little more than a list of links to your site's pages. This type of index page will not have enough content for search engines, nor will it give your users any information about the site or why they should explore it. Think instead of your home page as the lobby to a big company's headquarters. It would not be an empty room with a bunch of doors. Instead, the lobby provides basic information about the company in addition to those doors to the other parts of the company.

Large, complex sites may actually have a series of home pages, one for each section of the site. Amazon.com is laid out with a main home page that shows the different categories of products they offer, but then there is a home page for the book section of the site, devoted just to books, and a home page for the DVD section, and so on. Most government Web sites follow a similar pattern, with an overall home page for the entire governmental body and then separate, often quite distinct, home pages and sites for various departments or units of the organization.

Create an About You XML File

f you want to create a personal Web site, it seems logical to have an About You file, in which you tell readers about yourself and what you do. Your résumé can be neatly encapsulated into such an About You XML file. It is, after all, a series of data points about you.

A standard résumé contains a series of logical sections, including education, experience, and other skills. Each of these can become a parent element in the XML file, with child elements describing the schools attended and degrees obtained or job titles and companies for which you have worked.

By maintaining your résumé as an XML file, you can free yourself from having to deal with the formatting of the document. An XML file is going to be much easier to update and maintain than a traditional word-processing

document. Also, it can very easily be repurposed, so you could import the XML into Microsoft Word or Adobe Acrobat for printing in a traditional format or use XSLT to convert it to XHTML for display on the Web. You could even use Adobe InDesign to extract information from the résumé to use on a business card. By simply reordering the XML, you can have the presentational documents change automatically.

Keep in mind that all XML files need a root element, which in this case would most likely be something like resume. You could create a schema for your document as well, depending on how you plan to use it. Some applications that are XML-aware, such as Microsoft Word, deal with XML better if a schema is present than if it is not. Others, such as XSLT, will work fine with or without a schema.

Create an About You XML File

① Create a new file in your XML editor.

② Add an XML prolog.

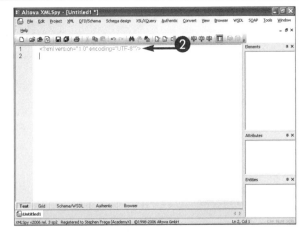

③ Type a root element, such as **resume**.

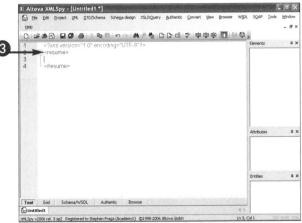

4 Type a child element.

5 Add data to the child element.

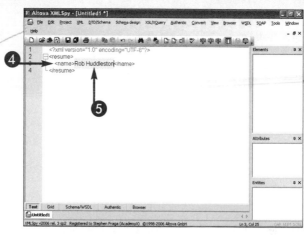

6 Add additional elements to fill out the résumé.

7 Click File → Save.

The file is saved.

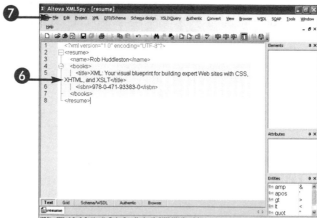

Apply It

Here's an example of what your About You XML file may contain:

```
<resume>
          <contactInfo>
                    <fullName>Your Name</fullName>
                    <email>Your email</email>
          </contactInfo>
          <objective>Sample objective text here...</objective>
          <education>
                    <collegeName>College Name</collegeName>
                    <degreeAndYear>Degree and Year Obtained</degree>
          </education>
          <experience>
                    <mostRecentJob>
                              <jobTitle>Title</jobTitle>
                              <employer>Employer</employer>
                              <description>Job Description</description>
                    </mostRecentJob>
          </experience>
     </resume>
```

Translate the About You File to XHTML

Creating a good About You page is something of an art. You need to tread a thin line between being informative and being too egotistical. Perhaps more important, you need to figure out how to provide the information that you want without being too boring.

At a minimum, the About You page should give your Web site visitors some idea as to why they should trust you to give them the rest of the information on the site. After all, one of the greatest advantages of the Web — the fact that anyone can publish anything — is also one of its greatest disadvantages. Traditional publishing can be trusted because there is an assumption that the work has been read and edited by experts beyond the author before going to print. The same is not true on the Web.

An About You page sets the tone for the rest of the site, so a humorous About You page is going to imply the use of humor in the remaining pages. It also allows you to set yourself apart from other sites that may provide similar information.

Many designers ignore or neglect the About You page, figuring that most site visitors will not bother going to it. Although that may be true for a certain percentage of users, you do want to be sure that your About You page is worth the time for those who do decide to view it.

If you have your pertinent personal information in an XML file, you can use XSLT to translate it to XHTML. That way, you only need to modify the XML file when the information changes and let the XSLT handle keeping the actual Web page up-to-date.

Translate the About You File to XHTML

① Create a new XLST file in your editor.

② Add an XML prolog.

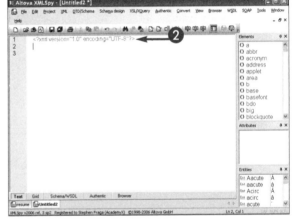

③ Add a root `xsl:stylesheet` element.

④ Add an `xsl:output` element.

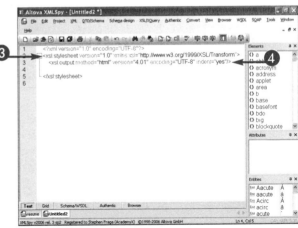

5 Add an `xsl:template` element.

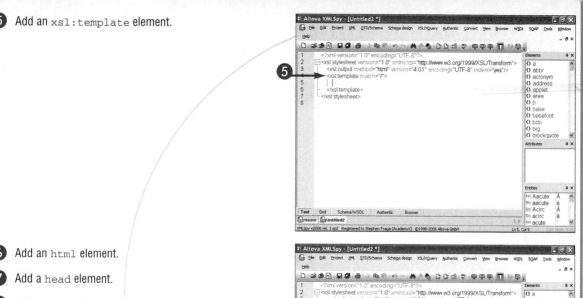

6 Add an `html` element.

7 Add a `head` element.

8 Add a `title` element.

9 Set the data of the `title` element to **About Me**.

10 Close the `title` and `head` elements.

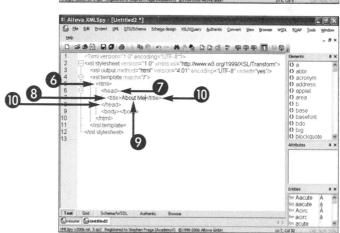

Extra

The graphical elements of the page can be inserted in one of three ways. Graphics that directly relate to the data in the XML file, such as a recent photo of yourself or screenshots of work products, should have references in the XML, with the appropriate image path and alternative text specified. Your XSLT can then insert the values of the image path and the alternative text into the XHTML it is constructing in the appropriate attributes.

More generic graphical elements, such as a site logo, should be inserted directly into the XHTML in your XSLT page. As these elements do not need to be updated every time the XML updates, there is no reason to reference them in the XML.

Graphics that merely add visual interest to the page, such as special bullets or rounded corners for elements, should be added to the page through a cascading style sheets' background image property. Remember that in the current version of CSS, each element can only contain a single background image, so you may find it necessary to occasionally add additional elements to your page to support extra images.

continued ➡

Many sites use the About Me page to double as a Contact Me page. In this case, the page will also need to contain whatever contact information you want to provide. At a minimum, you will want either a link to an email address or some sort of basic contact form, although the latter may be better off on a separate page, as it would not most likely relate to the information coming from the XML file.

Be careful about putting a link to an email address on your Web site, as it is fairly easy for spammers to locate the link and add that address to their lists.

You may also choose to include physical contact information, such as a phone number and mailing address. This is especially important if the site is intended to draw business or job offers to you. Although there are examples of very large sites that make finding physical contact information difficult (Yahoo! is an example), being willing to add this information will lend your site some additional credibility, as many people will be more likely to trust a site that provides it, and many individuals and organizations will not do business with sites that will not provide real-world contact information.

XHTML has an `address` element that is specifically designed to mark up a physical address on a Web page. Many designers will actually include all their contact information within the `address` block. By default, browsers will display information inside `address` in italics, but you can use the CSS `font-style` property, set to a value of `normal`, to override this.

Translate the About You File to XHTML *(continued)*

⑪ Add a `body` element.

⑫ Add a heading level one element.

⑬ Type **About Me**.

⑭ Close the heading element.

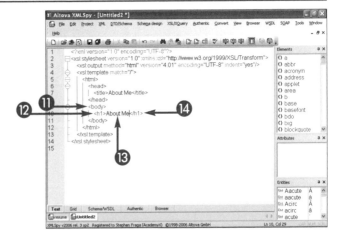

⑮ Add an `xsl:for-each` element.

⑯ Set the `select` attribute to the first child element of the About Me XML file.

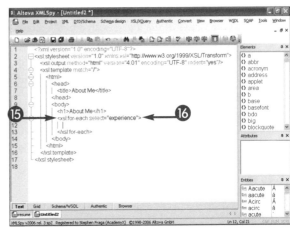

186

⑰ Add a paragraph element.

⑱ Use `xsl:value-of` to output the values from your XML file.

⑲ Close the `xsl:for-each` element.

⑳ Close the `body` element.

㉑ Close the `html` element.

㉒ Close the `xsl:template` element.

㉓ Close the `xsl:stylesheet` element.

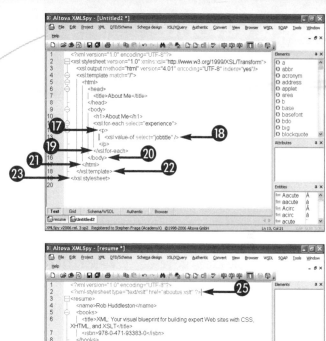

㉔ Open your About You XML file in your editor.

㉕ Add an `xsl-stylesheet` processing instruction.

Your XML file can now be transformed with the XSLT.

Extra

About Me pages can be an important source of additional keywords for search engine optimization. Your About Me page should include a description of yourself and the services you offer. That description should be carefully worded so as to include as many keywords as possible while still being human-readable. Be sure to use the appropriate XHTML elements for this content, including headings, as it will further enhance your search engine rankings.

You can discover what keywords you may want to use by performing searches on major search engines for people or services similar to yours. Google also provides a host of free Webmaster tools at www.google.com/webmasters, which includes the ability to see what terms people are using to actually find your pages. The site also contains other useful reports and information to help improve your rankings. You can also experiment with the Google Suggest tool at www.google.com/webhp?complete=1&hl=en, which provides terms related to the one you are typing based on what others are searching for at the time, and Google Trends at www.google.com/trends, which will show you the current most popular search terms.

Create a Favorite Movies XML File

Many personal Web sites contain lists of the designer's favorite movies, TV shows, books, or music. This list is an obvious candidate for an XML file because it is by definition nothing more than a list of data points.

Before simply creating the XML file, you need to consider what kinds of information about the movie you want to put on your page. You may simply want to list the titles, but you can also list the year the movie was released, its rating from the Motion Picture Association of America, or its running time. You could choose to specify its director, the main actors who starred in it, or even the studio that released it. All of this information can be looked up on the Internet Movie Database at www.imdb.com if you do not know it yourself.

If you see a lot of movies and have more time to work on your page, you may also choose to write a short review of the films. This could become the reason why visitors come to your site. Although there are many thousands of film review sites on the Web, finding one where you agree with the critic's choices can be challenging, so there is always room for one more voice.

A movies XML file will most likely have a fairly generic root element and then contain a set of movie elements, each of which will contain child elements for the title, rating, and whatever other information you choose to have. If you are going to have reviews in the file, you should enclose them in CDATA sections, so you do not have to remember to use character entities to escape characters such as the ampersand or quotation marks.

Create a Favorite Movies XML File

① Create a new XML file in your editor.

② Add an XML prolog.

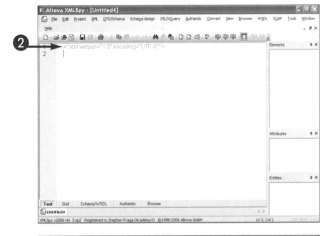

③ Add a root element.

④ Add a child element for the first movie, named something like `movie`.

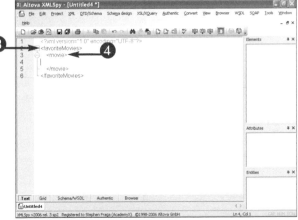

5 Add a `title` element as the child of the `movie` element.

6 Enter a movie title.

7 Close the `title` element.

8 Add other elements to store other details about the movie.

9 Close the `movie` element.

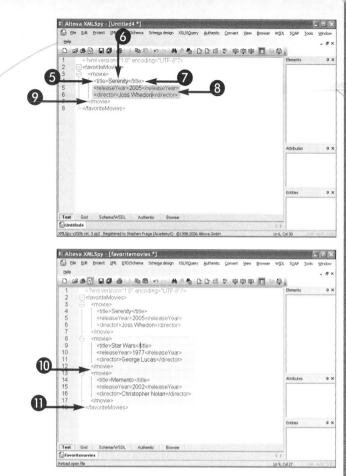

10 Repeat steps **4** to **9** to add more movies to the list.

11 Close the root element.

Your XML file is complete.

Extra

Experienced database developers will be tempted to try to create a relational setup with commonly referenced actors and directors. Although this would be standard practice in using a database to store movie information, you need to keep in mind that XML files are not relational databases but are rather plain text files. The analogy between XML and databases only goes so far. You will need to simply reenter repetitive data in the XML file. If you have a name that is being used very frequently, you could create an entity by which you could reference it, but this is more like storing the name in a variable than in a related table.

Although you will almost certainly need to create a CDATA section for the text of the review, other fields may benefit from it as well. CDATA sections prevent you from needing to use entities to reference illegal characters, so it may help in the film's title, which may include ampersands. You will need to decide whether the extra code required to write the CDATA versus the extra code needed for the entity is an acceptable tradeoff.

Translate the Favorite Movies File to XHTML

If you store your movie information in an XML file, you can quickly translate that to XHTML through XSLT and display it on the Web. As with other uses of XML and XSLT, this will make updating the page much easier, as all you will need to do is update the XML file when you add a new movie to the list.

In translating your XML to XHTML, you need to spend some time before you start to consider the visual design and layout of your page. The XSLT file can contain any static XHTML elements that you want, including banners with logos, navigation bars, images, and other common elements. Using cascading style sheets, you can format the page to look almost any way that you want.

You need to consider how you plan to actually display the movie information. Although the details of the movie coming from the XML file are data, a table would be perfectly acceptable. However, using unordered lists or possibly even headings and paragraphs styled with cascading style sheets may result in a nicer appearance.

You also need to decide how much information for your XML file you want to display on a single page. It is most likely unrealistic to display everything — title, director, actors, rating, reviews, and so on — for many documents on a single page. More often, you will want to display just the basic information about the movie, while possibly providing links to other pages that display the details of the movie and the review.

Translate the Favorite Movies File to XHTML

① Create a new XLST file in your editor.

② Add an XML prolog.

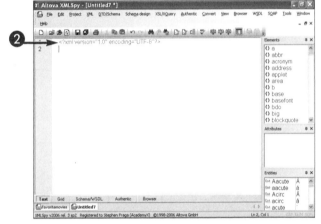

③ Add a root `xsl:stylesheet` element.

④ Add an `xsl:output` element.

⑤ Add an `xsl:template` element.

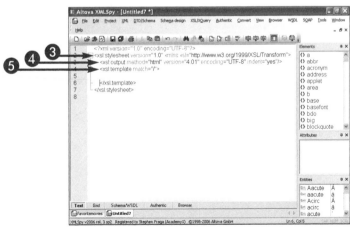

⑥ Add an `html` element.

⑦ Add a `head` element.

⑧ Add a `title` element.

⑨ Set the data of the `title` element to **Favorite Movies**.

⑩ Close the `title` and `head` elements.

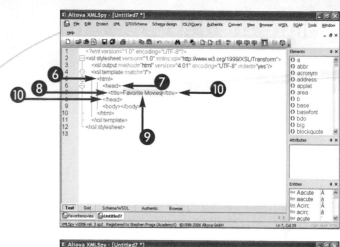

⑪ Add a `body` element.

⑫ Add a heading one element.

⑬ Type **Favorite Movies**.

⑭ Close the heading element.

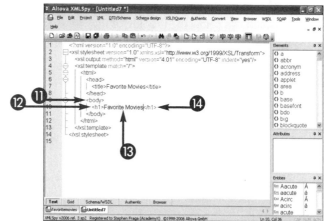

continued ➡

Extra

An extremely useful site for gathering information about movies is the Internet Movie Database at www.imdb.com. IMDB was originally created in the late 1980s — before the Web was even invented — by a group of people on an Internet discussion list who began compiling the movie data that was being passed around. Although the Web was still in its infancy in 1993, the first version of IMDB went online. It quickly grew into the largest resource of user-collected data about movies. Acquired by Amazon in 1998, it now covers TV and video game information as well.

You can search IMDB by movie title, the name of any cast or crew member, or other criteria. When searching for a movie, the Web site will list the actual title, the full cast and crew, MPAA rating, user reviews, worldwide release dates, and more. Most movie listings also provide links to images from the movies, and since its acquisition by Amazon, the site also provides links to that site to purchase those movies that are available on DVD.

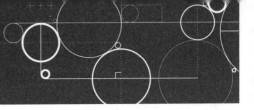

You should design your favorite movies pages with expansion in mind. Although you may start out only providing basic information about the films, you may later decide to add more details such as cast and crew names or reviews of the movie. Therefore, you will want to create a design that allows for future growth.

Listing your favorite movies in a simple table, for example, will not only be visually boring, but will also make adding long reviews difficult. Instead, designing the page so that the film titles appear as headings, with bulleted lists or paragraphs below the heading of the other information, gives you more freedom to add more information.

If you plan to list more than a few movies, you will also need to consider whether to have the movies all appear on a single page or create individual pages for each title. Keep in mind that XPath is easily powerful enough to allow you to filter each page based on the value of the title, so you could theoretically have a single XML file for all the movies and yet still display each as a separate file. If you do split the list into more than one file, you will also need to consider how your users will navigate through the titles. You can use XSLT to create a list of the titles that will link to each one, or you could use some sort of server-side technology to dynamically create the navigation and possibly even provide for search functionality.

Translate the Favorite Movies File to XHTML (continued)

⑮ Add an `xsl:for-each` element.

⑯ Set the `select` attribute to the first child element of the Favorite Movies XML file.

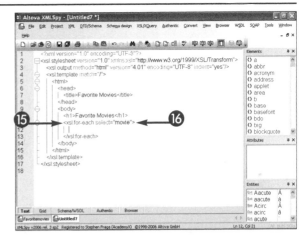

⑰ Add a paragraph element.

⑱ Use `xsl:value-of` to output the values from your XML file.

⑲ Close the `xsl:for-each` element.

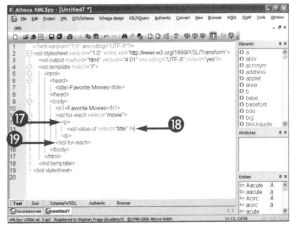

⑳ Close the `body` element.

㉑ Close the `xsl:template` element.

㉒ Close the `xsl:stylesheet` element.

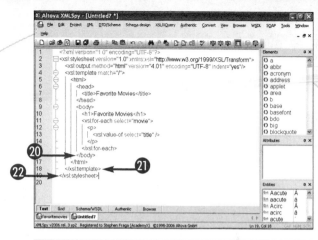

㉓ Open your Favorite Movies XML file in your editor.

㉔ Add an `xsl-stylesheet` processing instruction.

Your movies XML files page can now be transformed to XHTML.

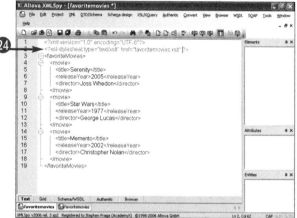

Extra

In order to create a drill-down interface, in which you display a list of movies on one page and then provide links to other pages that display the details about the movie, you will either need to create individual XHTML pages for each movie or use some sort of server-side processing to extract the details for display. Any of the modern server-side application languages, including Microsoft ASP.NET, Adobe ColdFusion, and PHP, could be written to parse the XML file and generate a details page based on the link that your user clicked.

There will certainly be a temptation to display visual elements from the movie, such as a picture or even the film's official poster, on your site. Be very careful when considering this not to violate copyrights. Movie studios are fiercely protective of their intellectual property, as you would most likely be too if you invested over a hundred million dollars in a product.

Add a Site Icon

Modern browsers enable Web developers to add their own custom site icon. The browser uses this icon on its address bar, displaying it to the left of the site's address rather than the normal browser icon. In addition, the site icon will be displayed on the Bookmarks or Favorites menu if the user adds a reference to the page.

Your site icon must be a 16 pixel by 16 pixel image. Although the image can be created in any graphics program, it must be saved as a special icon file with an .ico extension. Most major graphics editors have the capability to save an image as an .ico file. In addition, there are many tools available to create and save .ico files.

After you have the icon created, there are two ways to make it to appear. The simplest is to save it as favicon.ico

and upload it to the root directory of your Web server. Modern browsers will automatically look for it, and if they find it, they will use it.

The second method is to add a reference to the icon in a `link` tag in your XHTML document. In this case, the filename does not matter, as long as it has an .ico extension:

```
<link rel="icon shortcut"
type="image/vnd.microsoft.icon"
href="path_to_icon" />
```

This second method is useful for situations in which your Web hosting company does not allow access to the actual Web root, although these instances are rare.

Add a Site Icon

1 Open a new file in a graphics editor.

● In Adobe Photoshop, click File →
New.

● In the New dialog box, click OK.

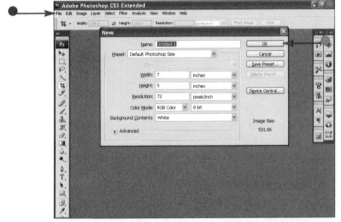

2 Set the size of the file to 16 pixels by 16 pixels.

● In Adobe Photoshop, click Image →
Image Size.

● In the Image Size dialog box, type 16 in the Width and Height boxes.

● Click OK.

The file is resized.

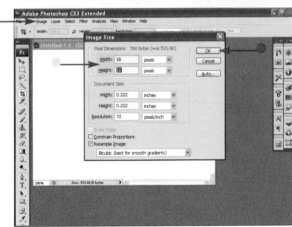

3 Create the icon.

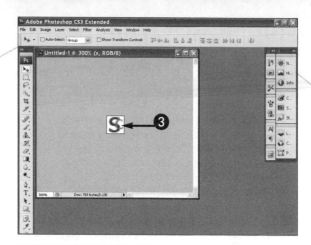

4 Save the icon as an Icon file type with a filename of "favicon."

In Adobe Photoshop, click File → Save As.

● In the Save As dialog box, type **favicon** and choose ICO as the type.

● Click Save.

Note: If your editor does not allow you to save as an .ico, you can use a free converter at www.html-kit.com/favicon/.

The file is saved.

Extra

Many modern browsers enable you to use GIF and PNG images in place of the ICO image. To use these formats, simply use the second method mentioned previously and use the XHTML link element to reference a path to the site icon. GIF images still need to be 16 pixels by 16 pixels, and the type attribute should be set to **image/gif**. PNG images also need to be 16 pixels by 16 pixels, with a type of **image/png**. GIFs must be 256 colors, whereas PNGs can be either 256 colors or 24-bit. Microsoft Internet Explorer does not fully support site icons in any format other than ICO, so be aware that using a GIF or PNG may cause the icon to not display in Internet Explorer, which will be used by the vast majority of most site's visitors. For this reason, it is still common practice to use the ICO format.

Also note that the favicon.ico file will be requested by the browser for just about every page request in your site, so your server logs may quickly fill with logged requests for it.

Put Some Advertising on Your Site

Given the time and effort required to create a Web site, it makes sense that many developers want to find some way to have the site generate revenue. The goal could be to simply bring in enough money to pay for the hosting fees, or it could be to make the site generate a profit. Whatever the reason, there are many ways that your site can potentially make money for you.

The most obvious method of making money is to sell something from your site, but this of course requires that you create the product and, if it is a tangible good, you will need to manufacture, warehouse, package, and ship the product as well. From a technical perspective, creating an ecommerce site that includes an online catalog and the ability to securely accept and process credit card payments is a daunting task.

For sites that do not have a product to sell, the obvious source of revenue is the sale of ads. Since their inception, many of the biggest and most successful sites on the Web have relied on ad revenue. Search engines, online mapping sites, and other service-oriented sites seem to give their services away for free but are in fact relying on users to click the ads that appear on these sites, and they get paid for each such click.

The easiest way of adding advertising to your site is to use an advertising service, such as the one provided by Google. Google's AdSense program scans the content of your page and automatically generates advertising from other businesses that are related to yours. Each time that a user clicks an ad, you receive a commission.

Put Some Advertising on Your Site

① In your browser, go to www.google.com/adsense.

② Click Sign Up Now to create an account.

③ After your application is processed, return to the AdSense page and log in.

④ Click the link of the AdSense product that you want to add to your site.

A page appears with code for you to add to your Web site.

5 Select the provided code.

6 Right-click and choose Copy.

7 Open the XHTML document on which you want the ads to appear in your editor.

8 Right-click in the code and choose Paste.

Now the Google-generated ads will appear on your Web site.

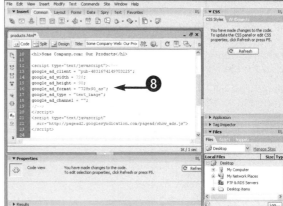

Extra

You can also sell advertising on your site yourself, but as with the ecommerce method, this requires a significant amount of setup. First, you need to design your site with the ads in mind. Your advertisers are going to demand that their ads be highly prominent on the page, so they will generally need to be placed at the top of the page, next to or even above your own banner. Ads can go elsewhere on the page, but advertisers will expect to pay much less if they do.

Second, you will need to be sure that you can accurately track the clicks on the banner. This can be done with server-side processing and usually works by having the banner link not to the advertiser, but rather to a page on your site that records the click and then forwards the user to the advertiser. Third, you will need to determine a pricing scheme. Fourth, you will need to find advertisers. This is probably the most difficult step, especially for sites that are not well-established or well-known. You should probably start with local businesses with whom you already have a relationship.

Find a Host

Large Web sites with a full-time information and technology staff will usually set up and run their own Web servers. However, this requires significant technical skill, is very costly to start up, and will need constant maintenance and supervision.

Most smaller online companies and individuals instead use the services of a Web-hosting company. These companies provide all the hardware, software, and technical expertise to maintain a constant Web presence. In exchange, you pay them a fee to host your site.

If you simply want a small personal site, you should first check with your Internet service provider. Most ISPs provide free hosting as part of their package. However, these hosting accounts tend to be very limited and usually do not allow for the use of your own domain name.

If you require more options or want to use your own domain, you will need to find a commercial Web host.

Fees for hosting range from a few dollars per year to many thousands of dollars per month. Obviously, the more you pay, the more services you receive. Most provide both monthly and annual payment structures.

At a minimum, a Web host provides you with a set amount of disk space, usually in the tens or hundreds of gigabytes, and a set amount of bandwidth that you can use per month. Most Web hosts offer support of one or more server-side scripting languages, such as Microsoft ASP or ASP.NET, Adobe ColdFusion, or PHP, as well as a variety of database storage options. They will likely provide you with an email account as well.

Which hosting provider you choose is ultimately a personal decision. You will benefit greatly by spending time comparison shopping amongst various hosts, comparing their prices and services to find the one that best suits your needs.

Find a Host

① In your browser, go to
   www.hostmysite.com.

Note: GoDaddy.com also offers
   Web-hosting services.

② Click Hosting.

③ Compare the available prices and plans.

④ Click Details to see more information
   about a plan.

5 After choosing the plan and payment option that you want, click Order Now.

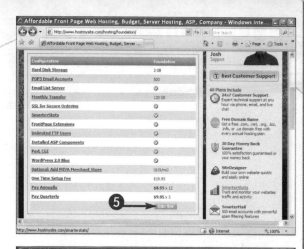

6 On the next few pages, choose the billing cycle option and select any additional services that you want.

7 Follow the online steps to check out.

Your hosting account is created.

Extra

As of June 2007, a search on Google for "Web host" returned 214,000,000 results. With so many hosts from which to choose, the process of selecting a host can be overwhelming. Many online groups and sites have been established to allow Web designers to chat about and review Web hosts, to try to narrow down the process and reduce the risk of signing up for a service that does not deliver on its promises.

Web Host Magazine, online at www.webhostmagazine.com, has a categorized search process for finding hosts and reading reviews about them. Another great source is WHRForums.com, an open community forum where other designers can share their experiences with various hosts. FindMyHost.com offers a wide array of links to Web hosts and includes a guarantee that it will assist you in dealing with problems with hosts that they have reviewed and approved.

Get a Domain Name

The easiest way for people to find and remember your site is to have your own domain name. Fortunately, purchasing a domain name is a fairly easy and surprisingly inexpensive task.

To register your own domain, you will first need to find a name that is not taken by someone else and then determine which top-level domain you want to use. Originally, there were three top-level domains open to the public: .com, .org, and .net. Later, the Internet Corporation for Assigned Names and Numbers (ICANN) created others, including .name and .biz. Every country has a two-letter country code as well, and several have made theirs available to anyone, regardless of whether they are a resident or citizen of the country. One of the better known of these is from the island of Tulavu, in the Pacific Ocean, which allows their .tv name to be used around the world.

In 1992, the National Science Foundation asked companies to bid to be granted a contract to develop the domain name system. One company, Network Solutions, entered the winning bid and thus became not only the developer of the system but the first registrar as well. They were later granted the right to charge for registrations, and they maintained a monopoly on the domain name registration system until 1999, when ICANN was created and the system was opened to anyone who wanted to become a registrar. Since then, thousands of domain registrars have come into business, and the prices to register domain names have dropped considerably.

Although registrars will attempt to convince you to use their service by offering packages of domain names, hosting, and other services, the key aspect for finding the one that you want is price. Just as with other services you may use, you will want to spend time comparison shopping to find the least expensive registrar.

Get a Domain Name

1 In your browser, go to www.networksolutions.com.

Note: GoDaddy.com also offers domain-registering services.

2 Type the domain name that you want to use.

3 Click the top-level domain that you want.

4 Click Search.

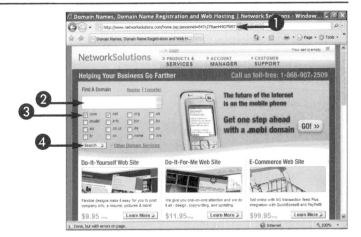

The site returns a list of domains that are available.

Note: If no domains are available with that name, Network Solutions offers you close alternatives or the chance to search again.

5 If the domain name that you want is available, click Add Selected Domain(s) to Order.

6 On the next page, choose if you want the domain to be private and click Continue.

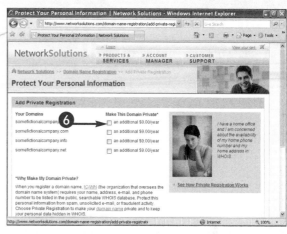

7 Choose other options and services and then complete the registration process to purchase your domain name.

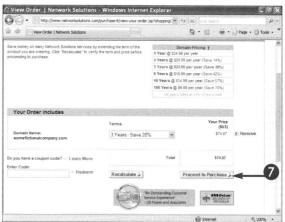

Extra

You need to inform your Web host about your domain name in order for your users to be able to use your domain name to find your site.

After you have registered the domain name, you will receive an email from your registrar that includes the names of the name servers where your domain name lives. You will need to log in to your hosting provider's control panel to enter this information.

Domain names take a day or two to propagate through the Web because the servers that convert the names to their corresponding IP addresses cache the information, so you will need to be patient when you first try to visit your site via its IP address.

Publish Your Web Site Using Windows FTP

In order for your Web site to be visible to other people, you will need to publish it. That is to say that you need to transfer the files from your local machine to your Web host's servers.

Although there are several different technologies available to transfer files, by far the most common is FTP (file transfer protocol). FTP has been used for many years to allow for the transfer of files between often incompatible operating systems and in fact predates the World Wide Web.

In order to use FTP, you will need to know the address of the server to which you want to transfer the files and have a username and password set up on the server.

Also, you will need an FTP client — software on your computer that you can use to create and maintain the FTP connection. If you are using Microsoft Windows, you can use its built-in FTP client. Windows FTP is automatically installed with Windows, so you do not need to do anything to get it to work.

The big disadvantage to Windows FTP is that it relies on the MS-DOS command window, so it can be very difficult to use if you are unfamiliar with DOS commands. However, it is lightweight, and the fact that it is available at no charge and requires no additional software installation or setup may outweigh the need to learn the admittedly arcane DOS commands.

Publish Your Web Site Using Windows FTP

① From the Start menu, select Run.

② Type **ftp**.

③ Click OK.

The Windows FTP window opens.

④ Type **open** *address_of_your_ftp_server*.

⑤ Press Enter.

⑥ Type your username.

⑦ Press Enter.

⑧ Type your password.

⑨ Press Enter.

The FTP server logs you in.

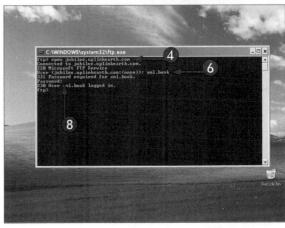

(10) Type **hash**.

(11) Press Enter.

(12) Type **lcd** and then the path to the folder on your hard drive that contains your Web page files.

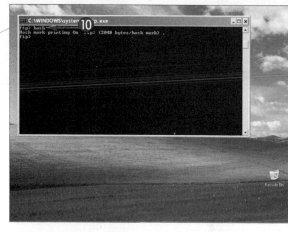

(13) Type **mput *.xml**.

(14) Press Enter.

All XML files in the current directory are uploaded.

(15) Type **Quit**.

(16) Press Enter.

The command window closes.

Extra

Some common commands you can use in Windows FTP are as follows:

open <server>	Opens a connection to a specified server
user <username>	Specifies a username to log in
dir	Displays a list of the files in the current directory on the server
cd <path>	Changes to a specified directory on the server
lcd <path>	Changes to a specified directory on the client
mkdir <directoryname>	Creates a directory on the server
hash	Displays hash symbols, or pound signs, to show the progress of a file upload or download
get <filename>	Downloads a file from the server
put <filename>	Uploads a file to the server
mget <*.extension>	Downloads all files with the specified extension
mput <*.extension>	Uploads all files with the specified extension
quit	Closes the connection and the command window
?	Displays a list of accepted commands

Publish Your Web Site Using Adobe Dreamweaver

dobe Dreamweaver CS3 simplifies the process of not only creating a Web site, but also of uploading it with its integrated FTP client.

In order to transfer files to the server in Dreamweaver, you must create a site. In Basic mode, you can simply follow the steps in the wizard to define your site. The last screen of the wizard prompts you for your FTP information, including your server address, username, and password. After the site is configured, you can expand the Files panel to full screen and have Dreamweaver create a connection. At that point, your local files will be displayed on the right side of the screen, and the files on the server will be displayed on the left.

To upload a file, you can select it and click the Put button or simply drag it to the left side of the screen. Downloading files is as easy as clicking the Get button or dragging to the right. You can create folders on the server by right-clicking the directory into which you want to create the new folder and choosing New Folder. Other file operations are the same as they are in Windows, so you can press F2 on your keyboard to rename a file or folder or use the Delete key to remove files. One extremely useful feature of Dreamweaver is that if you rename a file or folder, the program will automatically modify any files with a link to that file or files within the folder, helping to ensure that your links do not break.

Publish Your Web Site Using Adobe Dreamweaver

1 Open Adobe Dreamweaver.

2 Click Site → New Site.

  The Site Definition dialog box opens.

3 Give the site a name and click Next.

4 Specify if you are going to use a server language and click Next.

5 Click Edit Local Copies on My Machine, Then Upload to Server When Ready.

6 Provide the path to the files on your local hard drive.

7 Click Next.

8 Click this down arrow and choose FTP.

9 Type your server address.

10 Type your FTP login name.

11 Type your FTP password.

12 Click Next.

13 Click Done.

  The site is created.

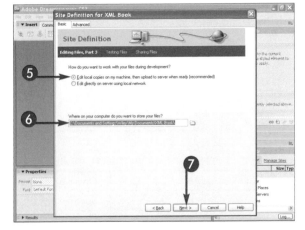

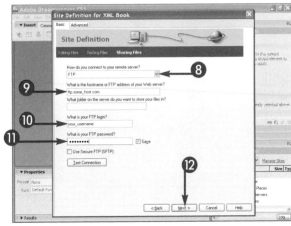

⑭ Click the Expand to Show Local and Remote Sites button on the Files panel.

The panel expands to full screen.

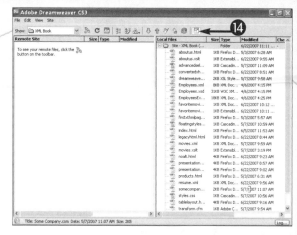

⑮ Click the Connects to the Remote Server button.

⑯ Drag files from the right to the left pane to upload them.

Note: *You can also drag files from the left to the right pane to download them.*

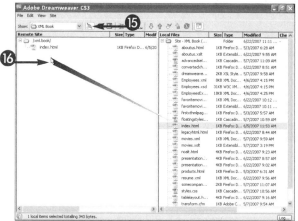

Extra

The Site management feature in Dreamweaver has several other very useful capabilities beyond those of most simple FTP programs.

Whenever you upload or download a file, Dreamweaver asks if you want to include dependent files, such as images and CSS documents, that the file being moved needs in order to be displayed correctly, which reduces the chances of accidentally forgetting those files.

Cloaking is a feature that enables you to specify either a folder or folders and all files with a certain file extension. Cloaked files will not be uploaded, even if their parent folder is dragged to the server window. This is helpful to make sure that original source files, such as those used by graphics editors or the files that were used to create PDFs, are not accidentally uploaded.

Using file synchronization, you can have Dreamweaver automatically upload all files that are newer on the local machine than the server, download all files that are newer on the server, or a combination of both. Web designers who work in teams will appreciate the Check In/Check Out feature that allows you to lock a file on the server when you download it, so another team member does not download an outdated copy and overwrite your work.

Publish Your Web Site Using SmartFTP

There are many free and low-cost FTP clients on the market. One very popular one is SmartFTP, produced by software maker SmartSoft. SmartFTP is freeware, so anyone can download and use it free of charge. SmartSoft makes versions of its product for Windows 2000, XP, 2003, and Vista.

SmartFTP supports secure connections. One of the criticisms of FTP in general is that everything, including the username and password, is transmitted in plain text and is quite easy to intercept. Secure FTP uses Secure Sockets Layer to encrypt the data transfer. Unfortunately, many servers are not set up to use Secure FTP, so you will need to confirm with your host if they use it. SmartFTP also has a very intuitive graphical user interface to minimize the learning curve when using it. It supports file synchronization, file compression, and file transfer integrity to make sure that files are not corrupted while in transit.

If you or your Web host uses a UNIX-based server, you will need to modify CHMOD properties to set the proper permissions on files that you transfer to the server. Many FTP applications either do not allow you to modify these properties or else use arcane command-line interfaces that make it difficult. With SmartFTP, you can set these permissions directly within the interface.

The program has an interface that closely resembles most other FTP programs. Once connected to the server, the local files will appear on half of the screen, and the remote files on the other half. You can simply drag files and folders from the local machine to the remote machine, or vice versa. SmartFTP will queue files for transfer, so you can select multiple files and start the transfer and then continue work on other items while the program uploads or downloads your files.

Publish Your Web Site Using SmartFTP

① In your browser, go to www.smartftp.com.

② Click Download.

③ Click the correct version for your computer.

• You are directed to the download site.

④ Click Download Now.

The File Download dialog box appears.

⑤ Click Run.

The file downloads, and the installation program launches.

⑥ Click Next.

⑦ Click I Accept the Terms of the License Agreement and click Next.

⑧ Click Typical.

⑨ Click Install.

The program installs.

⑩ Click Finish.

SmartFTP launches.

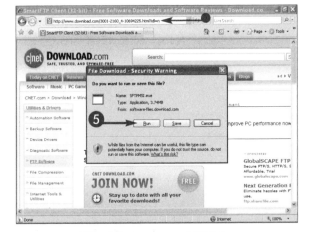

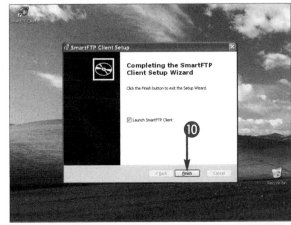

⑪ Click File ➜ New Remote Browser.

The New Remote Browser dialog box appears.

⑫ Type your server address.

⑬ Type your username.

⑭ Type your password.

⑮ Click OK.

The program connects to the server.

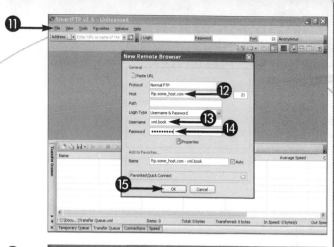

⑯ Click File ➜ New Local Browser.

The local browser window appears.

⑰ Drag files from the local browser to the remote browser.

The files upload.

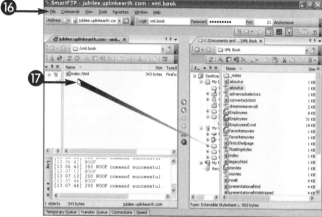

Extra

Most applications for creating, editing, and viewing Web pages and XML files are the same or nearly the same for both Windows and Macintosh. Both platforms have plain-text editors, Adobe Dreamweaver is nearly identical on both, and XMLSpy, although designed for Windows, will run on MacOS X via Virtual PC, Boot Camp, or Parallels.

In addition, there are many good FTP programs available for use on the Macintosh. One popular one is called Transmit, created by Oregon-based Panic (www.panic.com). It is a lightweight application that is very easy to install and use. Cyberduck is an open-source FTP client for Macintosh that includes many of the same features as other products. Both Cyberduck and Transmit are free.

Interarchy, created by Nolobe in Australia, is an extremely powerful FTP client for Macintosh that goes far beyond the capabilities of most other FTP programs. It includes the capability to script downloads to control them dynamically, on-the-fly file conversion and compression, and much more. It is not free, however.

Get Your Site Found by Search Engines

S earch engines remain the key method through which many users find Web sites. Search engines use software called *robots* or *spiders* that scan Web sites and catalog their contents, so the actual process of getting your site listed on a search engine is basically automatic. However, there are many things that you can do to increase your chances of getting a higher ranking in the search results.

Write Good Code

Search-engine spiders are reading your XHTML, and they give more weight to pages that use proper code than those that do not. Mostly, this is because pages that adhere to XHTML standards make more sense in their code than those that do not. Search engines will consider text in a heading level 1 tag to be more important than text in a paragraph.

Search engines do not read the entire document. Pages that follow XHTML standards tend to have less overall markup and more overall content, so the spider ends up seeing and cataloging a higher percentage of the content of the page on standards-based pages than on nonstandards-based pages.

Use Cascading Style Sheets

Using cascading style sheets for your formatting further reduces the amount of code in the XHTML document and further increases the chances that search engines will see and catalog the content of your page. Search engines do not care what your page looks like, but rather what it says, so pages that remove the presentational code from the document and place it in a CSS document will get better search rankings.

Content, Content, Content

Far too many Web developers focus on tricks to try to fool search engines rather than focus on what really matters: your page content. If really does not matter if you have the number one listing on Google if everyone who clicks the link immediately hits their browser's Back button and goes on to the next link because your site did not provide any useful content.

Make the Design Fit the Content

The Web is of course a visual medium, and what your site looks like is important. But what your site actually says is much more important. Compare the number of sites that you regularly use that are fairly ugly but provide useful content against the number of visually beautiful but content-light sites that you regularly visit. Almost certainly, the former is going to far outweigh the latter.

This is not to say that a site cannot be both extremely useful and visually stunning. But in order for that to work, you need to focus on the content first and then worry about the design. Good designs serve the content, whereas bad designs force the content into areas where it does not fit, does not make sense, or is not easy to use. It is extremely difficult to create a design first that will work well with the content you need, whereas it can be fairly easy to design around existing content.

A visually rich site with excellent content will not only get good search rankings, but it will also be a site that users who find it through a search engine will want to actually use and come back to.

Write Well

Grammar and spelling count. Search-engine spiders are just computers. Computer programs cannot decipher meaning from misspelled words, so they will not be properly cataloged. Humans can figure out what you mean if you misspell something or if you use bad grammar, but they will most likely become annoyed and try to find what they need elsewhere.

Write Well *(continued)*

Proofread all the content on your pages. Then have someone else proofread it for you. Although most Web-development applications include a spell checker, they should not be trusted because they will not catch a word that is misspelled in its context but actually correctly spells another word (such as the improper use of *their, there,* and *they're*). Only humans can catch those kinds of errors.

In addition to being an annoyance, misspellings and bad grammar present an unprofessional look for the company and the Web site developer, and they hinder the accessibility of the page.

Use Text, Not Images

Search-engine spiders and robots cannot see your page, and they cannot see images on it. Although there is nothing wrong with having images on the page, and in fact images can greatly enhance the look and feel of a page, you should not use an image in a place where text would be better. There are many designers who feel too limited by the lack of font choices on the Web and so place large blocks of text as an image so that it can be rendered in some special font.

The reality is that most users do not care what font you use, as long as it is readable. Rendering blocks of text as an image will make your page load much slower, but more importantly, none of the text on the image can be seen, read, or cataloged by a search engine. You could theoretically put the text in the `alt` attribute of the `image` tag, but search engines do not weigh keywords found in `alt` text very highly. Having the text on the page as text is the best way to ensure that search engines can see and catalog your page.

CSS Image Replacement

Some designers use a variety of tricks to use cascading style sheets to replace text on a page with an image. The basic theory is that you will place the text in the XHTML so that it can be read by search engines and screen readers and then use CSS to hide the text and display an image in its place. The code is fairly simple. First, enclose a `span` element within the main text element:

```
<h1 id="mainhead"><span>Some company's Web
page</span></h1>
```

Then use CSS to place an image as the background of the main text element:

```
h1#mainhead { background-image:
url(path_to_image.jpg); }
```

Then use CSS to hide the text:

```
h1#mainhead span { visibility:hidden; }
```

This is considered something of a hack, as you are technically adding code in the form of the span for purely presentational purposes, but it is commonly done and makes sure that you have the image you want for visual users and the text for nonvisual users.

Make Your Site Accessible to the Blind

Web accessibility is becoming a more important topic as government bodies begin mandating accessibility and as private industry realizes that disabled customers should not be ignored. It is also important to realize that search engine spiders read your page in the same way that a screen reader for the blind reads your page, so accessible pages will get higher search engine rankings than non-accessible pages.

Do Not Try to Trick the Search Engines

There is a cottage industry on the Web of companies that try to develop techniques to fool the search engines and get higher rankings for their clients. The search-engine companies consider these practices as a form of spam and will blacklist Web sites that get caught doing it. Some things to avoid are repeating words over and over on the page or in the keywords' `meta` tag and placing large blocks of text in heading tags. The search engines' software is getting more sophisticated and is largely designed to detect these types of abuses.

Web browsers are notoriously bad about parsing XHTML. In order to make the development of Web pages as easy as possible and to easily facilitate backwards-compatibility, browsers from the very early days of the Web have been designed to simply ignore bad or questionable code. This means that you can add any markup to your document that you want to, whether or not it is valid, and the browser will not return an error. When it encounters a tag, attribute, or attribute value that it does not recognize, it simply ignores it and goes on processing the page as if the offending code did not exist. Although beginners, who often become frustrated at the appearance of constant error messages, may find this lack of errors refreshing, experienced programmers know that troubleshooting errors is far easier than troubleshooting unexpected behavior.

It is therefore a good idea to always ensure that your markup validates as proper XHTML. Although there is currently no browser that natively validates XHTML, there are many free resources available that provide validation, including a section of the World Wide Web Consortium's site. The W3C validator enables you to validate pages that are currently online or provides a way by which you can upload pages to the site for instant validation.

The W3C validator is unable to validate pages at all that lack a correct DOCTYPE, as there is no way for the tool to know which syntax rules it should use without that. It will validate documents that use the HTML 4.01 Transitional, HTML 4.01 Strict, HTML 4.01 Frameset, XHTML 1 Transitional, XHTML 1 Strict, XHTML 1 Frameset, or XHTML 1.1 DOCTYPES.

Validate Your XHTML

① Open a Web browser.

② Navigate to http://validator.w3.org.

③ Click Validate by File Upload.

④ Click Browse.

⑤ In the File Upload dialog box, navigate to an XHTML document that contains a valid DOCTYPE and click Open.

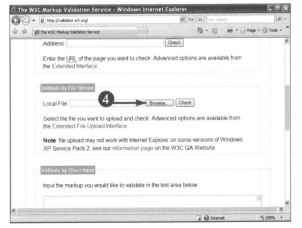

- The file path appears in the upload field.

⑥ Click Check.

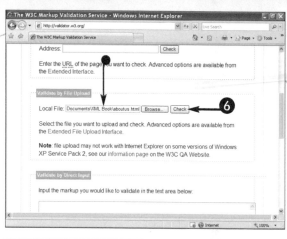

The validator returns validation results.

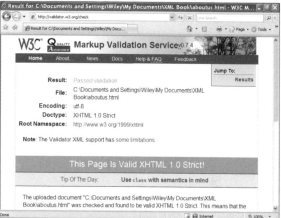

Extra

Because XHTML is really XML, you must always use character entities for ampersands, angle brackets, and double and single quotation marks. Ampersands in particular can often cause validation errors because although you may remember to use them in your code, they will frequently appear within Web site addresses as part of the query string — the data that is passed from one page to the next as part of the URL.

When you have an unescaped ampersand, the validator will give you four error messages. The first will say something like, "*Line 9 column 38*: cannot generate system identifier for general entity 'q.'"; the second will inform you that a "general entity 'q' [is] not defined and no default entity" exists. The third error will tell you, "reference not terminated by REFC delimiter," and the fourth will say "reference to entity 'q' for which no system identifier could be generated." All four of these errors, which will reference the same line, are saying that the validator sees your ampersand and interprets it as the beginning of a character entity — the only legal use for an ampersand — but that the entity does not exist and is not properly terminated by a semicolon (the third error).

Debug with Firebug

One of the nicest features of the Firefox browser is that it is highly extensible. Many hundreds of developers have created plug-ins or extensions for the browser to allow it to perform tasks beyond merely rendering XHTML and CSS. All of these extensions are provided free of charge. Many can be found on the official Firefox Add-ons page at http://addons.mozilla.org, and others can be found through a Google search.

A particularly useful Firefox extension is Firebug. According to the Firebug Web site at www.getfirebug.com, "Firebug integrates with Firefox to put a wealth of Web development tools at your fingertips while you browse. You can edit, debug, and monitor CSS, HTML, and JavaScript live in any Web page." Firebug can be installed with a single click from the Firebug Web site.

After it has been installed and Firefox restarted, Firebug will be accessible through the Tools menu.

Firebug enables you to step through the XHTML, CSS, and JavaScript on a page line by line and analyze it. As it is impossible to get the browser to actually return an error when you use invalid XHTML or CSS, stepping through your code with Firebug makes it much easier to track down and solve rendering issues. The browser will return errors with JavaScript, but they are often difficult to interpret and will often reference an incorrect line, so once again Firebug's ability to step through the code will simplify the process of determining the source of these errors.

Firebug also allows you to edit code directly within its interface and immediately see the changes in the browser window, eliminating the need to switch back and forth between the browser and your editor.

Debug with Firebug

❶ Using Firefox, browse to www.getfirebug.com.

❷ Click Install Firebug 1.0 for Firefox.

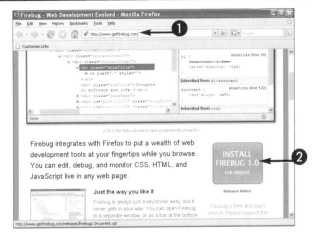

The Software Installation dialog box appears.

❸ Click Install Now.

The extension installs.

❹ Click Restart Firefox.

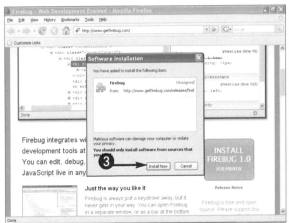

5 In Firefox, open a Web page that you want to debug.

6 Click Tools → Firebug → Open Firebug.

The Firebug window opens.

7 Click HTML.

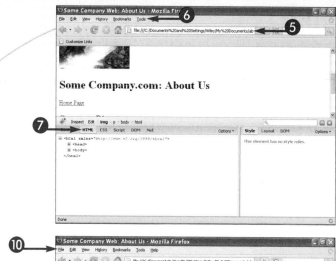

8 Click an HTML element.

The corresponding section of the Web page is highlighted, and any errors in the line are displayed in the right panel.

9 Edit the code.

The display updates.

10 Click File → Save Page As.

11 Click Save.

The edited page is saved.

Extra

As the popularity of Ajax, or Asynchronous JavaScript and XML, has grown, so too has the need for tools to assist in creating and editing Ajax. Firebug 1, released in early 2007, included a feature that allowed Firebug to monitor a page as it was altered on-the-fly by Ajax, making it one of the few tools available that enables developers to see and understand what is going on in an Ajax application in real time.

Firebug also includes a network monitor that you can use to analyze your Web page, file by file, to discover which assets of your page, such as CSS files, images, or JavaScript, may be slowing down your page's load time. Moving the mouse pointer over an image reference displays a thumbnail view of the image, and each asset file reference can be expanded to view the detailed HTTP header information.

Validate CSS

Creating valid cascading style sheets ensures that your page will render correctly in any standards-based browser, such as Firefox or Safari, and will simplify the process of modifying or hacking your CSS to render in nonstandards-based browsers such as Internet Explorer 6.

Invalid CSS is most often caused by misspelling property or value names, forgetting special symbols such as curly braces and semicolons, leaving off the pound sign on color values, or either not quoting values that need quotes or quoting values that do not need them. Any or all of these situations can confuse the browser when it attempts to render the page and will result in unexpected displays.

Before validating your CSS, make sure that you have already validated your XHTML. Browser-rendering problems are much more likely to be caused by invalid XHTML than by invalid CSS.

One simple, free tool for validating CSS is the W3C CSS Validation Service, which can be accessed at http://jigsaw.w3.org/css-validator/. This service allows you to check a CSS file, or the CSS embedded within an XHTML file, by entering a URL to the file, uploading a local file, or directly typing the CSS into a form on the page. The validator will analyze your CSS and either inform you that everything is fine or return a list of errors on the page, complete with line number references, so that you can fix them.

Although the errors are often highly technical, the W3C also maintains a documentation page for the validator that explains the errors. If your page does validate, the site will show you code that can be copied onto your page to display an icon showing that you have valid CSS.

Validate CSS

BY URL

1. In your browser, go to http://jigsaw.w3.org/css-validator/.

2. Enter a URL to a CSS file or a Web page that contains an embedded style sheet.

3. Click Check.

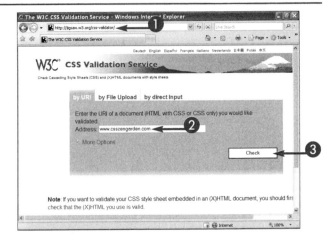

The results page is displayed, showing either a valid message or error descriptions.

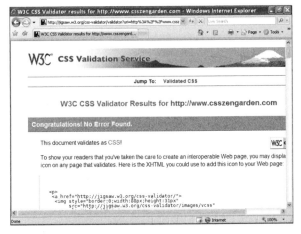

BY FILE UPLOAD

1 In your browser, go to
http://jigsaw.w3.org/css-validator/.

2 Click By File Upload.

3 Click Browse.

4 Navigate to and select a CSS file on
your local hard disk and click Open.

5 Click Check.

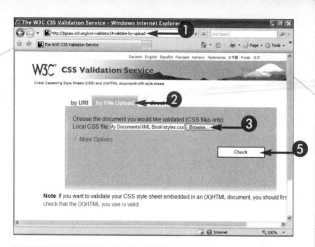

The results page is displayed,
showing either a valid message or
error descriptions.

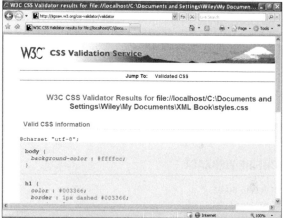

Extra

Adobe Dreamweaver CS3 includes a built-in validator that will not only check the validity of your code, but
will also point out potential browser incompatibility issues and provide a link to a Web page where you can
read about solutions to browser-specific CSS rendering bugs. To use this feature, open a CSS document in
Dreamweaver and then click the Check Browser Compatibility button on the toolbar. This will display the
Results panel. If the program detects errors in your CSS, you can double-click the error to go to the relevant
line of code. If it detects valid CSS that may nonetheless not render properly in a browser, it will display the
error and provide a link to the CSS Advisor Web site, where you can read about solutions to the problem.

Check Your Site's Accessibility

Web accessibility is becoming increasingly important as businesses realize that not making a site accessible means needlessly turning away potential customers. The United States and many other countries in the world have passed laws requiring that government agencies make their sites accessible.

There is a certain amount of additional code that needs to be added to your page for it to be accessible. The W3C's Web Accessibility Initiative (WAI) maintains a Web site at www.w3.org/WAI/intro/accessibility.php, which is an excellent resource for developers who want to make their page accessible. The WAI has also developed a series of checkpoints for Web developers to use to ensure the accessibility of their page, called the *Web Content Accessibility Guidelines* (WCAG), which are broken down into three priority groups.

After you have completed your markup, you will want to check to make sure that your site will be accessible. Two main online services exist to check for accessibility. WatchFire WebXACT is a free service that will check your page against the WAI's guidelines.

HiSoftware provides Cynthia Says, another free accessibility validator that not only checks your pages against the WCAG, but will also check for Section 508 compliance. Section 508 is the primary legal requirement for United States government agency Web sites.

An important limitation of both services is that they can only test for pages that have been uploaded to a Web server.

Validating your markup using WebXACT or Cynthia Says will help, but the best method for testing is to have a disabled user actually visit your site and attempt to use it, or in lieu of that, you can install screen-reading software on your computer and use it to test your pages yourself.

Check Your Site's Accessibility

USING WATCHFIRE WEBXACT

1 In your browser, go to http://webxact.watchfire.com/ScanForm.aspx.

2 Type in the address of the page that you want to validate.

3 Click Go!

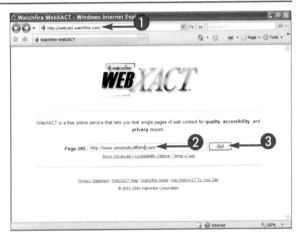

The results page is displayed.

4 Click Accessibility.

The page updates.

5 Scroll through the report and note any changes that need to be made to your page.

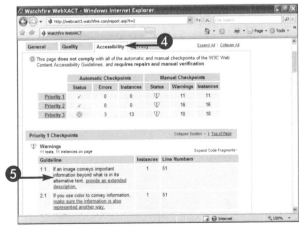

USING CYNTHIA SAYS

1. In your browser, go to www.cynthiasays.com.

2. Type in the address of the page that you want to check.

3. Click this down arrow and select the report mode that you want to use.

4. Click Test Your Site.

The results page is displayed.

5. Scroll through the report and note any changes that need to be made to your page.

Extra

The first step to ensuring that your page will be accessible is to make sure that you use proper XHTML markup. Screen readers, the devices blind users rely on to use their computers, read through your XHTML, and that reading will only make sense if you use the right tags in the right places. For example, you need to make sure that you use headings appropriately and do not skip heading levels. You should also be careful to not rely on color alone, so do not say, "Required fields are indicated in red below," but instead say, "Required fields are indicated by a red asterisk below." Use natural language, avoiding an overreliance on industry-specific jargon, "business speak," and acronyms. Remember that the `alt` attribute is required for every image; in order for your page to be accessible, you need to ensure that the `alt` text adequately and accurately describes the image and that unimportant images are placed on the page through CSS, where they will be ignored by screen readers.

Test Your Links

Anyone who has used the Web knows that broken hyperlinks are all too common. You need to be sure to test your links because users who encounter broken links on your pages will become frustrated and lose confidence in the site, possibly leading them to seek their information elsewhere. Also, broken links show that the designer did not care enough to take the time to make sure that her site worked, and it is possible that a link will technically work but actually lead to a site other than the one the designer intended. Often, this is due to a simple typo in creating the link in the first place. This can be just as frustrating for the user as a broken link, and because many adult sites use Web addresses that are intentionally close misspellings of popular sites, it can also be potentially embarrassing.

Many software packages provide link checkers, but none of them can be relied on completely. All are good about finding links that are actually broken, but none can find links that point to the wrong page, as they only have the capability to check that the resource to which the link points exists. There is obviously no way for a computer to make sure that the link is pointing to the right resource.

Therefore, the only truly reliable link checker is you or another human tester. Although this can be tedious, it is extremely important. You need to bring up your page in a browser and click every link on every page. Do not assume that just because you have a shared navigation bar that appears on every page that those links need only be tested on one page, as the paths required may be different, causing links on one page to work while the same links on another page are broken.

Test Your Links

① Open your Web site in a browser.

② Click a link on the home page.

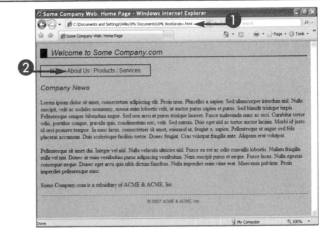

③ Click Back.

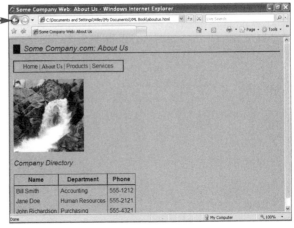

④ Click the next link on your home page.

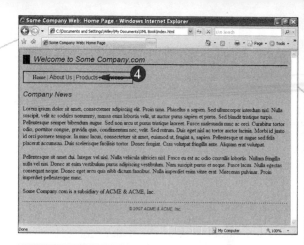

⑤ Repeat steps **3** and **4** for all the other links on your home page.

⑥ Repeat this process for every other page in your site.

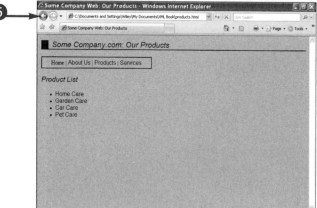

Extra

Most modern Web design applications, such as Adobe Dreamweaver and Microsoft Expression Web Designer, will automatically update links within a site if you move or delete a page. However, these features will only work if the file management is done within the program, so it is important to make sure that you always move, delete, or rename files within the interface of the program.

Many Web designers make the mistake of assuming that after their page is online, they are done testing links. This is not true, as the Web by its very nature is constantly changing. Links that worked when you first posted your site may not work weeks or months later. Therefore, it is important that you regularly return to your site and test your links. This is especially true for links to other sites, whose designers have no way of knowing that you link to their sites and therefore have no way of informing you if their sites' structure changes or if pages are removed altogether.

Avoid Common XML Mistakes

Postel's Law, named for an American computer software engineer named Jon Postel, states that computer software engineers should "be conservative in what you do (but) be liberal in what you accept." This theory is followed by most browser and XML parser developers. It basically means that software should be written to follow accepted standards as closely as possible, but on the other hand should allow for and attempt to parse input from sources that do not follow those standards. This can be best seen in the way that browsers treat XHTML. As you are aware, browsers will accept just about anything in an XHTML document and will simply ignore that which they do not understand.

Because XML has a much stricter syntax, XML parsers tend to be less forgiving about bad code. Although beginning developers can often become frustrated by error after error, experienced developers know that coding mistakes are an inevitable aspect of any development and that explicit errors are much easier to debug than unanticipated output.

Well-Formedness Errors

XML parsers always return fatal errors when your document is not well-formed, but there are times when you may have XML documents automatically generated that you assume will be well-formed but are not. Therefore, it is important to test your pages to ensure that they follow the rules of the XML syntax. Some common well-formedness errors are

- Missing closing tags. XML requires that all tags always be closed.

- Mismatched opening and closing tags due to tags that are not properly nested. XML elements must be closed in the opposite order in which they are opened.

- Mismatched opening and closing tags due to capitalization errors. XML is case-sensitive. The case of the opening element must match that of the closing element.

- Missing root element. All XML files must have a root element that contains all other elements.

- Attributes presented without a value or with an unquoted value. Attributes must have a value, and that value must be enclosed in either single or double quotation marks.

Validity Errors

Another common source of errors in documents relates to validity. When an XML document is well-formed, it should be compared against a schema to ensure its validity. This can be a more difficult error to detect, as the browsers will not check for validity by default. However, most commercial XML editors, including Altova XMLSpy, have the ability to check for validity.

Common validity errors include the following:

- Elements not presented in the correct order. The schema will define a specific order in which the elements must appear, and your XML files must match this order.

- Required elements missing altogether. Some elements may be defined in the schema as being required, and these must appear, in the proper context, in the XML.

- Elements not containing the correct type of data. Schemas allow developers to set specific data type requirements for XML files, and you need to make sure that you only populate elements with the correct type of information.

- Required attributes missing. If the schema makes an attribute required, you need to ensure that it is included.

- Attributes with the wrong type of data as their value. Just as you can set data types for elements, you can set data types for attribute values as well.

- Elements and attributes not matching the case as defined in the schema. When an element or attribute is defined in a schema, the case used in that definition must always be used.

- Not providing the proper reference to the schema in the root element of the XML. This can actually cause the validator to inform you that the file cannot be validated, so be sure that the path to the schema is correct.

Namespace Errors

Complex XML documents are more than likely going to rely on at least one, but possibly many, namespaces. If the namespace is not properly defined in the root element or if the namespace's prefix is mistyped or omitted altogether, the document will not be valid. You also need to ensure that any elements from the namespace are used properly, according to the namespace's schema.

Other Common Errors

Other common XML errors include the following:

- Including characters not supported by the specified encoding type. If you use UTF-8, for example, you must be sure that only legal characters within that encoding are used.

- Using undefined entities.   is a common entity in XHTML but is not native to XML and therefore can only be used if it is specifically defined in a schema or DTD, or if the HTML namespace is imported.

- Content before the root element's opening tag or after its closing tag. Only parsing instructions, comments, and whitespace can come before the root element's opening tag. Only comments and whitespace can follow its closing tag.

- Using illegal characters instead of their corresponding entities outside of CDATA. Most often, this would be an unescaped ampersand in a Web address.

- Comments that are not terminated. If you have an opening comment indicator and forget to close it, the entire rest of the document will be treated as a comment. Most likely, this will cause an error informing you that whichever tag immediately preceded the comment is not closed.

- Comments that begin or end with more than two dashes. Web designers sometimes like to set off their comments with a long string of dashes to make them easier to see. XML specifies that comments begin with an angle bracket, an exclamation point, and precisely two dashes, and end with precisely two dashes and an angle bracket. You also cannot have a sequence of dashes within the comment.

- Mixing content and presentation. Remember, XML is strictly content — all of your presentation is done through XSLT.

- Mixing content and processing. XML files are flat-text files. They only store information. They are not applications, in the sense that they cannot actually do anything to the data. All processing of the data needs to be done elsewhere.

Avoid Common XHTML Mistakes

E ven though browsers are happy to simply ignore any mistakes that you make in your XHTML, you should take care to avoid mistakes.

Pages with coding errors are harder to maintain. When you go back to look at your code later, you may not be able to correctly interpret your code if it contains errors. Also, the pages are more likely to break or fall apart when more content is added if improper markup is used.

Pages with errors may not be displayed correctly. Because browsers ignore any element that they do not recognize,

a misspelled element name may cause your page to render incorrectly. Missing closing anchor tags will cause the entire rest of the document to be a link. Cascading style sheets will most likely be applied incorrectly, or not at all, if your XHTML is incorrect.

Pages with errors will not be accessible. A very important aspect of Web accessibility is having the correct underlying code so that screen readers can properly interpret the page.

Basic Coding Errors

- XHTML elements and attributes not in lowercase. Traditional HTML was not case-sensitive, but because XHTML is based on XML, it is case-sensitive.

- Unclosed tags. HTML has a set of empty elements, including `br`, `img`, `hr`, `input`, `meta`, and `link`. These must be explicitly closed with a closing tag, or you must use a trailing slash in the tag.

- Attributes with no value. Certain attributes in HTML did not have a corresponding value. A common example is the attribute to preselect a check box or radio button, which was simply `"checked"`. In XHTML, attributes must have values, so this example would now need to be written as `checked="checked"`.

- Attribute values not quoted. All attribute values must be quoted. It does not matter if you use single or double quotes.

- Incorrectly nesting elements. All elements must be closed in the opposite order from which they were opened.

Common DOCTYPE Errors

- No document type declaration given or an incorrect one given. You need to make sure that you have a proper document type declaration as the very first line of your code. XHTML validators will be simply unable to test your page without the correct declaration.

- Improper coding to match the DOCTYPE. If you are using XHTML 1 Strict or XHTML 1.1 as your DOCTYPE, you must be sure that you do not use any presentational elements, such as `font`, or presentational attributes, such as `align`. XHTML 1 Strict and XHTML 1 Transitional do not allow the `target` attribute in anchor tags, but this is allowed in XHTML 1 Frameset and XHTML 1.1. XHTML 1 Frameset documents can only have a `body` element if it appears within a `noframes` element.

- No `xmlns` attribute in the root element. You must have an `xmlns` attribute in the root `html` element, pointing to the correct namespace for your DOCTYPE.

Other Coding Errors

- Skipping heading levels. If you only have one heading on a page, it must be h1. An h2 can only follow an h1 or another h2, h3 can only follow h2, and so on.

- Inline elements outside of block elements. Inline elements such as images and anchors for hyperlinks can only appear within block-level elements, such as paragraphs, divs, or table cells.

- Block elements inside inline elements. You cannot nest a block element inside an inline element. For example, if you are going to mark up some text with both a heading and a span, the span must be inside the heading, not vice versa.

- Unescaped characters. Ampersands that do not begin entities, angle brackets not being used to mark a tag, and double and single quotation marks not used around attribute values must be escaped using character entities.

- Missing, useless, or inaccurate alt text on images. All images in your XHTML must include meaningful alt text that accurately describes the image.

- Using an ID more than once. The value given in an ID attribute must be unique on the page.

Table Errors

- Missing headers. Tables should contain at least one row or column with header information to describe the data in the table.

- Missing captions and summaries. Tables should contain a meaningful description in the summary attribute of the table tag and should contain a caption immediately following the tag.

- Tables used for nontabular data. Many designers still rely on tables to display nontabular data. Most of the time, an unordered list will be more appropriate.

Hyperlink Errors

- Using "Click here." Reword links to use descriptive text instead.

- Not displaying links as visited. If you override the default display of links using cascading style sheets, you should be sure that you provide some different appearance for visited links so that your user knows what they have clicked.

- No "You are here" indicator. You should design your site's navigation to provide some sort of indicator for the page your user is on, either by changing the display of the link to the current page or providing breadcrumb navigation, or both.

- Link text that is not obvious. Your users should not feel that they are on a treasure hunt to find your links. Links within large blocks of text such as paragraphs should be underlined and an obviously different color from the rest of the text. On a related note, *never* underline text that is not a hyperlink.

Form Errors

If you have a form on your site, be sure to avoid these mistakes:

- Too long. Too many forms ask for a lot of information that is probably not that useful, such as salutations such as Mr. and Mrs.

- Requiring too much. Forms that have too many required fields are likely to turn customers away. For example, do not require a company name unless you are absolutely certain that you do not ever want a private citizen as a customer.

- Overvalidation. Forms that will only accept postal codes that follow the format used in the United States will preclude customers that live in Canada, for no good reason.

- Requiring specific formats. It is trivial to have a server-side script strip dashes out of a credit card number or parentheses out of a phone number. Let your users enter data in the format in any way that they choose.

- Not giving enough information. If you are going to have a user create a password and will require that password to be seven characters and include a number, make that clear to the user upfront. They should not have to submit the form and get an error back for something you failed to tell them.

Avoid Common CSS Mistakes

Many display issues surrounding cascading style sheets are actually avoidable by being aware of common mistakes and working around them from the beginning.

Coding Errors

- Selectors are case-sensitive. If you used mixed case in referencing an ID or class name in your XHTML, you must use the same mixed case in your CSS. Note that properties and values are not case-sensitive.

- Not closing curly braces. Each CSS declaration must have an opening and a closing curly brace.

- Quoting values. Only those values that contain more than one word, such as `"Times New Roman"`, should be quoted in CSS.

- Using the equals sign instead of a colon. In XML and XHTML, attribute names and their values are separated by an equals sign. Property names and their values in CSS are separated by a colon instead.

- Missing semicolons. Each property:value pair must be separated from each other pair by a semicolon. The final property:value pair in a declaration does not need a semicolon, but it is recommended that you include it so as to not forget it if you add additional properties later.

- Invalid properties. Designers with a background in older HTML sometimes find it difficult to move to CSS because many of the properties have different names. For example, the HTML `font` tag used the `face` attribute to set the font; in CSS, it is `font-family`.

- No units of measurement. There is no default unit of measurement in CSS, so one must be provided. The only exceptions are a value of zero, which is obviously the same regardless of the unit, and the `line-height` property, on which no unit is allowed.

- Whitespace errors. When using a class or ID selector, there cannot be a space between the period or pound sign and the name of the selector. Conversely, you must include a space when using contextual selectors and when using shorthand properties.

- Invalid class and ID names. A class or ID selector must begin with a letter and can contain only letters, numbers, and hyphens.

Color Errors

- Invalid named colors. There are only 16 valid color names: aqua, black, blue, fuchsia, gray, green, lime, maroon, navy, olive, purple, red, silver, teal, white, and yellow. Note that gray is spelled with an *A* and not an *E*.

- Forgetting the pound sign on hexadecimal color values. If you use hexadecimal to denote colors, you must begin the reference with a pound sign.

- Not enough contrast. Be sure to maintain enough contrast between your background and foreground, or text colors. This is an important accessibility issue.

- No background color set. You cannot assume that your user will have their computer set to display the background color as white. Therefore, you should always explicitly set it, even if you do want white.

Box Model Errors

- Setting a margin on inline elements. Only block elements have margins. You can apply padding to both block and inline elements.

- Trying to set `auto` as a value for `padding`. `auto` is allowed as a value for `width`, `height`, and `margin`, but not `padding`.

- Miscalculating the width or height of an element. In CSS, the `width` and `height` properties apply to the size of the content, not the entire box. So the actual width of the box is equal to its width plus the left and right padding, plus the left and right border widths, plus the left and right margin. Height is calculated in the same way. Forgetting to take these into account can create severely broken layouts, with elements overlapping or not floating properly when not given sufficient room.

Font Errors

- Using fixed font sizes. Microsoft Internet Explorer will not allow your user to resize the text if you set your font size using an absolute unit of measurement. Absolute units include inches, centimeters, millimeters, points, picas, and pixels. Relative units are percents, ems, and exes.

- Using real-world measurements. Inches, centimeters, millimeters, points, and picas should also be avoided, as they have meaning only in the real world. They are essentially meaningless on a computer screen because one inch on a small screen with a low resolution does not equal one inch on a large screen with a high resolution.

- Making text too small. It should be obvious that small text is hard to read, but this is one of the most common mistakes on the Web. Developers using Windows are often unaware that the default screen resolution on a Macintosh makes everything about 25% smaller, so small text on Windows will most likely be unreadable on the Mac.

- Not enough or too much line height. Having lines of text too close together is difficult to read, as is having lines too far apart. Proper line height is not an exact science, but an easy rule to follow is if you think the lines are too close or too far apart, then odds are good most users will as well.

- Trying to specify nonstandard fonts. The Web relies on system fonts, which means that the user's machine must have a font installed in order for the browser to use it. For practical purposes, this limits font choices on the Web to Arial, Courier, Times New Roman, and Verdana. A list of font choices should always be provided, including a generic font family such as sans, sans-serif, or monospace, in case a user happens to not have any of the listed fonts.

Pseudo-Class Errors

- Defining the link pseudo-classes out of order. Due to the way that they inherit, the four pseudo-classes for the anchor tag, `:link`, `:visited`, `:hover`, and `:active`, must be presented in that order.

- Botched references when using a pseudo-class and a class or ID. The proper way to reference an element that will use both a class and a pseudo-class is `a.current:link`, not `a:link.current`. The same applies to IDs: `a#home:link`, not `a:link#home`. The pseudo-class always comes last.

General Issues

- Designing for one browser. Although a very large majority of users rely on Internet Explorer, and increasingly high percentage of users do not. As Internet Explorer is notoriously buggy in its implementation of CSS, designing with only it in mind will cause you much grief. It is instead better to design for a standards-compliant browser first, such as Firefox, and then tweak your CSS as needed to correct the display in Internet Explorer. Testing your pages on as many browsers as possible is always recommended.

- Trying to create pixel-perfect sameness between browsers. The simple fact is that there will always be slight differences in the way your page looks across different browsers and different platforms. Keep in mind that the odds are extremely good that you are the only person who will ever be directly comparing your page in more than one browser — most users have one browser they use all the time. So as long as your page looks good and works well across browsers, it really does not matter if a particular image is a few pixels to the left in one browser.

Avoid Common XSLT Mistakes

Because XSLT documents are XML, all the syntax rules for XML must be followed in your XSLT documents. By far the most common mistakes in XSLT are simple XML well-formedness issues, such as forgetting a closing tag or improperly nesting tags.

However, there are some common XSLT-specific errors that you need to avoid.

Nested XHTML Mistakes

If your XSLT is going to generate HTML, you must make sure that the HTML is actually written following the XHTML syntax rules because the XSLT document needs to be properly formed. You therefore need to be sure that all tags are closed, attributes are given values and those values are quoted, and all tags and attributes are presented in lowercase.

Forgetting the Namespace

Your XSLT document must use the XSL namespace, so you need to be sure to define the namespace in the root style sheet element. Also, be sure to include the prefix before every element, in both the opening and closing tags, in every attribute, and in those attribute values that require it, such as data types.

Wrong Path to the Namespace

If you mistype the path to the XSL namespace, your document will not be properly transformed and will most often result in blank output. The proper path to the namespace is

```
http://www.w3.org/1999/XSL/Transform
```

This path is case sensitive, so be sure that *XSL* is all uppercase, and that the *T* in *Transform* is as well.

XPATH Errors

XSLT relies heavily on XPath, and mistakes in the latter will cause the former to generate errors or, more likely, return unexpected transformations. Common XPath errors include the following:

- Providing a relative path that does not match the starting point. When using XPath within an element that is nested in another element with an XPath expression, the inner element's path needs to be relative to the path in the parent. Commonly, beginning developers will want to provide XPath expressions that are always relative to the root of the XML file, which will either result in incorrect elements being transformed or no elements being found and thus transformed.

- Providing invalid expressions. When using XPath to perform calculations, you need to be sure that the elements used in the calculations will be legal. For example, you cannot perform math on elements that contain text, and you need to be sure that division problems will not attempt to divide by zero.

Avoid Common
Browser-Specific Mistakes

In theory, Web pages would be displayed in the exact same way on every browser on every computer platform. After all, if everyone writes the same XHTML and uses the same CSS, it logically follows that the page should be displayed the same. Unfortunately, anyone who has spent any time at all in Web design knows that this is not the way it works. Web browsers vary, at times greatly, in the ways in which they interpret and display documents. Odds are good that this will always be the case, and

as a Web designer, it is something that you simply have to accept.

Fortunately, there are some things that you can learn to do in your pages that will greatly reduce the chances of running into those browser-specific rendering issues. Although your page will likely never be displayed in exactly the same way across browsers, you can at least make it so that the rendering is close.

Do Not Code for Internet Explorer Specifically

One of the unfortunate realities of the Web is that the world's most popular browser is also the one with the most rendering issues. Although Microsoft has made great strides in recent years to make Internet Explorer adhere closer to standards, even Internet Explorer 7 has at times significant problems with certain aspects of cascading style sheets.

Designers who prefer to code so that their page looks good on Internet Explorer first and then modify the code to work in Firefox, Safari, and other browsers if time allows are making two big mistakes. First, those "other" browsers may account for 15 to 20 percent of your audience — not an insignificant number. Second, and perhaps more important, it is simply easier to code to standards first and then modify the page to work in Internet Explorer. You will find that you need to spend a lot less time making modifications to pages that look right in "minority" browsers first to get them to work in Internet Explorer than you will if you work the other way around.

Educate Yourself about Browser-Specific CSS Bugs

Every browser, even those that adhere closely to the standards, have occasional bugs in the ways that they render CSS. You need to be aware of at least the existence of these bugs so that you do not waste time trying to troubleshoot your code, thinking that there is an error in it when in fact there is not. The simplest way to become aware of a browser-specific bug is to make sure that you test your page in more than one browser. If you see a rendering problem that appears in one browser but not another, you can safely assume that the problem is with the browser and not your code. Then you can begin searching online resources for solutions or workarounds to the problem.

There are very few if any browser bugs that have not been thoroughly researched and documented online, and almost all have fixes available by slight modifications of your code. Generally, a Google search that includes the browser and a few words describing the problem will turn up resources to help you fix it.

Avoid Browser-Specific Plug-ins, Elements, and Properties

From the very early days of the Web, browsers have tried to set themselves apart from the competition by supporting plug-ins, HTML elements, and CSS properties that the other browsers do not. Most of the browser-specific tools that still exist today are for Internet Explorer, as the competition has mostly abandoned this approach to trying to compete. These sorts of Internet

Explorer–only options should be avoided, as they needlessly turn away customers who are either unable to use Internet Explorer, such as those on Macintosh computers, or simply prefer a different browser. In addition, there are almost always other, cross-browser means of achieving the same results.

Avoid Common Usability Mistakes

You need to always keep in mind that the Web is a user-centric environment. In a traditional "brick-and-mortar" business, the customer has invested time and gas to get to the store, so they are usually willing to put up with a certain amount of annoyance, such as waiting in a long line, to do business. On the Web, the customer has not likely invested much of anything in getting to your site, so they are far less likely to have patience for things that may frustrate them. In addition, a traditional business may have a bit more leniency because its competition is far enough away that

going to them would represent a bigger inconvenience to the customer. On the Web, your competition is never more than a few clicks away.

Following good coding practices will make sure that your page is easy for you to maintain and that it renders correctly on all browsers. Using CSS for presentation can ensure that your page looks good and loads quickly. However, neither of these guarantees a satisfying user experience. Some of the prettiest Web sites are some of the least usable.

Know Your Users

In order to design for your users, you need to know who they are. Existing companies have almost certainly already done the market research and will have the data available, but new startups need to invest in research and learn about their customers.

Test and Then Test Again and Again

Many of the common usability mistakes could have been handled by simple testing. Recruit members of your target audience and ask them to use your site. Be sure to get as wide a spectrum of your customers as you can, but avoid testers who do not represent your customer base. Do not give them specific tasks or instructions — they need to act like real customers. If they are having problems navigating the site or finding information, the fault is not with the tester, but rather with the design of the site. Get as much honest feedback as you can and make whatever adjustments are necessary. Then repeat the whole process.

Think Like a User

You need to approach the design of your site from your user's perspective, not yours. Do not refer to departments or locations by an acronym or abbreviation that would not make sense to any outsider. Although organizing the site along departmental lines would make sense internally and probably simplify the design and maintenance of the site, many users would probably find that confusing and difficult to navigate, so instead consider organizing your navigation based on what would make sense to someone in your target audience.

Unless your target audience is highly technical, avoid highly technical descriptions. Computer manufacturers fall into this trap all the time. The overwhelming majority of people have no understanding what a gigahertz or a megapixel is, but computer Web sites continue to use only those terms to describe their products, forcing customers to either guess and hope they get what they need or become frustrated and go to a traditional store, where they can have someone explain those terms to them.

Use Common Sense

Anyone who has used the Web for any amount of time has encountered Web sites that make basic usability mistakes and has most likely sat in front of his or her computer thinking, "Why would it do that? Did the person that designed this site ever actually look at it?"

If you think that something is strange, difficult to use, or just does not make sense, then trust your instincts and change it. Many times, the designers of a poorly implemented site did look at it, but either figured that the problem was not a big deal or did not bother to take the time to figure out a different solution.

Be Careful with Labels

Think about your labels and text links carefully. Poorly worded labels will confuse almost everyone. More common, however, is inconsistent labeling — having a link to "Contact Us" on one page and "Get in Touch with Us" on the next, even though both link to the same place.

Consider If You Have Too Much Information or Not Enough Information

People expect Web sites to give them the information that they need and will become frustrated if they continuously have to hunt through page after page of data to get what they want. On the other hand, they do not want to dig through loads of irrelevant information. There is a fine balance to be struck between providing too much and not enough information to your user.

Testing is the best way to discover the balance. If your testers are asking a lot of questions or are constantly hunting for more information, you should provide it upfront. If they seem to be getting lost or frustrated while wading through long detailed pages, narrow it down to what is really important.

Make FAQs Useful

A FAQ (Frequently Asked Questions) page is a common source of information on most sites. However, all too often the FAQ consists of a bunch of marketing-driven questions that the company wishes the users would ask, rather than a list of questions that the users really will ask.

In addition, far too many sites seem to think that if they have a FAQ, they can throw all other usability guidelines out the window, as customers will be able to just go to the FAQ whenever they get lost or frustrated. Instead, customers are likely to simply leave. The FAQ can be an important aspect of the site's help information, but it should be seen as a last resort. Ideally, very few customers should need to use FAQs because a properly designed site will alleviate the need to ask those questions.

Avoid a Cluttered Layout

It is difficult for most people to work in a crowded, cluttered office. Books that are nothing but dense blocks of text are hard to read and are off-putting. Computer applications that provide lots of buttons and controls all over the screen are harder to use. These principles apply to Web design as well. A crowded, cluttered page is going to be difficult to use and read. So include whitespace, and lots of it. Too many designers think that users will never move beyond the first page, so they feel that they need to get all the important information on there. Add to that the fact that many departments probably want a share of that real estate, including marketing, sales, and the CEO.

Keep in mind that you are designing a Web *site,* not a Web page. A well-designed site will get people off the front page and into the rest of the site, so there is no reason to cram that front page with too much information. In fact, a home page with limited data is more likely to encourage users to stick around and explore the rest of the site.

Understanding RSS

RSS stands for *Really Simple Syndication.* RSS enables you to define an XML document, using a standardized schema, and publish it as a Web feed that other users can subscribe to and either read through a dedicated application or publish on their own Web site.

The History of RSS

The first version of RSS, which stood for *RDF Site Summary,* was created at Netscape in 1999 by Ramanathan V. Guha. Guha had been working on a way to structure metadata for Web sites for several years, and this first version of RSS was designed for the My Netscape portal, an early personalized news and information site. Shortly thereafter, another developer named Dan Libby revised the RSS standard, renaming it in the process as *Rich Site Summary.*

Following AOL's acquisition of Netscape, the technology went through a period of open development by several competing interests. In 2002, the meaning of the acronym was formally changed to *Really Simple Syndication,* and a version 2 was released. However, another group continues to develop a slightly different standard based on the original RDF format, which is currently in version 1.

In 2002, the *New York Times* began offering an RSS feed of its headlines, and the technology took off from there.

Today, most major news sites have followed the *Times's* lead and offer RSS feeds, as do almost all blogs, many e-commerce sites, and others. Just about any site with frequently updated content can benefit from providing an RSS feed.

Subscribing to and Reading RSS Feeds

Reading, or "consuming" an RSS feed, requires an XML parser that understands the RSS schema. In the early days of its adoption, several specialized RSS readers or aggregators were available, but as the technology has become more widespread and popular, the ability to read RSS has been integrated into more and more applications. Today, most major browsers, including Firefox, Safari, and Internet Explorer 7, have built-in RSS readers. In fact, Firefox has the ability to add an RSS feed to its bookmark toolbar. Many major email clients, including Microsoft Office Outlook, also include integrated RSS readers. Each of these programs gives users the ability to subscribe to the feed, allowing them to receive updates to the feed's data automatically as it is made available.

Atom

A third branch of RSS development is Atom, which was developed to attempt to reconcile several issues with the RSS 2 specification. This group is now a part of the Internet Engineering Task Force. Like the other two competing RSS standards, Atom has advantages and disadvantages. Atom is generally considered to be more extensible than the RSS formats, but as the newer format, it is not as widely supported by aggregators.

As a developer, you essentially need to decide which standard you will use. Most RSS readers have decided to avoid the standards issue altogether and simply support all three, so the problems of having three competing versions are transparent to the end users.

Atom is used much more frequently on Weblogs, whereas news and other sites tend to use one of the RSS standards. Note that Atom is not an acronym but is instead merely the name of the standard.

All three RSS standards are XML documents, so the differences lie in their available elements. The decision to choose one syntax over another is mostly a personal preference. Remember that regardless of the one you use, your resulting document must be well-formed XML.

RSS 1 Syntax

If you choose to use RSS 1, you will have a root `rdf` element with, confusingly, an `rdf` namespace. Following that, you will have a channel element to describe the basic information about your feed, including a feed title and a general link for the feed. Next comes an `image` element for a feed logo and then a series of `item` elements. Each `item` element will contain a `title` element for the specific item, a `link` element with the path to the item's page, and a `description` element, which provides a brief summary of the item. These `item` elements will make up the bulk of your feed.

RSS 2 Syntax

RSS 2 uses a root `rss` element. Its first child will, like RSS 1, be a `channel` element, but unlike the version 1 standard, the `channel` element on most feeds will actually contain the entire rest of the feed, almost becoming a second, nested root element, although it exists for this reason because advanced users can create separate channels within the same document. The `channel` element will contain a `title` element for the feed, a `link` element to the feed's main page, a `description` or `summary` of the feed, a `language` to define the base language used in the feed, a `pubDate` and `lastBuildDate`, which are used by aggregators to know if the feed has been updated, and then some general information such as `docs`, `generator`, `managingEditor`, and `webMaster` elements. Following these elements, RSS 2, like 1, has a series of `item` elements for the actual data. These `item` elements will contain a `title`, `link`, and `description`, along with a `pubDate` and `guid` element, the latter providing a unique identifier for the item.

Atom Syntax

Atom uses a very different syntax from the two RSS formats. The root element of an Atom document is `feed`. Its child elements are `title`, `subtitle`, `link`, `updated`, `author`, and `id`, which describe the feed as a whole, just as in RSS 1 and 2. The main body of the document will be a series of `entry` elements, which will contain `title`, `link`, `id`, `updated`, and `summary` elements.

The RSS Logo

When Firefox first added RSS feeds to the browser, they developed a logo to represent feeds and released the logo under the GNU General Public License. The logo is a small orange square with white radio waves radiating from the bottom-left corner. In 2005, Microsoft announced that they were adopting the logo to represent RSS feeds in Internet Explorer and Outlook. Opera soon followed, making the little orange square the recognized standard for RSS. Web developer Matt Brett developed a Web site, Feed Icons at www.feedicons.com, to provide the logo in a variety of formats and colors to help facilitate its widespread use.

File Extensions

There is no agreed-upon file extension for RSS feeds. The most commonly used are .rdf, .rss, .atom, and, of course, .xml.

Create an RSS Feed

Creating an RSS feed for your site involves setting up an XML file to hold the information for your feed. You first need to decide which standard you will use. For the purposes of this task, I will use RSS 2, as it is generally the easiest syntax to work with.

In your XML document, remember after the opening channel to add `title`, `description`, and `link` elements that will describe your feed as a whole. As you add `item` elements, make sure that each `item` element also contains, at a minimum, a `title` for the item, a `description`, and a `link` to the page for the item. The title may or may not match the information from the XHTML title of the page.

After you have created the file, you will need to save it with an appropriate extension. For RSS 2, you should use either .rss or .xml. Then you will upload the file to your server — the exact location is unimportant.

You will want to validate your feed to make sure that you used the proper format. The free Feed Validator at www.feedvalidator.org will do this for you.

Finally, you need to let your users know your feed exists, so you will want to add a link to the feed document from your home page and any other appropriate pages. You can use a standard XHTML link and either use text or the RSS logo, which you can get free of charge from Feed Icons at www.feedicons.com.

Create an RSS Feed

① Create a new XML document in your editor.

● In Altova XMLSpy, click File → Open.

Select XML Document.

Click OK.

② Type an XML prolog.

③ Type an opening `rss` element.

④ Type **version="2.0"**.

⑤ Type an opening `channel` element.

⑥ Type a `title` element.

⑦ Type an appropriate title for your feed.

⑧ Type a `description` element.

⑨ Type an appropriate description.

⑩ Type a `link` element.

⑪ Type the path to your home page.

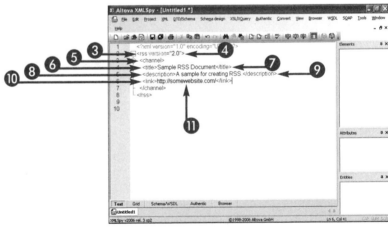

12 Type an opening `item` element.

13 Type a `title` element.

14 Type an appropriate title for the item.

15 Type a `description` element.

16 Type an appropriate description for the item.

17 Type a `link` element.

18 Type a path to the page for the item.

19 Close the `item` element.

20 Repeat steps **12** to **19** to add more items.

21 Click File → Save.

Give the document a name and click Save.

The file is saved.

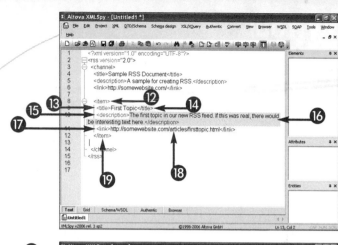

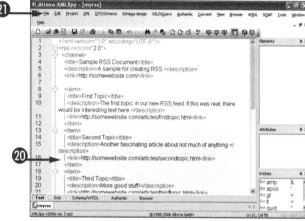

Extra

To have your RSS feed update automatically as your site's content changes, you will need to use server-side scripting. The exact syntax that you will need to use will vary depending on the language, but you need something that will scan your Web pages for changes, read through those pages, and generate the appropriate XML.

Most Web blogging software includes the ability to automatically generate RSS feeds every time that you update your blog. RSS is in fact one of the reasons why blogging has become so popular, as blogs on related topics can be easily aggregated, and it is possible to subscribe to blogs and know when they are updated without having to continually visit the actual site.

There are also commercial tools available to assist in creating RSS feeds. FeedForAll is a standalone application for creating feeds and can be purchased at www.feedforall.com, and DreamFeeder is an extension to Adobe Dreamweaver that enables that program to create RSS feeds from Web pages and can be purchased at http://rnsoft.com.

Show Your Photos with Flickr

A s the popularity and ease of use of digital cameras has expanded, so too has the desire to share photos on the Web. Although creating your own photo gallery requires nothing more than XHTML knowledge, many people would rather not have to create their own sites and want something simpler.

Flickr is the most popular of a set of Web sites that exist to allow users to share photos. In addition to simply posting photos, Flickr provides an online community to share pictures, automatic RSS feeds, and many related Web applications. Flickr is now owned by Yahoo!.

Flickr offers somewhat limited free accounts and much more feature-rich pro accounts, which cost a yearly fee. The main difference between the free and paid accounts is the number of photos that can be uploaded per month.

Signing up with Flickr involves using either an existing Yahoo! account or creating a new one. After you are signed up, you can immediately begin uploading and sharing photos. You can make uploaded photos available to the general public, or you can restrict access to certain other users. Flickr automatically makes an RSS feed available for the photo pages as well.

Flickr also provides a "badge," which enables you to create either an HTML or Flash widget so that you can display your Flickr photos on your own Web site. Setting up the badge involves going through a simple wizard interface on Flickr's site, at the end of which code is provided to copy and paste onto your page.

Users have the ability to comment on uploaded photos, creating the community aspect of the site.

Show Your Photos with Flickr

① In your browser, go to www.flickr.com.

② If you do not have a Yahoo! account, click Create Your Account, create an account, and then sign in.

OR

② If you do have a Yahoo! account, click Sign In and then enter your username and password.

After you are signed in, you will be taken to your personal home page within Flickr.

③ Click Upload Photos.

④ Click Browse.

⑤ Navigate to the photo that you want to upload.

⑥ Click Open.

⑦ Enter tags for the picture.

8 Set the privacy settings that you want.

Note: *Only public photos can be added to a badge.*

9 Click Upload.

The file(s) are uploaded.

10 Enter a title and description for each photo.

11 Click Save.

Extra

Any time you post content on the Web, you are making it available to a wide audience, so copyright infringement can become a concern. There are many myths out there about copyright, but the most important thing you need to know is that copyright protection is automatic. As soon as you create a unique work, it is protected by copyright.

Flickr is designed as a place to share photos, but that does not mean that copyright protections do not apply. Using the site's settings, you can restrict who has access to your photos. In addition, if you are going to make photos public, you can choose to apply a Creative Commons license to them, which sets restrictions on acceptable use of your images. Creative Commons offers a variety of restriction levels, from making the photo completely open as long as it is attributed to you, to restricting commercial use, and several others. Flickr provides a description of the Creative Commons choices at www.flickr.com/creativecommons.

continued

I n addition to using a Flickr badge, there are other tools available that enable you to display Flickr photos on Web sites. Because Flickr has an open application programming interface (API), anyone with programming knowledge can create tools to use Flickr photos.

One such tool is Splashr, available at www.splashr.com. Splashr gives you a set of about 30 templates. Using either a Flickr tag or tags, your username, or a photo group, Splashr will generate a presentation of the photos it takes from Flickr, and it provides copy-and-paste code for you to add the presentation to your site. It does not offer much in the way of customization, and the presentations tend to be large files.

Another tool is Badgr, available for download from www.mentalaxis.com/words/badgr. Badgr takes the Flickr

Flash-based badge concept one step further in that it provides considerably more customization options.

FlickrSLiDR, available at www.flickrslidr.com, is another tool that allows you to insert Flickr slideshows on your site. After you fill out a simple form, the page will generate a block of HTML code that you can paste into your editor.

Several other tools, listed at www.flickrbits.com, such as Chasr, FSViewr, and PictoBrowser, simplify the process of adding Flickr photos to your site. Flashr provides a programming object that enables you to access Flickr's API in ActionScript for Adobe Flash, and PHPFlickr is similar to Flashr but for PHP.

The Flickr API is itself well-documented and can be viewed at www.flickr.com/services/api/, complete with the necessary documentation and code samples, so you can create your own Flickr tools for noncommercial use if you are familiar with another programming language.

Show Your Photos with Flickr *(continued)*

⑫ In your browser, go to www.flickr.com/badge.gne.

⑬ Click An HTML Badge.

⑭ Click Next: Choose Photos.

⑮ Click Yours.

⑯ Click All of Your Public Photos.

⑰ Click Next: Layout.

⑱ Select the options that you want on the layout page.

⑲ Click Next: Colors.

⑳ Select colors to match the color scheme of your Web site.

㉑ Click Next: Preview & Get Code.

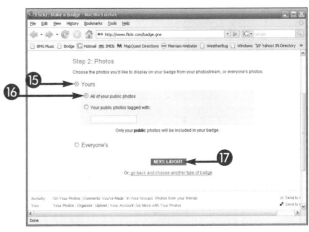

㉒ Select the code in the text area.

㉓ Right-click in the text area and click Copy.

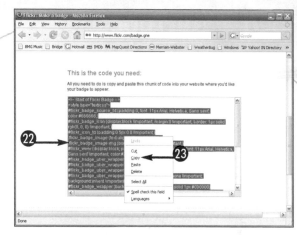

㉔ Open an XHTML document in your editor.

● In Adobe Dreamweaver, click File → Open.

   The document opens.

㉕ Paste the code from Flickr.

● In Adobe Dreamweaver, click Edit → Paste.

㉖ Click File → Save.

   The document is saved.

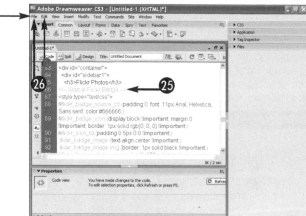

Extra

Inserting a Flash badge is as simple as inserting the HTML badge. You start at the same place, but on the first page of the badge wizard, you select Flash instead of HTML. The Flash badge gives you one less step, as the HTML one has the choice of several different layouts but the Flash badge has only one.

The big advantage of the Flash badge is that contains some simple animation. It randomly selects one of the images in the badge and enlarges it to fill the space of four of the thumbnails. After a few seconds, that image collapses back down, and another is randomly selected, repeating the process.

Your users will need to have the Adobe Flash Player installed on their computers in order to view the badge. However, as of March 2007, Flash Player has been installed on over 98.7% of Internet-connected computers worldwide, so very few of your users will have a problem viewing the badge. Most of those users who do not already have the Flash Player will be able to download and install it in a matter of a few seconds.

Embed a YouTube Video on Your Site

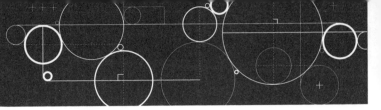

As broadband Internet access has increased and easier, cheaper alternatives to creating and editing video have become available, more Web sites are planning to incorporate video.

YouTube, now owned by Google, quickly established itself as a leading site for individuals to post video on the Web. YouTube relies on Adobe Flash Video, a widely accepted format that plays video through the Adobe Flash Player, currently installed on more than 98% of computers worldwide.

Uploading video to YouTube requires that you sign up for a free account. If you want to, you can also use an existing Google account. After you are logged in, you will be able to upload your video. YouTube accepts videos that were recorded in the .wmv, .avi, .mov, and .mpg formats, which it will compress and convert to Flash Video.

Due to the size of video files, it may take several minutes to upload your video. After the upload is complete, it can take several more minutes for YouTube to convert the file. After your video has been uploaded, YouTube will present you with the code that you need to embed the video on your site. You will simply copy and paste the code into your XHTML document.

YouTube will also present you with a My Videos page, from which you can preview and manage your videos. You have the ability to modify the title, description, and tags associated with the video. YouTube will also generate a still image from the video to display when the video is not playing, although according to their site, this can take up to six hours to appear after the video is uploaded.

Embed a YouTube Video on Your Site

① In your browser, go to www.youtube.com.

● If you do not have an account, you can click Sign Up to obtain one.

② Type your username.

③ Type your password.

④ Click Log In.

⑤ Click Upload.

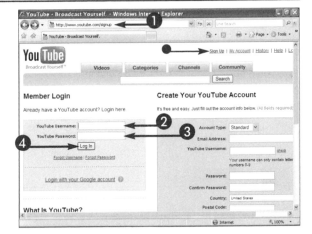

⑥ Enter a title for your video.

⑦ Enter a description of your video.

⑧ Enter appropriate tags for the video.

⑨ Click Upload a Video.

⑩ Click Browse.

⑪ Navigate to the video file that you want to upload, click Open, and then click Upload Video.

The video uploads.

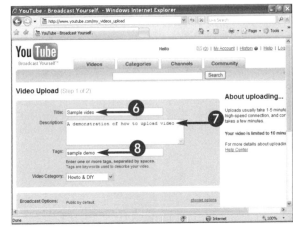

⑫ After the upload is complete, select the text in the text area.

⑬ Right-click in the text area.

⑭ Click Copy.

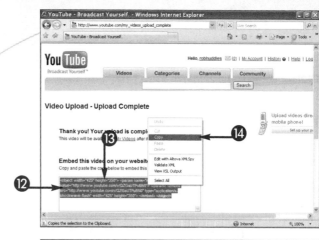

⑮ Open an XHTML document in your editor.

● In Adobe Dreamweaver, click File ➔ Open.

The document opens.

⑯ Paste the code from Flickr.

● In Adobe Dreamweaver, click Edit ➔ Paste.

⑰ Click File ➔ Save.

The document is saved.

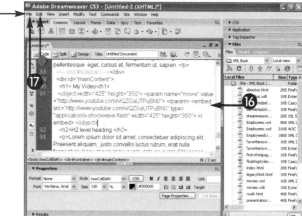

Extra

Creating and editing video is an extremely time-consuming process. After shooting the video, you will most likely want to edit it to some extent. There are many video-editing tools available, from freeware solutions aimed at amateurs to high-end professional tools. Most of these tools have a steep learning curve. Also, you should be aware that raw video files from your camera are going to be extremely large, so you will need to make sure that you have plenty of available hard disk space.

The process of compressing the video down to a file size that would be suitable to upload will decrease the quality. Then YouTube further compresses the video when it converts to the Flash Video format. Therefore, you should not expect extremely high-quality output.

If you have a copy of Adobe Flash, you can convert the video to the Flash Video format yourself, in which you will have much better control over the resulting quality. You can then place the video directly on your Web site, without using YouTube.

Show Your del.icio.us Links

ost Web users have a set of bookmarks of frequently visited sites. However, because these bookmarks are stored by the browser directly on your computer, it is not possible to directly access them from other computers or share them with other users.

The oddly named site del.icio.us describes itself as a "social bookmarking Web site." The basic premise is that instead of bookmarking pages in your browser, where only you can see them, you bookmark pages through the Web site instead. You can then view and use the bookmarks from anywhere and make them available to others.

Like other social sites on the Web, you need to begin by creating a free account. After you have signed up, the site will prompt you to download an extension for whichever browser you are using. The extension will add

del.icio.us buttons to your browser's toolbar. One will allow you to add bookmarks, and the other accesses your saved bookmarks. When you are on a site that you want to bookmark, you can click the button on the toolbar, and the link will be added to your del.icio.us bookmark account instead of to the browser's list of bookmarks. You also have the ability to add tags to the bookmark to make it easier for other users to find them.

The social sharing aspect of del.icio.us is one of its best features. You can go to the del.icio.us Web site and search for bookmarks that others have saved, thereby possibly discovering other sites related to your search topic.

del.icio.us makes the lists of links available via RSS, so any Web site can display the links from the bookmarks by consuming the RSS feed.

Show Your del.icio.us Links

1 In your browser, go to http://del.icio.us.

2 Click Get Started.

3 Fill out the form to create an account.

4 Click Install Buttons Now.

5 Follow the instructions to install the two needed buttons.

6 After the buttons are installed, browse to a page that you want to bookmark.

7 Click the Tag This button.

8 Click Save.

The new window closes.

9 Click the del.icio.us button.

The del.icio.us page opens.

10 Click the RSS button at the bottom of the page.

11 Right-click the browser's address bar.

12 Click Copy.

13 Open an XHTML document in your editor.

● In Adobe Dreamweaver, click File → Open.

14 Type an anchor tag.

15 Set the value of the `href` attribute to the address that you copied in step **12**.

16 Type appropriate link text.

17 Type a closing anchor tag.

18 Click File → Save.

The document is saved.

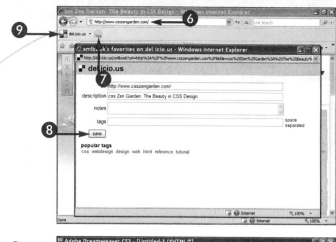

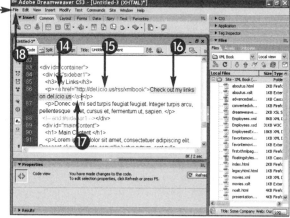

Extra

Many third-party tools have been created to work with del.icio.us. Some of the more useful tools are the browser-integration extensions, available for Firefox and Internet Explorer. These tools enable you to convert your existing browser bookmarks or favorites to del.icio.us bookmarks and to synchronize both, so bookmarks added to the browser will also be added to del.icio.us, and vice versa. There are also several operating system tools that give you desktop or task-tray integration with del.icio.us, so you can go to a bookmark without first having to open your browser.

The del.icio.us site has links to Save to del.icio.us buttons and Ajax-enabled tags to add to your site, to encourage your users to bookmark your site with del.icio.us.

If you have bookmarked sites with MP3 files, you can add the Play Tagger script, available on the del.icio.us site, to enable users to play the MP3s directly on your page, without your needing to add any additional code.

Embed a Google Map on Your Site

Since its release in 2005, Google's take on online maps has revolutionized the online mapping industry, and it very quickly established itself as the leading mapping site. Unlike other online maps that existed at the time, Google implemented their maps through Ajax, creating a much richer and more extensible interface. Google maps feature seamless scrolling, the ability to zoom in and out on locations, and the ability to switch to a satellite view to see the location as it actually appears.

Google makes most of its tools available for developers through the Google API, or application programming interface, and Google Maps is no exception. Any developer can place a live Google Map on her site, and, if she chooses, enable her users to scroll the map, zoom in and out, and switch between the map and satellite views. The code for implementing the maps on your page can be found at www.google.com/apis/maps. You will need to sign up for an API key, which places certain limits on the use of the maps, the biggest one being that the map can only be placed on pages within a single Web site. However, there is no limit to the number of keys one user can request.

After you have requested a key, you can copy and paste the code provided by Google into your XHTML page. The only difficulty is that the initial location shown on the map needs to be specified with longitude and latitude rather than a physical address. Developers familiar with JavaScript can implement the Geocoding feature, which enables you to enter a physical address, but the online documentation is not clear about how to integrate the Geocode script with the main maps script, so many beginning developers may find it easier to simply look up the longitude and latitude of their address instead.

Embed a Google Map on Your Site

① In your browser, go to www.google.com/maps.

② Click Sign Up for a Google Maps API Key.

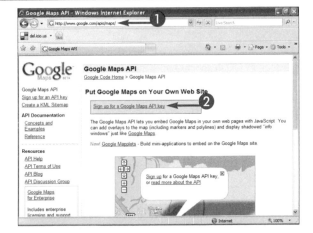

③ Read the terms of the service.

④ Click the check box stating that you read the terms.

⑤ Enter your Web site's address.

⑥ Click Generate API Key.

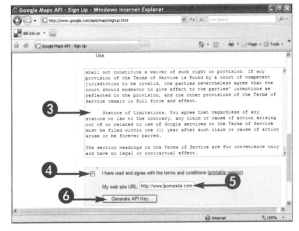

⑦ Select the sample code provided.

⑧ Right-click the selected code and choose Copy.

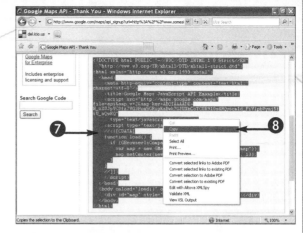

⑨ Open an XHTML document in your editor.

● In Adobe Dreamweaver, click File → Open.

⑩ Paste the code from Google at the spot on your page where you want the map to appear.

● In Adobe Dreamweaver, click Edit → Paste.

⑪ Change the latitude and longitude to your location.

⑫ Click File → Save.

The document is saved.

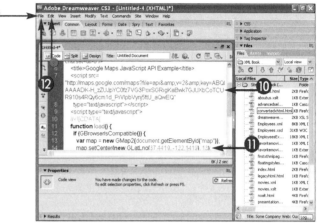

Apply It

You can add pan and zoom controls to your map by adding a few extra lines of JavaScript:

```
var map = new GMap2(document.getElementById("map"));
map.addControl(new GSmallMapControl());
map.addControl(new GMapTypeControl());
map.setCenter(new GLatLng(37.4419, -122.1419), 13);
```

Add Google Search to Your Site

Large sites can be overwhelming and difficult for users to navigate to get the information that they need. Therefore, adding search capabilities to your site will enhance its usability.

Creating your own search on a site would require building a database-driven Web application. Instead, you can use Google's Search API to enable this functionality for you. By copying some code provided by Google, you can add a Google Search box to any page on your site and give your users the ability to search just within your site or on the Web as a whole. The search is actually performed by Google, so you do not need any technical expertise.

Like many other Google applications, the Search API uses Ajax. Google currently provides six different search tools.

The simple Search box is similar to a search from Google's home page. A blog-restricted search will only search entries on your blog, and a custom search engine enables you to specify which sites should be searched and customize the look and feel of the search box to match your site. Google also provides a news bar to search headlines, a blog bar to search other peoples' blogs, and a blog comment form.

To implement one of the searches, you need to simply sign up for a Google account and then request an API key for a particular site. You will then be given sample code that can generally be copied and pasted directly onto your page. To use the simple search, you will not have to modify the code at all.

Add Google Search to Your Site

① In your browser, go to http://code.google.com/apis/ajaxsearch.

② Click Start Using the Google AJAX Search API.

③ Click I Have Read and Agree with the Terms and Conditions.

④ Enter your Web site's URL.

⑤ Click Generate API Key.

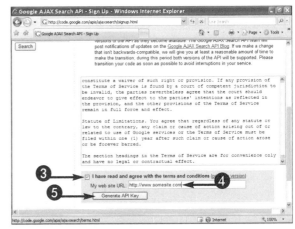

6 Select the sample code provided.

7 Right-click the selected code and choose Copy.

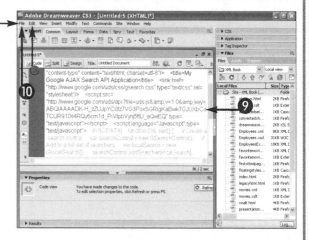

8 Open an XHTML document in your editor.

● In Adobe Dreamweaver, click File → Open.

9 Paste the code from Google at the spot on your page where you want to the search box to appear.

● In Adobe Dreamweaver, click Edit → Paste.

10 Click File → Save.

The document is saved.

Apply It

You can restrict the Google search to a specific site by using the `setSiteRestriction` method:

```
var siteSearch = new GwebSearch();
siteSearch.setSiteRestriction("yoursite.com");
searchControl.addSearcher(siteSearch);
```

XHTML Reference

The following is a complete list of the elements supported in XHTML 1, including suggested usage and supported attributes.

Current Tags

The following tags are used in the current specification.

Common Attributes

Unless otherwise noted, all XHTML elements accept the following attributes. They are always optional:

`id`: A unique identifier for the element.

`class`: A class selector for the element.

`style`: Applies an inline style to the element.

`title`: Sets a title for the element.

`lang`: Specifies the language of the element.

`xml:lang`: Specifies the language of the element. If both `lang` and `xml:lang` are given with different values, `xml:lang` will take precedent.

Also note that this appendix omits purely presentational attributes whose values are more properly represented by CSS, even if those attributes are still technically allowed under XHTML 1 Transitional.

<html>

The root element in every XHTML document.

Required for all documents.

The closing `<html>` tag must be the last tag in the document.

ATTRIBUTE

Note that the common attributes are not supported for this element, except for `lang` and `xml:lang`, which are recommended.

`xmlns`: Required. Specifies the namespace for XHTML. Its value will always be `http://www.w3.org/1999/xhtml`.

<head>

Defines the head section of the document.

Takes no attributes.

Required for all documents.

<title>

Sets the title of the document.

Must be a child of `<head>`.

Takes no attributes.

Required for all documents.

<meta>

Defines additional data about the document.

Optional.

Can be repeated.

As an empty element, it must be properly closed.

ATTRIBUTES

Note that the common attributes are not supported for this element.

`content`: Required. Defines the content of the information.

One of the following optional attributes must be given to define the scope of the content:

`http-equiv`: Sets a value for an HTTP header. Possible values are `content-type`, `expires`, `refresh`, and `set-cookie`.

`name`: Names the content. Possible values are `author`, `description`, `keywords`, `generated`, `revised`, or a user-defined value.

`scheme`: Provides more context for the browser to use in interpreting the data.

<link>

Links the document to a related external resource, most commonly CSS.

Must be a child of `<head>`.

Optional.

Can be repeated.

As an empty element, it must be properly closed.

ATTRIBUTES

Note that the common attributes are not supported for this element.

`rel`: Required. The relationship of the other document. Possible values include `alternate stylesheet`, appendix, bookmark, chapter, contents, copyright, glossary, help, index, next, prev, previous, section, shortcut icon, start, stylesheet, and subsection.

`href`: Required. The path to the external resource.

`type`: Required. The MIME type of the external resource.

`charset`: Optional. Defines the character encoding of the external resource.

`hreflang`: Optional. Sets the language of the external resource.

`media`: Optional. Sets the device on which the external resource should be displayed. Possible values are `all` (the default), `aural`, `braille`, `handheld`, `print`, `projection`, `tv`, `tty`, and `screen`.

`rev`: Optional. The opposite of `rel`, this attribute specifies the reverse relationship of the link.

<style>

Defines an embedded style sheet.

Optional.

Properly formed XHTML would require the contents of the `style` element to be enclosed in `CDATA`. However, browsers may not properly support this, so it is often ignored.

ATTRIBUTE

Note that the common attributes are not supported for this element.

`type`: Required. The MIME type of the contents. Will be set to `text/css`.

<base>

Sets a base hyperlink or target for the page.

Must appear within the head.

As an empty element, it must be properly closed.

ATTRIBUTES

Note that the common attributes are not supported for this element.

`href`: Required if `target` is not provided. Sets the base path for all hyperlinks.

`target`: Required is `href` is not provided. Sets the base target for all hyperlinks.

<frameset>

Defines a group of frames.

Only valid in documents using the XHTML 1 Frameset document type definition.

Appears in lieu of the body.

Can take itself as a child.

ATTRIBUTES

Note that the common attributes are not supported for this element.

All attributes are optional.

`rows`: Defines the size of the rows into which the browser window will be divided. Can be specified in either pixels, percentages, or a wildcard.

`cols`: Defines the size of the columns into which the browser window will be divided. Can be specified in either pixels, percentages, or a wildcard.

<frame>

Defines an individual frame in a frameset.

Only valid in documents using the XHTML 1 Frameset document type definition.

One `frame` element is required for each row or column defined in the parent frameset.

As an empty element, it must be properly closed.

continued ➡

ATTRIBUTES

The common attributes, as well as

`src`: Required. Defines the path to the document that will fill the frame.

`name`: Optional but recommended. Uniquely names each frame.

`scrolling`: Optional. Instructs the browser to allow or disallow scrolling on the frame. Possible values are `auto` (the default), `yes`, and `no`.

`noresize`: Optional. Instructs the browser to allow or disallow user resizing of the frame. The only legal value is `noresize`.

\<noframe>

Defines a section of the page to be displayed if the browser does not support frames. As only very old browsers do not support frames, its usefulness is questionable, although providing content in `noframe` can improve search engine results.

Takes no attributes.

Its first child must be `body`. Any XHTML that is normally allowed within the body is then acceptable.

\<body>

Defines the body of the document, which is all the content that will be displayed in the browser window.

Required for all documents with an XHTML 1 Strict and XHTML 1 Transitional document type. On XHTML 1 Frameset documents, `body` is only allowed within a `noframe` element.

Cannot be repeated.

ATTRIBUTES

All attributes are optional. `body` does not support any attributes beyond the common set.

\<a>

The anchor tag, used for hyperlinks and named anchors.

ATTRIBUTES

The common attributes, as well as

`href`: Required if creating a hyperlink. Defines the path to the target resource.

`name`: Required if creating a named anchor. Defines a name for the anchor, which can serve as the target of another link.

`accesskey`: Optional. Sets a keyboard shortcut to access the link.

`charset`: Optional. Advises the browser as to the encoding of the target link.

`coords`: Optional. A rarely used attribute for setting client-side image maps.

`hreflang`: Optional. Tells the browser the language of the target resource.

`rel`: Optional. Sets the relationship of the target. See the earlier description under `link` for possible values.

`rev`: Optional. Sets a reverse relationship. See the earlier description under `link`.

`tabindex`: Optional. Controls the order in which the field will gain focus if the user is tabbing through the page. Must be an integer between 1 and 32,767.

`type`: Optional. Advises the browser as to the content type of the target.

\<abbr>

Abbreviation, used to denote a piece of text that should be treated as an abbreviation. Screen readers will usually read the text as a word rather than sounding out each letter.

ATTRIBUTES

This element only supports the common attributes. Note that `title` should be used to designate the full text that is abbreviated.

<acronym>

Denotes an acronym in your page. Some browsers may use special display properties, such as a dotted underline, when rendering acronyms. More importantly, most screen readers will read the acronym as a word, rather than sounding out each letter, so it is more appropriate for "NATO" than for "USA."

ATTRIBUTES

This element only supports the common attributes. Note that `title`, while technically optional, should always be used to designate the full text that is abbreviated.

<address>

Denotes the address block on a page, usually consisting of the physical address of the company.

By default, browsers will display text within this tag in italics.

ATTRIBUTES

This element only supports the common attributes.

<area>

Sets coordinates for an image map clickable region.

Must appear within a `<map>` tag set.

As an empty tag, it must be properly closed.

ATTRIBUTES

The common attributes, as well as

`alt`: Required. Specifies alternative text for the region.

`coords`: Required. Sets the coordinates of the corners of the shape of the region.

`href`: Required. Sets the target resource's location.

`shape`: Required. Defines the shape of the region. Possible values are `circle`, `rect`, and `poly`.

`accesskey`: Optional. Sets a keyboard shortcut for accessing the region.

`disabled`: Optional. Disables the region, making it unclickable. The only legal value is `disabled`.

`name`: Optional. Names the region.

`nohref`: Optional. Specifies that the region has no associated link.

`tabindex`: Optional. Defines the region's order when the user is tabbing through the page. The value must be an integer between 1 and 32,767.

<bdo>

Bi-directional, used to change the direction of text from left-to-right to right-to-left, or vice versa.

ATTRIBUTES

The common attributes, as well as

`dir`: Required. Defines the direction. Legal values are `rtl` and `ltr`.

<blockquote>

Used to describe a large quotation from another source.

By default, text within the `blockquote` will be indented from both the left and right margins.

ATTRIBUTES

The common attributes, as well as

`cite`: Optional. Provides a reference to the resource being quoted.

Creates a line break in a block of text.

As an empty element, it must be properly closed.

ATTRIBUTES

This element only supports the common attributes.

<button>

Creates a button.

Can only appear within `<form>`.

ATTRIBUTES

The common attributes, as well as

`type`: Required. Sets the action for the button. Possible values are `submit`, `reset`, and `button`.

`accesskey`: Optional. Sets a keyboard shortcut for accessing the region.

`disabled`: Optional. Disables the region, making it unclickable. The only legal value is `disabled`.

`name`: Optional. Names the region.

`tabindex`: Optional. Defines the region's order when the user is tabbing through the page. The value must be an integer between 1 and 32,767.

continued ➜

`<caption>`

Denotes the caption of a table.

Must be used within `<table>` and must be the first child of that element.

ATTRIBUTES

This element only supports the common attributes.

`<cite>`

Marks a citation in the text. Browsers will display text in italic by default.

ATTRIBUTES

This element only supports the common attributes. The `title` attribute should be used to provide a reference to the original source.

`<code>`

Used to mark a block as code, usually in onscreen tutorials. Text will be displayed using a monospaced font by default.

ATTRIBUTES

This element only supports the common attributes.

`<col>`

Denotes a column of a table.

Used to add styles for the column.

Must appear within `<table>`, after `<caption>` but before other code except `<colgroup>`.

As an empty element, it must be properly closed.

ATTRIBUTES

The common attributes, as well as

`span`: Optional. Defines the number of columns being defined.

`<colgroup>`

Used to group a set of `col` tags together.

Must appear within `table`, after `caption` but before any other code.

Requires one or more `col` elements as children.

ATTRIBUTES

The common attributes, as well as

`span`: The number of columns to which the `colgroup`'s settings will apply.

`<dd>`

Definition list definition, which marks the definition portion of the list item.

Must appear within `<dl>`.

ATTRIBUTES

This element only supports the common attributes.

`<del>`

Marks text as being deleted; browsers will display the text with strikethrough.

ATTRIBUTES

The common attributes, as well as

`cite`: Optional. Provides a reference, often the identification of the person authorized to delete the text.

`datetime`: Optional. The timestamp of the deletion.

`<dfn>`

Marks the definition of a word.

Note that this is not used within the definition list, but rather in normal text.

ATTRIBUTES

This element only supports the common attributes.

<div>

A division, or logical section of your page, usually for style purposes.

ATTRIBUTES

This element only supports the common attributes.

<dl>

Denotes a definition list.

ATTRIBUTES

This element only supports the common attributes.

<dt>

Sets the term for an item in a definition list.

Must appear within <dl>.

ATTRIBUTES

This element only supports the common attributes.

<em>

Marks a word or words for emphasis.

Most browsers will render text within <em> in italics.

ATTRIBUTES

This element only supports the common attributes.

<fieldset>

Denotes a collection of related form fields.

Must be used within <form>.

Browsers will draw a visual border around the <fieldset>.

ATTRIBUTES

This element only supports the common attributes.

<form>

Marks a form.

All form controls must appear within the tag set.

ATTRIBUTES

The common attributes, as well as

`action`: Required. The path to the resource that will process the form.

`method`: Required. Instructs the browser as to how the data from the form should be sent. Possible values are `get` and `post`.

`accept-charset`: Optional. Specifies a list of acceptable character encodings for the values being entered in the form.

`enctype`: Optional. The encoding type used to send the data. Possible values are `application/x-www-form-urlencoded`, which is the default; `multipart/form-data`, which must be used if uploading files via the form; and `text/plain`.

`name`: Optional. A unique name for the form, used by JavaScript.

<h1>

Heading level 1.

ATTRIBUTES

This element only supports the common attributes.

<h2>

Heading level 2.

ATTRIBUTES

This element only supports the common attributes.

<h3>

Heading level 3.

ATTRIBUTES

This element only supports the common attributes.

continued ➡

Current Tags *(continued)*

<h4>

Heading level 4.

ATTRIBUTES

This element only supports the common attributes.

<h5>

Heading level 5.

ATTRIBUTES

This element only supports the common attributes.

<h6>

Heading level 6.

ATTRIBUTES

This element only supports the common attributes.

<hr>

Creates a horizontal rule, a visible line across the page.

ATTRIBUTES

This element only supports the common attributes.

<img>

Used to add images to the page.

As an empty element, it must be properly closed.

ATTRIBUTES

The common attributes, as well as

`src`: Required. The path to the source image file.

`alt`: Required. Text equivalent to the image.

`ismap`: Optional. Defines the image as a server-side image map. Rarely used.

`longdesc`: Optional. Provides a path to a document that describes the image in detail.

`lowsrc`: Optional. Provides a path to a lower-resolution, and presumably smaller, image file that the browser can display while the larger image is downloaded. Rarely supported by modern browsers.

`usemap`: Optional. Provides a reference to a map element on the page.

<iframe>

Creates an inline frame, or "window," in the page into which another XHTML document can be displayed.

Note that although this is a frame, it is used within an XHTML Transitional or Strict document, not a Frameset, and appears within the <body>.

ATTRIBUTES

The common attributes, as well as

`src`: Required. The path to the document to be displayed within the frame.

`longdesc`: Optional. Provides a path to a document that describes the frame in detail.

`name`: Optional. An identifier for the frame.

`scrolling`: Optional. Determines whether scrollbars will appear if needed in the frame. Possible values are `auto` (the default), `yes`, and `no`.

\<input>

Creates text field, check box, radio, hidden, file, and image form controls, as well as buttons, within forms, depending on the specified type.

Must appear within the `<form>` tag.

As an empty element, it must be properly closed.

ATTRIBUTES

The common attributes, as well as

`type`: Required. Sets the type of the form control. Possible values are `button`, `checkbox`, `file`, `hidden`, `image`, `password`, `radio`, `reset`, `submit`, and `text`.

`name`: Required. A name for the form field.

`value`: Required if `type="checkbox"`, `type="radio"`, or `type="hidden"`. Optional for `type="text"`, `type="submit"`, and `type="reset"`. Not supported on other types.

`alt`: Required alternative text if `type="image"`. Not supported by other types.

`accept`: Optional. List of MIME types to allow. Only used with `type="file"`.

`accesskey`: Optional. Sets a keyboard shortcut to give the field focus.

`checked`: Optional. Preselects the field. Only used with `type="radio"` or `type="checkbox"`.

`disabled`: Optional. Causes the field to be unselectable.

`maxlength`: Optional. Sets a maximum number of characters that may be entered in the field. Only applies to `type="text"` and `type="password"`.

`readonly`: Optional. For `type="text"`, causes the text in the field to be unchangeable by the user. Must be used with a value.

`size`: Optional. Physical width of the field. May also be set through CSS.

`src`: Optional. Provides a path to the image. Only used with `type="image"`.

`tabindex`: Optional. Controls the order in which the field will gain focus if the user is tabbing through the page. Must be an integer between 1 and 32,767.

`usemap`: Optional. If `type="image"`, provides a path to the map element.

\<ins>

Marks text to be inserted into a future draft of a document.

ATTRIBUTES

The common attributes, as well as

`cite`: Optional. Provides a reference, often the identification of the person authorized to insert the text.

`datetime`: Optional. The timestamp of the insertion.

\<kbd>

Marks text that should be keyboarded in; usually used in tutorials.

Browsers will display text in a monospaced font, such as Courier, by default.

ATTRIBUTES

This element only supports the common attributes.

\<label>

Denotes text as a label, used on form fields.

Must appear with `form`.

ATTRIBUTES

The common attributes, as well as

`accesskey`: Optional. Sets a keyboard shortcut to give the associated field focus.

`for`: Optional. If the `label` tag is not wrapped around the text and the form control, you can use the `for` attribute to associate the two. The `for`'s value will be equal to the ID of the control.

\<legend>

Marks text as a label for a `fieldset`.

Must appear as the first child of `fieldset`.

ATTRIBUTES

The common attributes, as well as

`accesskey`: Optional. Sets a keyboard shortcut to give the associated field focus.

continued →

Current Tags *(continued)*

\<li\>

Denotes an individual item in an unordered or ordered list.

Must appear within either ol or ul.

ATTRIBUTES

This element only supports the common attributes.

\<ol\>

Marks an ordered, or numbered, list.

Must contain one or more \<li\> tags for the items.

ATTRIBUTES

This element only supports the common attributes.

\<map\>

An image map.

Requires one or more child area elements.

ATTRIBUTES

The common attributes, as well as

name: A name that is used to associate images with this map code.

\<optgroup\>

Groups a set of option tags within a form's select list.

Windows-based browsers display optgroup as a bold, unselectable item; Macintosh-based browsers create submenus.

Must appear within select and must contain one or more option tags.

ATTRIBUTES

The common attributes, as well as

label: Required. The text to display in bold (for Windows) or as the top-level menu (for Macintosh).

\<object\>

Used to embed external files, usually multimedia such as Flash or QuickTime.

ATTRIBUTES

The common attributes, as well as the following. All attributes are optional.

accesskey: Defines a keyboard shortcut to access this object.

archive: URLs to relevant resources.

classid: Sets a Windows Registry key for the plug-in needed for the object.

codebase: Defines the location of the code for the object. Primarily used for Java applets.

codetype: The MIME type of the code referenced in the classid.

data: The path to the object's data.

declare: Defines an object that should be declared rather than instantiated.

name: Names the object.

noexternaldata: Denotes that the object requires no data.

standby: Text to display while the object loads.

tabindex: Controls the order in which the object will gain focus if the user is tabbing through the page. Must be an integer between 1 and 32,767.

type: The MIME type of the object's data.

<option>

Sets individual items within a `select` list.

Must appear within either `select` or `optgroup`.

ATTRIBUTES

The common attributes, as well as

`value`: Required. The value of the selected item.

`label`: The text to display to the user. If not provided, `value` will be used.

<p>

A paragraph of text.

ATTRIBUTES

This element only supports the common attributes.

<param>

Sets parameters for controls in an object.

Must appear within `object`.

As an empty element, it must be properly closed.

ATTRIBUTES

The common attributes, as well as the following. All attributes are optional.

`name`: A unique name for the parameter.

`type`: The MIME type of the parameter.

`value`: The parameter's value.

`valuetype`: The MIME type of the parameter's value.

<pre>

Denotes preformatted text.

Text within these tags will respect whitespace.

Very rarely used.

ATTRIBUTES

This element only supports the common attributes.

<q>

Designates a short quotation used within text.

Some browsers will automatically place double quotation marks around the text.

ATTRIBUTES

The common attributes, as well as the following. All attributes are optional.

`cite`: A reference to the source of the quotation.

<samp>

Used to show code samples.

Browsers will display text using a monospaced font.

ATTRIBUTES

This element only supports the common attributes.

<script>

Designates a block of code containing some kind of client-side script, usually JavaScript.

Legal in either the head or the body.

ATTRIBUTES

The common attributes, as well as

`type`: Required. The MIME type of the script. Usually `"text/javascript"`.

`source`: Optional. A path to an external script block. Note that if used, the `script` tag will be empty. However, it is not legal to close it with a trailing slash. Instead, you must provide an explicit closing `script` tag.

continued →

<select>

Creates a drop-down menu form control.

Must be used within `form` and must contain one or more `option` or `optgroup` tags.

ATTRIBUTES

The common attributes, as well as

`name`: Required. The name of the control.

`accesskey`: Optional. Sets a keyboard shortcut to give the field focus.

`disabled`: Optional. Causes the field to be unselectable.

`multiple`: Optional. Allows for multiple selections. The only legal value is `multiple`.

`size`: Optional. The number of options to display onscreen. Only valid if used with `multiple`.

`tabindex`: Optional. Controls the order in which the field will gain focus if the user is tabbing through the page. Must be an integer between 1 and 32,767.

<span>

Used to apply a style definition where no other tag exists or makes logical sense.

ATTRIBUTES

This element only supports the common attributes. Most frequently, you will apply either an `id` or `class` (or possibly both) to reference a selector in your CSS.

<strong>

Strongly emphasized text.

Browsers display text within `strong` using a bold typeface.

ATTRIBUTES

This element only supports the common attributes.

<sub>

Subscript, which displays text below the baseline.

ATTRIBUTES

This element only supports the common attributes.

<sup>

Superscript, which displays text above the normal line of text.

ATTRIBUTES

This element only supports the common attributes.

<table>

Designates a table.

Must include one or more `tr` elements.

Can optionally include a single `caption` element, a single `thead` element, a single `tfoot` element, and a single `tbody` element, none of which need to appear together.

May include one or more `colspan` and `col` elements.

ATTRIBUTES

The common attributes, as well as the following. All attributes are optional.

`cellpadding`: The padding within the cell of a table. As not all browsers support the CSS `padding` property for table cells, this is still commonly used.

`cellspacing`: The space between cells of a table. Until browser support for `margins` on table cells or `table-collapse` improves, this will continue to be commonly used.

`summary`: A text description of the table. Used to improve accessibility.

\<tbody\>

Defines a set of rows as the body of the table.

Useful for applying styles to a section of the table.

In some browsers, tables with `tbody` will scroll, and others provide better printed output.

Must appear within `table`.

ATTRIBUTES

This element only supports the common attributes.

\<td\>

Table data, used to designate a cell of a table.

Must be used within `tr`.

Any elements allowed within `body` are allowed within `td`.

ATTRIBUTES

The common attributes, as well as the following. All attributes are optional.

`abbr`: Sets an abbreviated version of the cell's contents, to be read by a screen reader.

`colspan`: Sets the number of columns across which this cell should span.

`headers`: Defines the headers for this cell. The value is a space-separated list of the `id`s of the appropriate header cells.

`nowrap`: Instructs the browser to not wrap the text within the cell, even if horizontal scrolling may occur.

`rowspan`: Sets the number of rows that this cell should span.

`scope`: Specifies if this cell provides header information. Possible values are `row`, `col`, `rowgroup`, and `colgroup`.

\<tfoot\>

Defines a row or rows as the footer of the table.

Some browsers will allow for greater control of the table if using this along with `thead` and `tbody`. For example, most tables will repeat the contents of `tfoot` at the bottom of each page if a very long table is printed.

Also useful for applying styles to the table.

Must appear within `table`, and oddly, after the `thead` but before the `tbody`, although the browser will render it below the `tbody` rows.

ATTRIBUTES

This element only supports the common attributes.

\<th\>

Used in place of `td` for header cells in a table.

Default display of `th` content is bold and centered.

Must be used within `tr` and usually within a `thead` section.

ATTRIBUTES

The common attributes, as well as the following. All attributes are optional.

`abbr`: An abbreviated version of the text of the header.

`colspan`: Sets the number of columns across which this cell should span.

`nowrap`: Instructs the browser to not wrap the text within the cell, even if horizontal scrolling may occur.

`rowspan`: Sets the number of rows that this cell should span.

`scope`: Specifies the range of cells to which this header applies. Possible values are `row`, `col`, `rowgroup`, and `colgroup`.

\<textarea\>

Defines a multiline text field.

Must appear within `form`.

ATTRIBUTES

The common attributes, as well as

`name`: Required. The name of the field.

`cols`: Optional. The physical width of the text area, in characters.

`rows`: Optional. The physical height of the field, in rows of text.

continued ➡

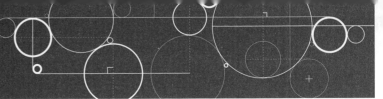

Current Tags *(continued)*

<thead>

Used in conjunction with `tbody` and `tfoot` to define logical sections of a table.

Must appear within `table`.

ATTRIBUTES

This element only supports the common attributes.

<tr>

Defines a table row.

Must be placed within `table`, `thead`, `tbody`, or `tfoot` and must contain one or more `th` or `td` tags.

Text or other content cannot be placed directly within a `tr`.

ATTRIBUTES

This element only supports the common attributes.

<ul>

Sets an unordered, or bulleted, list.

Must contain one or more `li` tags for each item of the list.

ATTRIBUTES

This element only supports the common attributes.

<var>

Designates text as being a variable, such as in a program.

Displays as italic by default.

ATTRIBUTES

This element only supports the common attributes.

Deprecated Tags

XHTML 1 deprecated many tags from older versions of HTML, meaning that they are no longer considered part of the specification and should not be used. Primarily, these tags represent presentational code — tags that exist solely to describe how something should be displayed, rather than its logical place in the structure of the document. Using the XHTML 1 Transitional `DOCTYPE` technically allows for the use of many of these tags, whereas XHTML 1 Strict and XHTML 1.1 disallow them altogether.

<applet>

Used to embed a Java applet. Replaced by `<object>`.

<b>

Designates text to be displayed as bold. Replaced by either `<strong>` or CSS.

<basefont>

Sets a default font for the document. Replaced by CSS.

<bgsound>

Adds a background sound to the document. Never an official part of the HTML specification; only works in Internet Explorer.

<big>

Makes text one size bigger. Replaced by CSS.

<blink>

A Netscape-only tag that causes text to blink. Never officially recognized by the specification.

<center>

Centers a block of code on the page. Replaced by CSS.

<dir>

Creates a directory list. Replaced by `<ul>`.

<embed>

Used to embed external media files. Replaced by `<object>`.

<font>

Sets the size, color, and/or typeface of text. Replaced by CSS.

<i>

Sets text as italic. Replaced by either `<em>` or CSS.

<isindex>

Early method of identifying that a document should be indexed by search engines.

<keygen>

Early, Netscape-only attempt at securing form submissions. Never supported by any other browser.

<layer>

Early, Netscape-only block element for styles and positioning. Replaced by `<div>`.

<marquee>

Microsoft's answer to `<blink>`, which creates scrolling text. Although many non-Microsoft browsers (including Firefox) support `<marquee>`, it has never been part of any specification. Cross-browser, standards-based scrolling text can be achieved through JavaScript and CSS.

<menu>

Another early list type. Replaced by `<ul>`.

<multicol>

Netscape-only tag for generating multicolumn text.

<nobr>

Designates a block of text that will not wrap, even if it results in horizontal scrolling.

<noembed>

Set content, usually text, that would appear if `<embed>` failed.

<nolayer>

Set content to display if `<layer>` was not supported (that is, in all non-Netscape browsers). Universal support for `<div>` makes this meaningless.

<noscript>

Designated alternative content for browsers when `<script>` was not widely supported.

<s>

Same as `<strike>`.

<small>

Renders text one size smaller. Replaced by CSS.

<spacer>

Creates specified amount of space in Netscape; primarily used to hold together complex table layouts. Replaced by CSS.

<strike>

Strikethrough text. Replaced by CSS.

<u>

Underlines text. Not recommended, as it confuses users who may think that the text is a hyperlink; can be achieved if you want to through CSS.

<wbr>

Indicates potential word breakpoint. Used within `<nobr>`.

CSS Reference

The following is a reference to the commonly used properties and values in CSS 1 and 2. Note that styles used exclusively for alternative media types such as aural and Braille are excluded.

Font and Text Properties

Font and text properties provide for control over the appearance of text on the page.

`font-family`: Specifies the typeface to be used. Any font can be named. If the font name contains more than one word, it must be enclosed in quotation marks. It is generally recommended that a comma-separated list of fonts be provided.

`font-size`: Allows for setting the size of text. Units of measurement supported include pixels, points, picas, percentages, ems, exes, inches, centimeters, and millimeters, although pixels and percentages are recommended. The unit of measurement must always be given.

`font-style`: Sets the text in italic. Possible values are `normal`, `italic`, and `oblique`, although the last is rarely supported.

`font-variant`: Allows for setting text in small caps. Possible values are `normal` and `small-caps`.

`font-weight`: Makes the text bold or unbold. Possible values that are nearly universally supported are `normal` and `bold`. The specification also states values of `bolder`, `lighter`, and `100, 200, 300, 400, 500, 600, 700, 800,` and `900`, theoretically allowing the designer to give various degrees of boldness, but no browser currently supports any of these values.

`font`: Shortcut property that allows the designer to give values for `font-style`, `font-variant`, `font-weight`, `font-size`, `line-height`, and `font-family` in a single property.

`text-align`: Sets the horizontal alignment of text on the page. Possible values are `left`, `right`, `center`, and `justify`.

`text-decoration`: Sets or removes underlining and other decorative text effects. Possible values are `none`, `underline`, `overline`, `line-through`, and `blink`.

`text-indent`: Indents the first line of a block of text by the specified value.

`text-transform`: Changes the case of text. Possible values are `none`, `capitalize`, `lowercase`, and `uppercase`. `capitalize` makes the first letter of each word uppercase; `uppercase` sets every letter in uppercase.

`line-height`: The space between lines in an element.

`word-spacing`: The space between words within an element.

`letter-spacing`: The space between characters within an element.

`vertical-align`: The vertical alignment of an element. Note that not all browsers support `vertical-align` fully, and in particular, many do not support it within table cells.

Color and Background-Color Properties

Use the `color` property to set the foreground or text color and `background-color` to set the background color. Any XHTML element within the `<body>` tag, including `<body>` itself, can take either of these properties.

Colors can be specified as RGB values, named colors, or hexadecimal, with the latter being the preferred method. If using hexadecimal, the value must always be preceded by a pound sign (#).

The CSS Box Model defines the area in which elements exist and is made up of three basic sections: padding, borders, and margins.

Padding

Padding defines the space within an element. Any element, either block or inline, can take padding.

`padding-top`: The amount of space above the element, before the border.

`padding-bottom`: The amount of space below the element, before the border.

`padding-right`: The amount of space to the right of the element, before the border.

`padding-left`: The amount of space to the left of the element, before the border.

`padding`: The shortcut property that allows you to specify all four padding values at once. If a single value is given, it will be used for all four sides. Two values specify padding for the top/bottom and left/right, and four values set padding for top, right, bottom, and left, in that order.

Borders

Borders are visual boxes around elements. Any element can take borders.

Borders consist of three properties: the visual style, the color, and the width. Borders can be set for each side individually, or using shortcuts, for all sides at once.

BORDER STYLES

Modern browsers support the following values for `border-style`. Older browsers may not support all of these, but should degrade nicely to a solid border:

`none`: No border will be drawn.

`hidden`: Except in tables, this is the same as `none`. In tables, the property will suppress borders when used along with `border-collapse`.

`solid`: A single line.

`double`: A double line. The browser determines the space between lines.

`dotted`: A series of dots make up the border. The exact shape and position of the dots is up to the browser.

`dashed`: A series of dashes, with the exact position determined by the browser.

`groove`: A line with shading to create a slight indented 3D effect. The shading is determined by the browser.

`ridge`: The opposite of `groove`, `ridge` uses shading to create a raised appearance.

`inset`: The browser shades two sides of the border to create the effect of the box being lowered below the page. As with other properties here, the exact shading is left to the browser.

`outset`: The opposite of `inset`, with the box apparently raised above the page.

BORDER PROPERTIES

`border-top-style`: Sets the style for the top border.

`border-bottom-style`: Sets the style for the bottom border.

`border-right-style`: Sets the style for the right border.

`border-left-style`: Sets the style for the left border.

`border-top-width`: Sets the width for the top border.

`border-bottom-width`: Sets the width for the bottom border.

`border-right-width`: Sets the width for the right border.

`border-left-width`: Sets the width for the left border.

`border-top-color`: Sets the color for the top border.

`border-bottom-color`: Sets the color for the bottom border.

`border-right-color`: Sets the color for the right border.

`border-left-color`: Sets the color for the left border.

`border-style`: A shortcut property that enables you to set the style of the border for all four sides at once. If one value is given, it will be used for all four borders; two values set the top/bottom and left/right borders, and four values set each individually, in the order top, right, bottom, left.

continued →

Box Model Properties *(continued)*

border-color: A shortcut property that enables you to set the color of the border for all four sides at once. If one value is given, it will be used for all four borders; two values set the top/bottom and left/right borders, and four values set each individually, in the order top, right, bottom, left.

border-width: A shortcut property that enables you to set the width of the border for all four sides at once. If one value is given, it will be used for all four borders; two values set the top/bottom and left/right borders, and four values set each individually, in the order top, right, bottom, left.

border-top: A shortcut property that enables you to set the properties for the top border in a single line. The properties are specified as width, style, and color in a space-separated list.

border-bottom: A shortcut property that enables you to set the properties for the bottom border in a single line. The properties are specified as width, style, and color in a space-separated list.

border-right: A shortcut property that enables you to set the properties for the right border in a single line. The properties are specified as width, style, and color in a space-separated list.

border-left: A shortcut property that enables you to set the properties for the left border in a single line. The properties are specified as width, style, and color in a space-separated list.

border: A shortcut for specifying all the properties for all four sides of the border at once. Properties are given as a space-separated list in the order width, style, color.

Margins

Margins define the space around an element. Only block elements can take margins.

margin-top: The amount of space above the element.

margin-bottom: The amount of space below the element.

margin-right: The amount of space to the right of the element.

margin-left: The amount of space to the left of the element.

margin: The shortcut property that allows you to specify all four margin values at once. If a single value is given, it will be used for all four sides. Two values specify the margins for the top/bottom and left/right, and four values set the margins for top, right, bottom, and left, in that order.

Other Box Properties

width: Sets the width of an element. The default is 100%, but any valid unit will work. Inline elements cannot use width.

height: Sets the height of an element. The default is equal to the height of the content, but any valid unit will work. Inline elements cannot use height.

display: Controls how the element is displayed onscreen. Values are none, which essentially removes the element from the page; block, which causes the element to be displayed in its own space and can take widths and margins; and inline, causing the element to appear within a line with elements before and after it.

List Properties

The following properties control the appearance and layout of lists:

list-style-type: Sets the style for the bullet or number. Common values are none, disc, circle, square, decimal, lower-roman, upper-roman, lower-alpha, and upper-alpha.

list-style-image: Replaces the bullet with an image, using a URL to the graphic file.

list-style-position: Sets the indentation of the list. outside, the default, creates a list with hanging indents, and inside wraps subsequent lines of the list item all the way to the margin.

Background Image Properties

In CSS, any element can take a background image. Note that images that are important for the content of the page should be inserted using the XHTML `<img>` tag.

`background-image`: The URL to the image being used as a background.

`background-repeat`: Sets the tiling of the image. Possible values are `repeat` (the default), `repeat-x` (only tiles vertically), `repeat-y` (only tiles horizontally), and `no-repeat`.

`background-position`: The position of the image, relative to the top-left corner of the element.

`background-attachment`: A value of `fixed` causes the image to remain in place, even if the browser window is scrolled, whereas a value of `scroll` (the default) causes the image to scroll up and down with the browser window.

`background`: A shortcut property for specifying other background properties. A single value can be given for image or color, or more than one property can be given in a space-separated list.

Layout Properties

The following properties are used by designers to control the layout of elements on the page:

`float`: Causes an element to allow other elements to float next to it. Accepted values are `left`, `right`, and `none` (the default). Standards-based browsers require that `position:relative` be provided when using `float`.

`clear`: Causes an element to not float, if the prior element allowed it to. Values are `left`, `right`, `both`, and `none` (the default).

`position`: Allows you to define how the element should be positioned on the page. The default value for position is `static`.

`relative`: Allows you to move the element in relation to its original position on the page. An element using relative position remains in the flow of the document, so other elements will not move into its original space. Using `position:relative` requires that you also specify either `top`, `left`, `right`, or `bottom`. As noted earlier, most browsers require this property if also using `float`.

`absolute`: Allows you to place an element anywhere on the screen. Absolutely positioned elements will be removed from the flow of the page, and other elements will not stay out of their way, often causing overlapping content. Using `position:absolute` requires that you also give values for its position from a corner of the parent element, using either `top` and `left`, `top` and `right`, `bottom` and `left`, or `bottom` and `right`.

`fixed`: Places an element on the screen that will not move, even if the browser window is scrolled. Some browsers, including Internet Explorer 6, do not support `position:fixed` and will simply ignore it. (Internet Explorer as of version 7 supports `position:fixed`.)

`visibility`: Controls whether or not elements can be seen onscreen. Values are `visible` and `hidden`. Unlike `display:none`, an element set to `visibility:hidden` will still be "seen" by other elements on the screen, so their space will be respected.

`z-index`: Sets the stacking order of elements that overlap. The value can be any integer from 0 to 32,767, with elements with higher numbers appearing on top of elements with lower numbers.

`overflow`: Controls how content should be displayed if a height is given that is smaller than the content. The default is `visible`, which means that all content will be shown, although some browsers will still respect the height in regards to drawing the bottom border and placement of other elements. Other values include `scroll`, which causes a scrollbar to appear whether or not it is needed; `auto`, which creates a scrollbar only when needed; and `hidden`, which crops the content at the given height.

XSD Reference

The W3C XML Schema Definition (XSD) language has a set of predefined elements and attributes. The following is a reference for the language.

The Schema Namespace

Your schema's root element needs to establish the schema namespace. Although the actual prefix used is technically optional, most developers rely on `xs`. The location of the schema is http://www.w3.org/2001/XMLSchema. Note that this path is case-sensitive.

The Root Element

XSD documents are written in XML and, as such, require a root element.

xs:schema

The root element of your document. It will take a required `xmlns` attribute to establish the namespace.

Element Declaration Elements

The majority of an XML Schema document is made up of elements that declare the XML document's elements and their attributes or provide internal documentation within the schema.

xs:element

Defines an element within the schema.

The `xs:element` may contain `xs:annotation`. If no type attribute is provided, it must have either `xs:simpleType` or `xs:complexType` as a child.

ATTRIBUTES

All attributes are optional.

`abstract`: Restricts instance documents to elements in this element's substitution group. Allowed values are `true` and `false`, with the latter the default.

`default`: A string that sets the default value if the element is empty.

`block`: Restricts usage of the element. Possible values are `#all`, `extension`, `restriction`, and `substitution`.

`final`: Controls which elements can use this as the head of a substitution group. Possible values are `#all`, `extension`, and `restriction`.

`form`: Defines whether or not this element is in the schema's target namespace. Possible values are `qualified` and `unqualified`.

`id`: Sets a unique identifier for the element.

`maxOccurs`: Sets the maximum number of times the element can be used in a document. Possible values are an integer or the string unbounded, which signifies that the element can occur unlimited times.

`minOccurs`: Sets the minimum number of occurrences for an element.

`name`: The name of the element. If omitted, the `xs:element` must be empty and have a `ref` to another element declaration.

`nillable`: Allows the element to have a value of `nil`.

`ref`: The name of an element declared by a top-level `xs:element`.

`substitutionGroup`: Qualified name of a global element for which this element may be substituted.

`type`: The data type of the element.

Element Declaration Elements *(continued)*

xs:attribute

Defines an attribute.

The element may contain an `xs:annotation` element. If no type is provided, it may contain an `xs:simpleType` child.

ATTRIBUTES

All attributes are optional.

`default`: A default value for the attribute if the instance document does not set it explicitly. Cannot be used with `fixed`.

`fixed`: Sets the value of the attribute, which cannot be overridden by the instance document. Cannot be used with `default`.

`form`: If set to a value of `qualified`, the attribute must be in the target namespace. If `unqualified`, it must not be.

`id`: A unique identifier for the attribute.

`name`: The name of the attribute. Cannot be used with `ref`.

`ref`: A reference to an attribute defined by a top-level `xs:attribute`. Cannot be used with `name`.

`type`: The data type of the attribute.

`use`: Restricts the usage of the attribute. The default value is `optional`, giving authors of the instance document the choice of whether to use it. You may also use `prohibited`, which does not allow the attribute to be used, or `required`, forcing its use.

xs:notation

Defines a notation in the schema, usually embedded documentation.

ATTRIBUTES

All attributes are optional.

`id`: A unique identifier for the notation.

`name`: The name of the notation.

`public`: A public identifier for the notation.

`system`: A system identifier.

Element Type Definition Elements

When declaring elements in a schema, you can use the following to define its type.

xs:complexContent

Used within a `complexType` definition to set mixed-type elements.

The element must contain either `xs:restriction` or `xs:extension`, and may contain `xs:annotation`.

ATTRIBUTES

All attributes are optional.

`id`: A unique identifier for the type.

`mixed`: A value of `true` allows mixed content, and a value of `false` does not.

continued ➞

XSD Reference
(continued)

xs:complexType

Defines an element that contains other elements, attributes, or both.

The contents of the `xs:complexType` will be the valid child elements of the parent `xs:element`.

ATTRIBUTES

All attributes are optional.

`abstract`: Restricts instance documents to elements in this element's substitution group. Allowed values are `true` and `false`, with the latter the default.

`block`: Restricts usage of the element. Possible values are `#all`, `extension`, `restriction`, and `substitution`.

`final`: Controls which elements can use this as the head of a substitution group. Possible values are `#all`, `extension`, and `restriction`.

`id`: Sets a unique identifier for the element.

`mixed`: Values of `true` or `false`.

`name`: The name of the element. If omitted, the `xs:element` must be empty and have a `ref` to another element declaration.

xs:extension

Used inside either `xs:simpleContent` or `xs:complexContent` to define the type of the element.

ATTRIBUTES

All attributes are optional.

`base`: Gives the qualified name of the base type being extended.

`id`: A unique identifier for the extension.

xs:list

Used within `xs:simpleType` to provide a list of possible types.

ATTRIBUTES

All attributes are optional.

`id`: A unique identifier for the list.

`itemType`: The type from which the list will be derived.

xs:restriction

Derives a new type from the provided base.

ATTRIBUTES

All attributes are optional.

`id`: A unique identifier for the restriction.

`base`: The name of the base type.

xs:simpleContent

Used within `xs:complexType` for elements whose content is a simple data type, such as `xs:string` or `xs:integer`.

ATTRIBUTE

`id`: Optional. A unique identifier for the content.

xs:simpleType

Sets a new simple data type for elements, which means that the element can only contain text, and not other elements or attributes.

ATTRIBUTES

All attributes are optional.

`final`: Prevents subtyping of the simple type.

`id`: A unique identifier for the type.

`name`: The name of the type.

Element Type Definition Elements *(continued)*

xs:union

Used within an `xs:simpleType` to allow multiple types for the element.

ATTRIBUTES

All attributes are optional.

`id`: A unique identifier for the union.

`memberTypes`: A space-separated list of the allowed types.

Content Model Definition Elements

The following elements allow you to define whether declared elements in your XML document should be optional or required and how often they may appear.

xs:all

Indicates that every element listed as its child must appear and can only appear once. The order of the children is irrelevant.

ATTRIBUTES

All attributes are optional.

`id`: A unique identifier for the element.

`maxOccurs`: The maximum number of times the group of elements can occur. The default is 1, and only 0 or 1 can be specified.

`minOccurs`: The minimum number of times the group can occur, either 0 or 1.

xs:any

Sets a general group of elements that may or may not occur.

ATTRIBUTES

All attributes are optional.

`id`: A unique identifier for the element.

`maxOccurs`: The maximum number of occurrences of the elements. Any positive integer can be used, or you can set `unbounded`.

`minOccurs`: The minimum allowed occurrences of the elements.

`namespace`: The namespace from which the elements can be drawn. The special value of `##any` allows elements from any or no namespace; `##other` allows elements from any namespace other than the current one; `##targetNamespace` allows any element from the schema's namespace; `##local` indicates elements that are not in any namespace. You may also specify a Uniform Resource Identifier (URI) to a namespace, and any of the above values can be listed together.

`processContents`: Determines whether or not the elements used need to be declared. The values are `strict` (the default), which forces declaration; `skip`, which allows undeclared elements even if they are invalid; and `lax`, which only forces validation for declared elements but allows undeclared ones.

continued ➡

Content Model Definition Elements *(continued)*

xs:anyAttribute

Used within an `xs:complexType` element, `xs:anyAttribute` allows the element to use any attribute from the namespace(s) declared in its `namespace` attribute.

ATTRIBUTES

All attributes are optional.

`id`: A unique identifier for the element.

`namespace`: The namespace or namespaces from which allowed attributes can be derived. See the description above for the `xs:any`'s `namespace` attribute for a list of acceptable values.

`processContents`: The same attribute, with the same values, as in `xs:any`.

xs:attributeGroup

Used as a global element to define a new group of attributes. In this case, it would have a required `name` attribute and contain one or more child `xs:attribute` or `xs:attributeGroup` elements.

Can also be used as a child of itself, in which case if would take a required `ref` attribute to reference an `attributeGroup` created elsewhere.

ATTRIBUTES

`id`: Optional. A unique identifier for the group.

`name`: Required if used globally.

`ref`: Required if used as a child of another `xs:attributeGroup`.

xs:choice

Allows any element or group in its children to appear.

ATTRIBUTES

All attributes are optional.

`id`: A unique identifier for the attribute.

`minOccurs`: The minimum number of required instances of the child elements.

`maxOccurs`: The maximum occurrences of the child elements.

xs:group

Used globally, it defines a group to be referenced elsewhere. Used as a child of `xs:complexType`, it indicates that the contents of the group to which it refers should appear at this point in the document.

ATTRIBUTES

`id`: Optional. A unique identifier for the attribute.

`name`: Required if used globally.

`ref`: Required if used as a child of `xs:complexType`, in which case it is a reference to a named group defined by a top-level `xs:group` element elsewhere.

`minOccurs`: The minimum number of required instances of the child elements.

`maxOccurs`: The maximum occurrences of the child elements.

xs:sequence

Defines a set sequence of child elements, which must occur in the order given.

ATTRIBUTES

All attributes are optional.

`id`: A unique identifier for the element.

`minOccurs`: The minimum number of required instances of the child elements.

`maxOccurs`: The maximum occurrences of the child elements.

Schema Assembly Elements

The following elements allow you to piece together a schema from component parts.

xs:import

Allows you to import schemas into other schemas to allow the use of more than one namespace.

ATTRIBUTES

All attributes are optional.

`id`: A unique identifier for the element.

`namespace`: The namespace URI for the schema being imported. Can be omitted if the imported schema does not use a namespace.

`schemaLocation`: The URI of the schema being imported.

xs:include

Allows you to include the contents of one schema in another, usually for simple organization of very large documents. It is different from `xs:import` in that included schemas must use the same namespace.

ATTRIBUTES

`id`: Optional. A unique identifier for the element.

`schemaLocation`: The required URI of the included document.

xs:redefine

Similar to `xs:include`, this allows the inclusion of external schemas. However, the elements being included can override type, model group, and attribute group declarations from the including document, which is not permitted with `xs:include`.

ATTRIBUTES

`id`: Optional. A unique identifier for the element.

`schemaLocation`: The required URI of the included document.

Simple Type Constraint Elements

The next group of elements allows you to set constraints on element usage.

xs:enumeration

Used with `xs:restriction` to define new types by specifically listing them.

ATTRIBUTES

`id`: Optional. A unique identifier for the element.

`value`: Required. A single valid value of the type specified by the parent `xs:restriction`. More than one value can be created by using multiple `xs:enumeration` elements.

xs:fractionDigits

Used within `xs:restriction`, this allows for derivation from `xs:decimal` by setting the number of non-zero digits that may follow the decimal point.

ATTRIBUTES

`id`: Optional. A unique identifier for the element.

`fixed`: Optional. Can be `true` or `false`. If `true`, then types further derived from this type may not override its value. The default is `false`.

`value`: Required. A positive integer or zero.

continued ➞

xs:length

Sets the *exact* number of characters allowed in xs:string, xs:QName, xs:anyURI, and xs:NOTATION types. If used with a list, it sets the number of items of the list. If used with xs:base64Binary and xs:hexBinary, it sets the number of bytes in the data.

ATTRIBUTES

id: Optional. A unique identifier for the element.

fixed: Optional. Can be true or false. If true, then types further derived from this type may not override its value. The default is false.

value: Required. A positive integer or zero.

xs:maxExclusive

Sets the maximum value allowed value for xs:decimal, xs:float, xs:double, xs:date, xs:duration, xs:dateTime, xs:time, xs:gDay, xs:gMonthYear, xs:Month, and xs:gYear. Instances must be *less than and not equal to* the value given in the element.

ATTRIBUTES

id: Optional. A unique identifier for the element.

fixed: Optional. Can be true or false. If true, then types further derived from this type may not override its value. The default is false.

value: Required. Any simple type value.

xs:maxInclusive

Similar to xs:maxExclusive, with the difference being that this element does allow values equal to, as well as less than, the value provided.

ATTRIBUTES

id: Optional. A unique identifier for the element.

fixed: Optional. Can be true or false. If true, then types further derived from this type may not override its value. The default is false.

value: Required. Any simple type value.

xs:maxLength

Sets the maximum allowed length of an element. It applies to the same types as xs:length. See the earlier description of xs:length for details on the types to which it can be applied and special notes.

ATTRIBUTES

id: Optional. A unique identifier for the element.

fixed: Optional. Can be true or false. If true, then types further derived from this type may not override its value. The default is false.

value: Required. A positive integer or zero.

xs:minExclusive

The opposite of xs:maxExclusive, it sets a minimum value that must be *greater than but not equal to* the value.

ATTRIBUTES

id: Optional. A unique identifier for the element.

fixed: Optional. Can be true or false. If true, then types further derived from this type may not override its value. The default is false.

value: Required. Any simple type value.

xs:minInclusive

The opposite of xs:maxInclusive.

ATTRIBUTES

id: Optional. A unique identifier for the element.

fixed: Optional. Can be true or false. If true, then types further derived from this type may not override its value. The default is false.

value: Required. Any simple type value.

xs:minLength

The opposite of `xs:maxLength`.

ATTRIBUTES

`id`: Optional. A unique identifier for the element.

`fixed`: Optional. Can be `true` or `false`. If `true`, then types further derived from this type may not override its value. The default is `false`.

`value`: Required. A positive integer or zero.

xs:pattern

Allows you to create new types using regular expressions.

ATTRIBUTES

`id`: Optional. A unique identifier for the element.

`value`: Required. A regular expression to define the type. If you are unfamiliar with regular expressions, check *Beginning Regular Expressions* by Andrew Watt, published by Wrox.

xs:totalDigits

Sets the number of non-zero digits allowed in `xs:decimal`, including both before and after the decimal.

ATTRIBUTES

`id`: Optional. A unique identifier for the element.

`fixed`: Optional. Can be `true` or `false`. If `true`, then types further derived from this type may not override its value. The default is `false`.

`value`: Required. A positive integer or zero.

xs:whiteSpace

Tells the validator how to treat whitespace.

ATTRIBUTES

`id`: Optional. A unique identifier for the element.

`fixed`: Optional. Can be `true` or `false`. If `true`, then types further derived from this type may not override its value. The default is `false`.

`value`: Required. Valid values are `preserve`, in which case whitespace is significant; `collapse`, in which case tabs, carriage returns, and line feeds are replaced by a single space, and multiple spaces are collapsed into one; and `replace`, which replaces tabs, carriage returns, and line feeds with a space.

Schema Documentation Elements

Schemas provide for a set of elements to enable them to be self-documenting.

xs:annotation

Ignored by validators, this element allows you to add metadata to the document. It will have one or both of two child elements: `xs:appinfo` or `xs:documentation`.

ATTRIBUTE

`id`: Optional. A unique identifier for the element.

xs:documentation

Human-readable information about the schema. Any XML, XHTML, or plain text is allowed.

xs:appinfo

Machine-readable information about the document. It will contain well-formed XML, such as XSLT, a schema of the schema, or anything else.

ATTRIBUTE

`source`: Optional. Rather than placing the XML inside the `xs:appinfo` element directly, you can use this attribute to point to an external source.

ATTRIBUTES

`source`: Optional. Points to an external documentation source.

`xml:lang`: Optional. Specifies the language of the documentation.

XSLT Reference

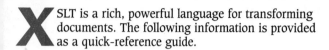

SLT is a rich, powerful language for transforming documents. The following information is provided as a quick-reference guide.

XSLT documents need to define a namespace, pointing to http://www.w3.org/1999/XSL/Transform. It is widely accepted to use the `xsl` prefix for the namespace.

Root Elements

As an XML document, the style sheet must contain a root element. There are two root elements supported by the language; personal choice alone will dictate which one you use.

<xsl:stylesheet>	<xsl:transform>
The more commonly used root element of the XSLT document.	The other allowed root element. Whether you use it or `xsl:stylesheet` is personal preference.
ATTRIBUTES	**ATTRIBUTES**
`xmlns`: Required. Defines the namespace.	Same as those listed for `xsl:stylesheet`.
`version`: Required. Sets the version of XSLT being used.	
`id`: Optional. Uniquely identifies the element.	
`extension-element-prefixes`: Optional. Space-separated list of prefixes used in the document.	
`exclude-result-prefixes`: Optional. A space-separated list of prefixes that should not be copied to the result document.	

Top-Level Elements

The following elements must be direct child elements of the root of the style sheet.

<xsl:attribute-set>	**ATTRIBUTES**
Sets a group of attributes that can be used elsewhere in the document. The element will contain one or more `xsl:attribute` elements.	`name`: Required. Names the set for later reference. `use-attribute-sets`: Optional. Adds attributes from another attribute set to this one.

\<xsl:import\>

Imports another XSLT document into this one. In the event of conflicts, the document into which the style sheet is being imported will take precedence. If used, `xsl:import` must be the first child element of the root, appearing before any other top-level elements.

ATTRIBUTE

`href`: Required. The URI to the imported style sheet.

\<xsl:key\>

Defines keys to be used elsewhere in the `key()` function.

ATTRIBUTES

All attributes are required.

`name`: The key's name.

`match`: An XPath expression specifying which elements have this key.

`use`: An XPath expression that gives the values of the keys.

\<xsl:output\>

Determines the exact format of the transformed document. Although this element is technically optional, it is considered best practice to always use it, even when outputting to XML, the default.

ATTRIBUTES

All attributes are optional.

`method`: The method of the output. Valid values are `text`, `xml`, `html`, or potentially other values supported by the parser.

`version`: The version of the output. For HTML, you should use `4.01`. For XML, `1.0`.

`encoding`: The encoding used by the processor, usually either ISO-8859-1 or UTF-8.

`omit-xml-declaration`: If `yes`, the resulting document will not contain the XML prolog. This can be helpful for HTML output, as some browsers will incorrectly parse HTML if the prolog exists. The default is `no`.

\<xsl:preserve-space\>

Allows you to set which elements in the result document should not have their whitespace stripped. By default, elements that contain only whitespace will have their text nodes removed.

ATTRIBUTES

`elements`: Required. A list of the elements to which this should be applied.

\<xsl:template\>

The key element in XSLT. It will contain a template that the processor will use to construct the output. It will contain the output.

ATTRIBUTES

All attributes are optional.

`match`: An XPath expression to get the nodes to which the template will be applied.

`priority`: A number to give precedence to a template if more than one template may match a given node.

`name`: An identifier for the template.

`mode`: Causes the template to only match if the calling instruction's `mode` attribute has the same value.

`standalone`: Adds the standalone attribute to the XML prolog. Valid values are `yes` and `no`.

`doctype-public`: The public identifier for the document type declaration of the result document.

`doctype-system`: A system identifier for the doctype.

`cdata-section-elements`: A space-separated list of elements whose contents should be output inside CDATA. Useful if outputting XHTML where you should use CDATA for style and script blocks.

`indent`: If `yes`, the processor should insert whitespace into the document to make it more readable. The default is `no`.

`media-type`: The output's MIME type, such as text/html.

continued ➡

Top-Level Elements *(continued)*

<xsl:decimal-format>

Provides a pattern to be used by the `format-number()` function to convert numbers to strings. Not usually necessary when working in English, but may be needed for other languages.

ATTRIBUTES

All attributes are optional.

`decimal-separator`: The character to separate integers from decimals. The default is a period.

`digit`: The character to represent a digit in format patterns — # by default.

`grouping-separator`: The character that separates groups of digits. In English, this is usually a comma every three digits, which is the default.

`infinity`: A string to represent infinity. The default is `Infinity`.

`minus-sign`: A character to represent negative numbers. The default is a hyphen.

`NaN`: A character or string to represent not a number. `NaN` is the default.

`name`: An identifier for the element. Used by the `format-number()` function to know that it should use this element.

`pattern-separator`: The character to separate positive and negative subpatterns. The default is a semicolon.

`per-mille`: The character for `per-mille`. The default is ‰.

`percent`: The character for percentages. The default is %.

`zero-digit`: The character to represent zero. The default is 0.

<xsl:include>

Includes the contents of another style sheet. No precedence is created, unlike `xsl:import`.

ATTRIBUTE

`href`: The URI to the included document.

<xsl:namespace-alias>

Replaces a namespace URI in the style sheet with a different namespace URI in the result document.

ATTRIBUTES

Both attributes are required.

`stylesheet-prefix`: The prefix of the namespace in the style sheet.

`result-prefix`: The prefix of the namespace in the result.

<xsl:param>

Defines a global variable that can be set outside the style sheet or whose value can be changed with the `with-param` element. The value of the parameter can be referenced with the syntax `$name`, where the name is defined by the `name` attribute.

ATTRIBUTES

`name`: Required. The name of the `param`.

`select`: An XPath expression that produces the `param`'s value. If the `xsl:param` element is empty, this attribute must be given. If the element is not empty, it cannot be used.

<xsl:strip-space>

Sets which elements in the source should have whitespace stripped from them.

ATTRIBUTE

`elements`: Required list of the elements from which whitespace should be stripped.

<xsl:variable>

Sets a local variable within the style sheet. Unlike `xsl:param`, the value of the variable cannot be set from outside of the document. In fact, after it is set, it cannot be reset at all. The variable can be referenced using `$name`.

ATTRIBUTES

`name`: Required. The name of the variable.

`select`: An XPath expression that sets the value. If the `xsl:variable` element is empty, you must have a `select` attribute; if it is not, you cannot use this attribute.

The following elements provide processing instructions to the parser.

<xsl:apply-imports>

Processes the current node using imported templates.

Takes no attributes.

<xsl:apply-templates>

Instructs the processor to apply a given named template at this spot in the document. It may have child `xsl:sort` and `xsl:with-param` elements.

ATTRIBUTES

Both attributes are optional.

`select`: An XPath expression returning a node-set.

`mode`: If present, only templates with a matching `mode` attribute will be processed. If absent, templates with a `mode` attribute will not be processed.

<xsl:attribute>

Adds an attribute to an element in the resulting document. The contents of the element must result in a string that is a valid attribute for the resulting element.

ATTRIBUTES

`name`: Required. The name of the attribute.

`namespace`: Optional. The namespace of the attribute.

<xsl:call-template>

Invokes a template by name.

The element can contain one or more `xsl:with-param` elements to pass values to parameters in the template being called.

ATTRIBUTE

`name`: Required. The name of the template being called.

<xsl:choose>

Performs one or more of a set of actions. This is the function performed by `if-else` statements in traditional programming languages.

The element takes no attributes but must contain one or more `xsl:when` elements with an optional `xsl:otherwise` element.

<xsl:comment>

Inserts a comment into the results document.

Takes no attributes.

<xsl:copy>

Copies the current node to the results document. It does not copy the node's contents or attributes, just the node itself. However, child `xsl:attribute` elements can be used to copy the node's attributes, and child `xsl:value-of` elements can copy its contents.

ATTRIBUTE

`use-attribute-set`: Optional. Adds attributes from the named attribute set.

<xsl:copy-of>

Copies the result of the `select` expression to the results document. This copies the specified node, as well as the node's attributes, children, namespaces, and so on.

ATTRIBUTE

`select`: Required. An XPath expression to the node to be copied.

<xsl:element>

Creates an element in the results document.

ATTRIBUTES

`name`: Required. The name of the element.

`namespace`: Optional. The namespace for the element.

`use-attribute-sets`: Optional. A reference to attribute sets to be used in the element.

<xsl:fallback>

Defines a template to be used if the processor does not recognize the element's parent element.

Takes no attributes.

continued ➡

Instruction and Processing Elements *(continued)*

<xsl:for-each>

The XLST looping mechanism.

ATTRIBUTE

select: An XPath expression. The contents of the xsl:for-each will be executed once per instance of the results of the expression.

<xsl:if>

Another, more limited XSLT conditional statement. You can provide a single test, and the contents will be executed only if true. There is no else or else if construct in XSLT, so you must use xsl:choose instead in those cases.

ATTRIBUTE

test: Required. An XPath expression that returns a Boolean.

<xsl:message>

Sends its contents as a message to the processor. The exact messages that can be sent are processor-dependent.

ATTRIBUTE

terminate: Optional. Instructs the processor to halt after the message if set to yes.

<xsl:number>

Inserts a formatted number into the results document.

ATTRIBUTES

All attributes are optional.

count: A pattern that specifies which nodes should be counted.

format: Determines how the list is numbered. Values include 1, which returns 1, 2, 3, and so on; 01, which returns 01, 02, 03, and so on; A, which returns A, B, C, and so on; a, which returns a, b, c, and so on; i to return i, ii, iii, and so on; and I, resulting in I, II, III, and so on.

from: A pattern that identifies the node on which to begin counting.

grouping-separator: The character that will separate groups of digits.

grouping-size: The number of digits in each group.

lang: The language code in which the number should be formatted.

letter-value: The default is traditional, but you can set this to alphabetic to force I to start the sequence I, J, K, and so on rather than I, II, III, and so on.

level: The levels of the source document tree that should be considered in determining the current node's position. Valid values are single, all, and multiple.

value: An XPath expression that returns the number to be formatted.

<xsl:otherwise>

The optional last child of xsl:choose, this provides a default instruction to be processed if all xsl:when statements are false.

Takes no attributes.

<xsl:processing-instruction>

Inserts a processing instruction into the resulting document.

ATTRIBUTE

`name`: Required. The target of the processing instruction.

<xsl:sort>

Sorts the resulting values. Given as the child of `xsl:apply-templates` or `xsl:for-each`. Multiple `xsl:sort` elements may be given to sort on more than one criteria, as in sorting by last name and then first name.

ATTRIBUTES

All attributes are optional.

`select`: An XPath expression setting the key for the sort. If not given, the current node will be used.

`data-type`: Setting a value of `number` will cause the processor to not sort numbers as strings.

`lang`: Sets the language by which the sorting should work.

`order`: Either `descending` or `ascending`. The default is `ascending`.

`case-order`: Specifies whether the sorting should pay attention to the case of the data. Values are `upper-first` and `lower-first`. The default is language-specific.

<xsl:text>

Adds pure text to the output file. Normally, this is not necessary, as pure text within an element will be treated as such. However, it is useful to force the output of whitespace, which may otherwise be ignored.

ATTRIBUTE

`disable-output-escaping`: Optional. Setting this to `yes` (the default is `no`) means that characters that would normally be output as escaped entities, such as the angle brackets, would instead be output as the actual characters.

<xsl:value-of>

Outputs the value or contents of the element, text, attributes, processing instructions, and just about anything else.

ATTRIBUTES

`select`: Required. An XPath expression to the node being output.

`disable-output-escaping`: Optional. See the earlier description for this attribute under `xsl:text`.

continued ➡

\<xsl:when>

Provides a test for an `xsl:choose` statement. Its contents will be processed if the test is true. One or more `xsl:when` elements may be the child of `xsl:choose`. They will be evaluated in order, but the evaluation will terminate as soon as one is true.

ATTRIBUTE

`test`: Required. An XPath expression that returns a Boolean.

\<xsl:with-param>

Passes a named parameter to a template. Can be the child of `xsl:apply-templates` or `xsl:call-template`.

ATTRIBUTES

`name`: Required. The name of the parameter being called.

`select`: Optional. An XPath expression to form the parameter's value. If used, `xsl:with-param` must be empty; if not, then it must have contents to determine the value.

XSLT Functions

In addition to fully supporting XPath functions, XSLT has the following additional functions.

`current()`: Returns the current node. Will generally function exactly like a single dot in XPath.

`document(string)`: Returns the root node of a supplied XML document.

`element-available(string)`: Returns `true` if the supplied argument is a recognized element.

`format-number(number, string pattern [, decimalFormat element])`: Converts a number to a string. The first argument is the number to be converted, the second a pattern for conversion. The optional third argument references an `xsl:decimal-format` element.

`function-available(string)`: Returns `true` if a function, supplied as an argument, exists.

`generate-id()`: Returns a string that can be used as a value in an ID. The same string will always be produced for the same node.

`key(string)`: Returns all nodes with a key with the name given.

`system-property(string)`: Returns the value of the named property.

`unparsed-entity-uri(string)`: Returns the unparsed entity with the specified name.

XPath Reference

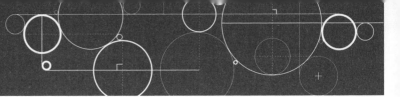

XPath provides a syntax for identifying specific pieces of information in your document. The following is a reference to the key aspects of the language.

XPath Data

XPath reads XML documents in a tree structure. Each node of the tree will exist in one of the following seven types.

Root

Each document must have a root node, or root element. For XPath, the root will contain a comment node for each comment presented outside the root, one processing instruction node for each processing instruction, and a single element node for the root itself.

Element

Each element in the document is represented by an element node. This node will contain a name, namespace, parent node, list of children, comment nodes, processing instructions, and text. It may also have a collection of attributes.

Attribute

The attribute node contains the name, namespace, value, and parent element of the attribute.

Text

Each text node is the string of text between opening and closing tags of an element.

Namespace

Namespace nodes are the namespace of an element.

Processing Instruction

This contains the target, data, and a parent node.

Comment

Comments are represented by their own nodes, with a reference to the parent.

Data Types

XPath expressions will return a value in one of the four following types.

Boolean

A `true` or `false` value.

Number

All numbers are 64-bit floating point numbers, ranging from 4.9406564584146544e-324 to 1.79769313486231570e+308. There are also the special values of `Inf` for positive infinity, `-Inf` for negative infinity, and `NaN` for not a number, which is returned for undefined mathematical functions such as dividing by zero.

String

A sequence of Unicode characters. Literals must be enclosed in quotation marks, either single or double according to the preference of the author. You must use the `concat()` function to combine strings, as XPath does not provide for an operator to do so. Strings can be zero-length.

Node-set

A collection of XML nodes, such as elements or attributes. Most location paths in XPath return node-sets.

XPath expressions that return *node-sets,* or locations to specific elements, attributes, or other data in your document, will need to be expressed as a location path, using one of the following syntaxes. Locations are separated by forward slashes, similar to the UNIX style of referencing file paths.

Axes

The axis sets the direction of the path. The axis is separated from the location by two colons.

There are thirteen axes in XPath, as follows.

CHILD

All children of the current node.

DESCENDANT

All nodes contained within the element, regardless of how many steps down.

DESCENDANT-OR-SELF

Any descendant of the current node, including itself.

PARENT

The parent element of the current node.

ANCESTOR

The root and all elements that contain the current node.

ANCESTOR-OR-SELF

All ancestors of the current node, including itself.

FOLLOWING-SIBLING

All nodes that follow the current one with the same parent.

PRECEDING-SIBLING

All nodes with the same parent that precede the current one.

FOLLOWING

All nodes beginning after the end of the current node, not including attributes and namespaces.

PRECEDING

The exact opposite of `following`.

ATTRIBUTE

All attributes of the current node, not including `xmlns`.

NAMESPACE

All namespaces in the current scope.

SELF

The current node.

Abbreviated Syntax

`.` (one period): Current node.

`..` (two periods): Parent node.

name: The child element with that name.

`//`: All descendants of the current node, including the node itself.

`@name`: The attribute of the current node.

Predicates

Additional tests, enclosed in square brackets, that follow a node text and usually return a Boolean.

continued

XPath Functions

XPath defines 27 functions. XPath expressions will fill in omitted arguments with default values or the current node and do not require that the arguments passed be a specific data type.

boolean(object) Converts its argument to a Boolean. Zero and `NaN` are `false`; all other numbers are `true`. Empty node-sets and empty strings are `false`; non-empty node-sets and strings are `true`.	**lang(string languageCode)** Returns `true` if the string is written in the language specified in the second argument. The closest element that is the node itself or an ancestor with an `xml:lang` attribute determines the language of the string.
ceiling(number) Returns the smallest integer greater than or equal to the provided argument.	**last()** Returns the number of nodes in the current node-set.
concat(string1, string2, …) Combines the given strings into a single string from left to right.	**local-name()** Returns the current node's local name, or the part of the element after the colon if a namespace is given.
contains(string1, string2) Returns `true` if `string2` exists within `string1`. The test is case-sensitive.	**name()** Returns the name, including the namespace, of the current node.
count(node-set) Returns the number of nodes in the provided set.	**namespace-uri()** Returns the namespace URI of the current node.
false() A Boolean that always returns `false`.	**normalize-space(string)** Strips leading and trailing whitespace from its argument.
floor(number) Returns the greatest integer less than or equal to the number.	**not(boolean)** Reverses its argument, so if a true expression is passed to it, it will return `false`, and vice versa.
id(string | node-set) Returns a node-set containing all elements with the specified IDs.	

number(object)

Converts the argument to a number. Strings are converted by stripping whitespace and then picking the closest mathematical value to the string, or more likely to NaN. Booleans are converted to 1 if `true`, 0 if `false`. Node-sets are converted to the string value and then follow the rules for converting strings.

position()

Returns a number equal to the position of the current node in the node-set.

round(number)

Rounds the number to the closest integer.

starts-with(string1, string2)

Returns `true` if `string1` begins with `string2`. The test is case-sensitive.

string(object)

Converts the given value to a string. Node-sets are converted to the first string value of the set. Integers are converted to their English form, using a minus sign if negative. Non-integers are converted using a decimal point. A Boolean `true` value is converted to the word *true* and `false` to *false.*

string-length(string)

Returns the number of characters in the given string, including whitespace.

substring(string1, index [, length])

Returns the substring of `string1`, beginning at `index` and continuing to `length`. Note that strings are counted with a first character as 1, not 0 as in many other languages. If `length` is omitted, the substring continues to the end of `string1`.

substring-after(string1, string2)

Returns the substring of `string1` that occurs after the first instance of `string2`. It will return an empty string if `string2` is not in `string1`. The test is case-sensitive.

substring-before(string1, string2)

Returns the characters of `string1` that precede the first occurrence of `string2`. The test is case-sensitive.

sum(node-set)

Converts each node to a number and returns the total.

translate(string1, string2, string3)

Searches `string1` for characters found in `string2` and replaces them with `string3`.

true()

Returns a `true` value.

INDEX

INDEX

INDEX

INDEX

INDEX